AF541094

Human Rights
Issues and Perspectives

Jawahar L Kaul,

2023
Regency Publications
A Division of
Astral International Pvt. Ltd.
New Delhi – 110 002

First Published, 1995

Reprinted, 2023

ISBN: 9788186030172

Disclaimer:

Every possible effort has been made to ensure that the information contained in this book is accurate at the time of going to press, and the publisher and author cannot accept responsibility for any errors or omissions, however caused. No responsibility for loss or damage occasioned to any person acting, or refraining from action, as a result of the material in this publication can be accepted by the editor, the publisher or the author. The Publisher is not associated with any product or vendor mentioned in the book. The contents of this work are intended to further general scientific research, understanding and discussion only. Readers should consult with a specialist where appropriate.

Every effort has been made to trace the owners of copyright material used in this book, if any. The author and the publisher will be grateful for any omission brought to their notice for acknowledgement in the future editions of the book.

Published by : **Regency Publications**
A Division of
Astral International Pvt. Ltd.
– ISO 9001:2015 Certified Company –
4736/23, Ansari Road, Darya Ganj
New Delhi-110 002
Ph. 011-43549197, 23278134
E-mail: info@astralint.com
Website: www.astralint.com

Dedicated to
the memory of
Late Prof. Ramesh Chandra

Justice Ranganath Misra
Chairperson

राष्ट्रीय मानव अधिकार आयोग
National Human Rights Commission

सरदार पटेल भवन, संसद मार्ग, नई दिल्ली-110 001 भारत
फोन : (का) 011-3340891 फैक्स : 91-011-3340016 (आ) 011-3018085

Sardar Patel Bhavan, Sansad Marg, New Delhi-110 001 INDIA
Phone : (O) 011-3340891 Fax : 91-011-3340016 (Res.) 011-3018085

Foreword

I am delighted to have been called upon by the Editor, Dr. Jawahar L. Kaul to write a foreword for *Human Rights—Issues and Perspectives*, a series of articles in book form dealing with different facets of human rights.

The Universal Declaration of 1948 recognises the inherence of a wide set of rights for every human being the world over. Ever since man stepped into organised society and came to be confronted with superior powers, either manual or legal and came to suffer oppression, struggle for emancipation started and continued through the centuries.

The Editor is right in saying that it should however, not be presupposed that after the adoption of international codes and national laws on human rights, the protection of human rights has finally been safeguarded. Human Rights would be respected in a community if the perception of its members of such rights is clear and a culture of human rights has generated. Such a situation can be found only in a violence-free society providing appropriate growing ground for the delicate plant of human rights to thrive. As long as there is not a high perception leading to generation of a culture of human rights, it would indeed be difficult to take human rights out of the teaching sphere into a living reality.

The theme in each of the articles is related to the domain of human rights and the contributors have taken pain and great care to project the essence of the matter. I sincerely hope that this book would play a helpful role in improving general perception of human rights and the readers would find it interesting.

(Ranganath Misra)

Preface

While I write this preface, I am conscious of vast and multifarious *corpus juris* on the human rights. We are also aware of the impact of change through new technology, the population explosion, globalisation of production and trade, mass poverty, environmental degradation and the emerging new global order, which should in effect provide new challenges for the emerging norms of human rights. All this has thrust a newer perspective upon human rights law, with demands for new norms and more effective protection.

Human rights, it must be re-emphasized are not new. They have been part and parcel of every jurisprudence, although in varying degrees. Human rights being assertions, each assertion setting forth a right that all individuals have by virtue of the fact that they are human. These assertions have significantly reinforced at different periods of history, explicit demands for either definite Bills of Rights or such similar constitutional safeguards to protect those freedoms. What has however, added new dimensions to human rights is theorizing from social organisation to law, in support of a definite normative regime encapsulating a wide variety of rights under the common rubric of human rights, although not always without protest or even being successful. That is precisely the reason that even now we find a classification between rights receiving 'absolute protection', rights receiving 'quasi-absolute protection' and rights receiving 'relative protection'. It is true with the international norms as also with the national human rights law; the argument that such a distinction is more artificial than real, notwithstanding. By postulating such a distinction the organs of protection legitimates abuse of human rights.

The evidence of the importance being attributed to the human rights movement and ideology should be clear from an overview of the United Nations activities in the human rights realm. Over the years there has been a remarkable proliferation of UN human rights law. The (1948) United Nations Declaration on Human Rights, (1966) Covenant on Civil and Political Rights, and the (1966) Covenant on Economic, Social and Cultural Rights represent the core documents in human rights. Not only has the UN dealt with particular kind of rights but it has also dealt with particular groups of people requiring specialized treatment, be it the women, children, refugees or detained persons or even minorities. Therefore human rights has become a major factor in extending UN activities in diverse areas. While the result of UN activities remain uncertain because of supervening conditions, however, at the institutional level, various UN instruments have had important educational value in setting standards on human rights, to raise the level of people's expectations as to how they should be treated and to some extent to raise the level of treatment of individuals by governments. Further such instruments offer at least some possibility for recompense to those who fall victim to human rights violations.

When we look into the progress of human rights law over the years, we come across a slow and steady transformation of 'moral claims' and 'soft rights' into 'positive rights' and 'greater assertion' of protection of human dignity in all its forms. We are also witnessing protests against laws and policies which are contrary to human dignity and development of human personality. Indeed in this we are told that human rights law, unmindful of the concern with fate and welfare of man is doomed to be an exercise in self deception. In the process an entirely new thinking in relation to the exercise of state power has come into existence. It is increasingly being felt that state power should be judged against a new set of ideals, aspirations for democracy and economic and social welfare and respect for dignity and sanctity of human beings. The stress is no longer on the dialect between liberty and authority but on the dialect between individual and community. This becomes all too evident when we set ourselves into the normative texts and constitutional interpretations relating to human rights and fundamental freedoms. The whole exposition revolves around the rights to freedom as well as various rights to welfare. Indeed the new approach aims at transmuting social goals into the law of human rights. What is suggested is that the observance of human rights and fundamental freedoms can be guaranteed as a matter of course, only by creating political, economic, social, cultural as well as juridical conditions facilitative of human rights and fundamental freedoms.

The movement for integration of international standards into the mainstream human rights law has been ever increasing. Striving for convergence between minimum international standards and national human rights law has been the hallmark of judiciary, social scientists, political activists and other non-governmental organizations, of course not always with success. Whether one looks into the rights of children, women, environment or protection of other rights, the national policies and laws are analysed in the light of international standards. The international norms have become the reference points for introducing innovations in the mainstream human rights law for protection of human rights and fundamental freedoms. Indeed a whole consciousness for changing national laws and practices for the better is fast emerging.

However, despite this consciousness and vast proliferation of human rights law setting standards, imposing obligations, violations of human rights recur, their perpetrators undettered. Contextual justifications for not fulfilling the obligations continue pouring in. States continue showing disrespect to the dictates of furtherance of human dignity and social welfare. For, too many practices and laws derogatory of human dignity continue unabated. The race for economic development has sidelined the concerns for human development. The fate and welfare of man stands at the altar of states' swords. Clearly the imperatives of fulfillment of human rights and dignity decry much more than what is apparent or what is offered.

The present collection of essays provide insights into the normative framework of human rights and the emerging issues concerning protection of human rights, which have over the years assumed importance. Not only do these essays delve into theoretical expositions, various drawbacks in the mainstream human rights law, judicial discourses, but they also highlight the challenges before the mainstream human rights law in general and in India in particular. Indeed the process of education on the complexities of protection of human rights in general, and in India in particular should continue, which these essays do. It is however, naive to suppose that on such a complex subject as human rights, the present work is a complete statement. On the contrary these essays should invite comments and criticism, of course with courtesy and respect. If they do, the authors and the editor would be more than content, for, it would reinforce the process of understanding and dialogue, on the subject theme.

The origin of this collection of essays is a casual discussion. It all happened when my colleagues Dr. K.P.S. Mahalwar, Dr. P.C. Juneja, and I got involved in a discussion about the sad demise of Prof. Ramesh Chandra, Founder Dean and Professor, Faculty of Law, Maharshi Dayanand University, Rohtak. We soon found ourselves so overwhelmed with the contribution of Prof. Ramesh Chandra in the overall development of our Faculty, that we decided to bring out a commemorative volume of essays in honour of Late Prof. Ramesh Chandra. The choice of a theme for such a volume was easy, as Human Rights was a theme very dear to Prof. Ramesh Chandra, hence this title. Also contributions from other authors on the subject theme would be easily forthcoming. Dr. Mahalwar and Dr. Juneja have however, been gracious enough to allow me to be the editor of this collection of essays.

Prof. Ramesh Chandra had joined this Faculty in quite difficult circumstances which were then prevailing in our university. One needs great courage to leave a premier institution like Delhi University to opt for our Faculty which was relatively unknown at that time. But one's loss is another's gain. Prof. Ramesh Chandra's long experience at Allahabad, Shimla and Delhi Universities served him well to lay down the foundation for the future progress of our Faculty. It was under his patronage that our Faculty started Postgraduate and Doctoral Programmes in Law. Being very enthusiastic about Five Year Law Course, he was instrumental in starting this course in our Faculty, which eventually became the first one to have a Five Year Law Course. Over the years these courses have progressed so well that we have the satisfaction of working in such an institution. Having worked with such a distinguished Colleague and Guide (he was our research supervisor too) for a long time and having been overwhelmed with his dedication and oneness of purpose, this work is dedicated to the memory of Prof. Ramesh Chandra.

In the preparation of this volume the primary credit goes to the authors of various essays, who very promptly responded to my request of sending their contributions on the subject theme. Incidentally some of the authors have been colleagues of Prof. Chandra at Delhi and elsewhere also. The questions raised by these authors are, I believe, of surpassing importance for creating a consciousness and commitment for promotion and protection of human rights in general and in India in particular. I express my sincere gratitude to all these authors. As Alston tells us that "the honouring of a master is a gesture which brings glory to those who accomplish it more than to him to whom it is addressed".

I am grateful to Justice Ranganath Misra for writing a foreword to this volume. I am also thankful to Professor(s) C.P. Sheoran, Ranbir Singh, P.C. Juneja; Dr. K.P.S. Mahalwar and Dr. P.S. Lathwal for their cooperation in the project. However, by mentioning only these names I do not mean to ignore the warmth and affection of my other colleagues. Neena Vashist provided assistance in editorial work, which is gratefully acknowledged. Mr. Arun K. Verma of Regency Publications deserves accolade for publishing this volume in the minimum of time. He has also saved me a lot of problems involved in the publication job. Anupam Dhar graciously allowed me to use all facilities available at his office, which is thankfully acknowledged. Last but not the least, my wife Vijay Kaul deserves a special mention for inspiring me to undertake and complete this task.

JAWAHAR L. KAUL

August 27, 1995

Department of Law
Maharshi Dayanand University
Rohtak 124 001

Contents

Part III: Human Rights and Judicial Discourse

Part IV: Human Rights and the Child

Contributors

Cottrell, Jill. Faculty of Law, University of Hong Kong, Hong Kong.

Dalal, A.S. Lecturer, Department of Law, Maharshi Dayanand University, Rohtak 124001.

Ghai, Yash. Faculty of Law, University of Hong Kong, Hong Kong.

Jaswal, P.S. Reader, Department of Laws, P.U. Chandigarh. 160014

Jaswal, Nishta. Reader, Department of Laws, P.U. Chandigarh 160014.

Juneja, P.C. Professor of Law, Maharshi Dayanand University, Rohtak 124001.

Kaul, Jawahar L. Reader, Department of Law, Maharshi Dayanand University, Rohtak 124001.

Kumar, Naresh. Lecturer, Department of Law, Maharshi Dayanand University, Rohtak 124001.

Lathwal, P.S. Lecturer, Department of Law, Maharshi Dayanand University, Rohtak 124001.

Madhavan, Geeta. Advocate High Court of Madras, Madras. Formerly Lecturer, Department of Legal Studies, University of Madras.

Mahalwar, K.P.S. Reader, Department of Law, Maharshi Dayanand University, Rohtak 124001.

Sanjaoba, Naorem. Professor, Head and Dean, Faculty of Law, Gauhati University, Guwahati 781014.

Raina, B.K. Lecturer, Department of Law, University of Jammu, Jammu Tawi 180004.

Raina, S.C. Reader, Department of Law, University of Jammu,. Jammu Tawi 180004.

Sharma, Sudesh. K. Reader, Department of Law, University of Jammu, Jammu Tawi 180004.

Shahabuddin, Ansari. Lecturer, Department of Law, K.G.K (P.G.) College, Moradabad. U.P.

Singh, Mahendra P. Professor and Dean, Faculty of Law, University of Delhi, Delhi 110007

Singh, Parmanand. Professor of Law, University of Delhi, Delhi 110007.

Singh, Ranbir. Professor of Law & Dean, Faculty of Law, Maharshi Dayanand University, Rohtak 124001.

Vashist, Neena. Lecturer, Department of Law, Maharshi Dayanand University, Rohtak 124001.

Verma, S.K. Professor of Law, University of Delhi, Delhi 110007.

PART I

HUMAN RIGHTS: EMERGING NORMS

1

What are Human Rights?†

*Parmanand Singh**

Introduction

The popularity of the concept of human rights in current politics, the rapid growth of law relating to international protection of human rights and frequent appeal to human rights for social change, curbing governmental lawlessness, social oppression and human needs satisfaction has been so overpowering, that the language of human right has become an empty-catch all under which any political or moral values can easily be subsumed. Today every good or value, every benefit and every support and every claim against blows of misfortune, tyrannical or sadistic uses of power is being asserted by the people in the guise of human rights. Since appeal to human rights is being employed as a stimulant to people's emotions, a list of these rights can easily be derived from deprivations, privations, brutalities and atrocities. If the rights have to be "human" then man is the measure and there is no reason that a limit should be placed to the claims made in the guise of human rights.

In popular conception of human rights this concept only requires positive social, political and judicial action to support the claims said to be rooted in 'humanity' and 'personal

† Paper presented at the National Seminar on Human Rights Development and Democracy held at Banaras Hindu University from 29–31, March 1995.

* Professor of Law, Campus Law Centre, Faculty of Law, University of Delhi, Delhi-110 007.

dignity'. The language of human rights has acquired such a momentum through a long line of judicial decisions, that the age-old divide between civil and political rights and social and economic rights is completely being bridged and all claims of rights are asserted under the rubric 'human rights'. Even the Protection of Human Rights Act 1993 defines human rights as rights 'relating to life, liberty, equality and dignity of the individual guaranteed by the Constitution or embodied in the International Covenants and enforceable by the Courts in India.[1]

In India today every one talks of human rights by bringing ordinary people in public focus. In this sense the language of human rights has become a resource for populism and for doing politics. As has been aptly put by Upendra Baxi, "poverty alleviation programmes, even when they show some concern for the 'poor' are largely directed to meet the needs of party political regimes, and the gap between the rhetoric on war against 'poverty' and the reality in terms of changing the life-conditions of the 'poor,' is very often a function of coherence of political ideologies, ways of organisation of party cadres, and the leadership styles."[2] An editor of a leading newspaper has recently remarked that mere populism without action can hardly bear any fruit in satisfying basic human needs. On the contrary populism results in the loss of credibility and the legitimacy of the State.[3] Baxi views the problem of human rights as the problem of development, a "process of planned social change through continuing exercise of public power."[4]

Another approach is to link human rights with the development policies of the Indian government. Critics of the political economy contend that a model of economic development based on multinational capital and privatisation of economy will have a negative impact on human rights contributing to "increased inequalities, dismantling of social services with adverse effects on the poor, and restrictions on trade union rights." Implementation of development projects will have a negative impact on the local population, particularly indigenous people. The new economic policy will have the "tendency to centralise the decision-making powers."[5] Rajni Kothari believes that the new philosophy of trade "would increase unemployment, lead to a model of modernisation that will push the people to the brinks of survival, erode worker's rights and further depress the conditions of migrant women and child labour."[6] Another critic points out that our government is prepared to "hand over the country to foreign sharks and their Indian business cohorts, whose sole interest would be quick profit and not the benefit to the common."[7] A.R. Desai's grudge is that "the development policies adopted by the Indian rules have resulted in destroying the ethnic identities, social structure and cultural ethos of the indigenous people who have been reduced into agrarian serfs, bonded labourers, agricultural proletariat, marginalised poor cultivators or uprooted unemployed citizens."[8]

There are others who argue that 'development' creates 'poverty' and negates human rights. Poverty, therefore is not a "growth problem alone; it is a structural and attitudinal problem as well."[9] The UNICEF State of the World's Children Report 1995 also subscribes to this view. It states:[10]

> Whereas it is obvious that free market economic systems are capable of generating economic growth, it is far from obvious that they are capable of creating just, civilized and sustainable human society. And in the recent commitment to free market economic policies . . . supported by the World Bank, and the International Monetary Fund, insufficient account had been taken of the effects on the poor or vulnerable or on the environment.

The Marxist scholars also share the view that liberalisation has failed to generate income to the society as a whole by mobilising revenue for the satisfaction of the basic human needs. For instance Bhiku Parekh,[11] argues that in a capitalist model of development human rights serve as an ideological legitimation to mask social and economic inequalities in the society. These rights are mere illusions incapable of being enjoyed by a vast majority of the community who are utterly disadvantaged by the capitalist domination and market economy. Baxi also argues that in a civil society the exercise of liberty creates space for domination by some over others and thus law becomes repressive and violative of human dignity.[12]

While political commentators want Indian market economy to have a 'human face,' the legal scholars argue for dissolving the antinomy between civil and political rights (or fundamental rights) and social and economic rights (or directive principles). For example, in a recent article Rajeev Dhavan describes the directive principles as a "massive 'socialist' empowerment of the State" for securing social and economic rights and argues for dispelling the myth that 'socialism' and 'human rights' are incompatible. To him at the "root of the problem lies the troubling assertion that while CPR inhere in human beings, ESR are the gift of the State. It is the patronising theory of human rights which is responsible for the fragmented approach to human rights which treats ESR and CPR as falling into two distinct trade-off categories." Dhavan believes that ESR have "become a matter of politics and planning" because even in public interest litigation cases involving economic and social rights the "judges are backing off where the government or expert committee have advised against action or inquiry."[13]

Are New Rights Different from Traditional Liberties?

In legal and moral theory the concept of rights first appeared on the stage of thought in the guise of natural rights. Such philosophers as Hobbes, Lock and Rosseau and such acute political philosophers as the leaders of French and American Revolution had a clear conception of rights that must be assured to men if they were to live with security and dignity. According to the doctrine of natural rights of the seventeenth and eighteenth century man was believed "to have a fixed and unalterable nature, to be endowed with reason, which gave him certain rights without which he ceased to be a human being."[14] These natural rights summed upon in the Lockean formula of "life, liberty and property". The moral requirement was to act with respect for persons. The idea of respect for persons was interpreted as freedom for interference by others. Thus, rights against arbitrary coercion, physical restraint, freedom of speech and association and right against discrimination were concerned with the protection of the individual person against governmental power. The natural rights had a metaphysical or moral status derived from human nature or God or Reason or other Supra-legal sources and belonged to men as part of their intrinsic nature. The doctrine of natural rights had greatly influenced the drafting of British Bill of Rights (1689), Declaration of Independence (1776) and Declaration of Rights of Man and Citizen (1789) and formed part of the U.S. Constitution. The doctrine of natural rights viewed man as a self-determining and self-directing agent living in an environment that offered him ample resources and opportunities to pursue his own goals and choose his own actions free from interference by others.

Natural rights thus represented the struggle of men against various forms of intrusions and oppressions. These rights placed great emphasis on liberty, freedom and independence. But since this doctrine was theoretically suspected from the start it never acquired intellectual respectability and failed to exploit the ground it had won. Towards the end of eighteenth century Jeremy Bentham the founder of classical utilitarianism and analytical positivism mounted an attack on the doctrine of natural rights. Bentham argued that the doctrine of natural law or rights could settle nothing. The only proper basis for determining how people should live was the principle of utility. He held that laws and rights could be evaluated by reference to principle of utility and not by reference to a misleading belief in the existence of natural rights. Rights were, according to him, not a matter of moral or political legitimacy but owed exclusively to positive law.[15] This view of rights-as-defined by law has been made famous by the hens of Bentham such as John Austin, Hans Kelsen and H.L.A. Hart.

The legal positivists transformed natural rights by first refining the concept of civil liberties and establishing a catalogue of specific rights and then by developing the procedural apparatus to secure these rights. Like the natural rights, the traditional individual rights to freedom of speech, assembly, due process and so forth were defined as right to freedom from interference from others. Most of the common law rights formulated in such concepts as negligence, tort, defamation, liability, are defined as prohibitions against interference with individual freedom. The same is the case with constitutional rights, called fundamental rights. Most of the fundamental rights guaranteed by the Indian Constitution are controlled by a negative verb forbidding the state to 'deny', 'abridge', 'violate' 'infringe', 'deprive', 'discriminate' the specific rights. These rights rarely require a positive social or political action to endowment with positive social goods and services.

According to Iredell Jenkins,[16] human rights are different from traditional individual rights in as much as they "tend to take the form of claims *to* or *for* something. Their function is to assure to people certain goods, benefits and support for which they experience an urgent need, to which they feel entitled, and which they are unable to procure by their individual effort."[17] The essence of what is happening here is that the concept of "right" is being enlarged to include not only means but also ends. "What men are now claiming as a right is not merely that they be left unhindered in their pursuit of values but that these values be bestowed upon them."[18] The extension of rights in this way has enlarged the duties of the State which is now charged with obligation to satisfy basic human needs.

Jenkins holds that the origin of "human rights is quite similar to that of natural rights: each is born of desperation and dedicated to action. But there are also important differences that will have important consequences. The doctrine of human rights appeals chiefly to the feelings of men, while that of natural rights spoke more seriously to their minds."[19] He believes that the doctrine of human rights "marks a return to that of natural rights but without the metaphysical foundation of the latter."[20]

The long passage from natural to legal human rights has been poignantly summed up by Jenkins thus:[21]

> "The concept of natural rights teaches us that any doctrine of rights must have a firm theoretical basis. Since rights are means to the achievement of human good, a correct catalogue of rights depends upon a sound theory of human nature and the human situation. Without such a theory, determination of what claims constitute rights becomes a purely subjective and haphazard operation; all we can do is to attend to the manifold demands that men

voice, estimate the extent of their support, and try to satisfy those that are the most widely and vociferously urged. This is obviously a hit and miss procedure, substitutions clamor (if not violence) for reason and discontent for justification."

In India today the judges are exactly adopting a "hit and miss" procedure when every fresh week they are declaring a new human right employing the elusive language of 'human dignity' and equating 'dignity' with basic human needs. But the traditional theory of individual rights teaches us that mere declaration of rights are in vain without an effective apparatus to implement them. The idea of rights involves the notion that men must be able to invoke these rights when they stand in need of them.

Right and Will Theory

As has been stated above, some moral and political theories hold that the only rights are rights to freedom which require only duties of non-interference. Most of these rights as liberties connect closely to the will theory of rights. This theory holds that rights mark out an area within which a person's will is decisive. In other words rights make the enforcement of another's duty dependent on one's exercise of will. This theory presupposes the correlativity of rights and duties in Hohfeldian sense and treats rights as power of waiver over someone else's duty.

H.L.A. Hart who is the contemporary exponent of will theory emphasises the correlativity of rights and duties and places great emphasis on liberty as a fundamental value. He asserts: "If there are any moral rights at all, it follows that there is at least one natural right, the equal right of all men to be free."[22] Thus all rights are derived from a basic right to equal liberty. Rights make sense only in a system where people are left free to lead their own lives and be responsible for their own decisions and actions. Only when a person's action interferes with the equal liberty of others, that he can be restrained by law. Many traditional civil liberties such as freedom of speech, religion and property can be derived from a basic right to equal liberty placing high value to the freedom of action and freedom from interference. Apparently the rights to welfare or well-being cannot be justified by the will theory of rights.

The contemporary belief in 'human rights' involves the idea of rights to freedom as well as various rights to welfare or right to assistance of others. Hence freedom ceases to be a distinct value in the sense of *freedom of action* or *freedom of will*. The notion of freedom takes within its fold *freedom of action* as well as *freedom from pain and suffering*. Or even *freedom from hunger, noise, disease, want and so forth*. The modern doctrine of human rights, therefore, seeks fresh grounds and content of right: so that the deficiencies of the established theories of rights are exposed and the unmet needs and neglected values are accommodated within the doctrine of rights. The new concept of human rights is also impelled by the logic that the idea of rights as embodying freedoms and liberties, and especially marked liberties only encourages acquisitive capitalism and 'rugged' individualism.

Rights as Respect for Persons

Susan Moller Okin defines human rights as a 'claim to something (whether a freedom, a good or a benefit) of crucial importance for human life'. According to her "there are at least three kinds of important human needs—to basic physical goods, to physical security, to being treated with respect."[23] Milne also defines human rights as implying a duty to act with respect for persons. He argues that "human rights are simply what every human being owes to every other human being and as such represent universal moral obligation."[24] Thus if human rights are viewed as respect for human being, such rights will include right to life, to freedom from arbitrary coercion and to be respected as human person. The Courts in India have also derived a catalogue of human rights from the notion of 'human dignity' implied by a right to life. In many cases 'human dignity' has been defined in terms of basic need satisfaction. In some cases, however, the concept of 'dignity' of the individual has been viewed as an aspect of personal liberty. For example, *Kartar Singh* v. *State of Punjab*,[25] Justice K. Ramaswamy has held that liberty aims at freedom not only from arbitrary restraint but also to secure such conditions which are essential for full development of human personality. Thus human dignity has become an empty-catch all under which both a basic right to liberty or freedom in the sense of a right not to be interfered with and also rights to well-being such as food, shelter, health, work, education, etc. can easily be subsumed.[26]

As long as the concept of human rights is confined to freedom from pain and suffering due to arbitrary coercion, torture or tyrannical abuse of power there seems to be no theoretical difficulty because these rights can adequately be secured by recognised procedures and remedies and by the application of the principle of rule of law and governmental accountability. Theoretical problems would perhaps arise when 'human rights' is viewed as embodying claims to positive benefits such as food, shelter, medical assistance, decent living, clean air, an efficient transport system and the like. Some of these rights can hardly be secured through affirmative litigation. In other words these beneficial rights might receive social or judicial acknowledgement without being adequately protected by established duties on the part of others.

Neil Mac Cormick[27] has offered a very interesting theory of rights to justify the concept of human rights as embodying both the right to freedom and right to welfare or assistance of others. He has offered a modern version of interest theory of rights by attacking the idea of the correlativity of rights implied by will theory and legal positivism. Mac Cormick's principal argument is that the will theory obscures the fact that duties are imposed in order to protect rights. According to him, rights can *exist* without being adequately protected by established legal rules and procedures. The purpose of rights is not to protect individual assertion or exercise of will but certain *interests* or *benefits*. A person has a right whenever the advancement of his interest has received social recognition. Such recognition itself is a good reason for imposing a *duty* or for providing assistance to those in need. If we apply Mac Cormick's theory we would say that the *existence of rights is independent of whether they are enforced or not.* One can talk of rights without exactly determining who has the duty and how such duty can be protected.

The effect of Mac Cormick's *interest* or *benefit* theory would be that when a judge ascribes a right to someone to adequate means of livelihood, shelter, clothing, medicare, job, minimum level of welfare and so on, he is in fact holding that the interest represented by such a right 'ought' to be protected. That a particular right can have no practical application in the sense of its justified enforcement, does not invalidate a right. Rights have an objective existence and are derived from the recognised nature of human beings and their needs.

Rights to welfare are not 'rights not to be interfered with,' but 'rights to be positively assisted.' In case of constitutional right such assistance has to be given by the State. But in modern political theory there has been a long-running dispute among the political philosophers concerning the relationship between liberty and equality. In other words can people be made more free, and at the same time can a more equal distribution of resources be achieved?

For example if people have liberty to do whatever they like (especially in the context of market liberties implied by a liberalised economy), the traditional doctrine of liberty requires that the State should not interfere in the exercise of these liberties nor can the State require the fortunate ones to co-operate in staffing the services required to supply positive social goods to those in need except perhaps through taxation. At the same time State is obligated to organise the national effort in order to satisfy basic human needs and to protect men against their mistakes and misfortunes.

If health care, education, food, and housing and other necessities and amenities of life are declared to be human rights and the State is obligated to fulfil these needs, without being able to secure the contribution of the members of the society according to their ability, then we are involving ourselves in a series of contradictions. If in the face of liberalisation of economy government has to manage its own affairs like a business enterprise in a competitive economy we will have democracy of the market place rather than a democracy of social justice notwithstanding the contemporary rhetoric for human rights. And to many critics of India's political economy, the new philosophy of trade has not sprung from the Indian soil or from popular conviction but it is an alien transplantation which according to the ruling powers is irreversible. Put in more legal terms it is futile to hold that it is compulsory for the State to supply positive goods and services to the poor and the victimised and then to hold that all citizens have certain liberties which the State cannot or is unwilling to violate or abridge.

Philosophers such as Robert Nozick[28] would argue that a theory of rights requiring positive assistance of others would violate the individual rights to liberty and property which are also based upon the idea of respect for persons. Nozick maintains that liberty and equality are incompatible ideas. Any attempt to achieve equality (in the sense of equality of resources or welfare) would require constant interference with liberty. To Nozick respect for persons means to respect the distinctness of persons. The idea of distinctness of persons entails an exclusive right of each person in his labour and his own person and no right in the person or labour of others. If a person acquires something by his own labour by a free and voluntary transaction without the use of force or fraud then he has the exclusive right to that thing. This implies a right to liberty and right to property. Nozick's theory which is also based upon the basic idea of respect for persons would reject any idea of rights which entails a duty on someone to assist those in need because such a theory will violate the value of "distinctness of a person." It would appear, therefore, that a society and State which gives overriding consideration to free market transactions implied in a liberalised economy, would treat money and liberty as the highest values for pursuing good and worthwhile life. 'Rights to welfare' or 'positive equality' would only be a 'rhetoric' or 'benevolent paternalism' in such a society.

Conclusion: Treating People as Equals

What rights people should have would thus, depend upon the basic question: What is truly valuable and good? What goals and aspirations would be truly worthwhile? What ways of living would count as excellence in a human being? Only when we arrive at a conception of a good and worthwhile life, we might think as to what kinds of law, legal apparatus and institutions will encourage the attainment of the desired goals and aspirations. If we choose a life of public concern and participation as superior to a life of material acquisition, then we have to renovate the modern civil society and create a society of caring and compassionate individuals willing to assist others in need.

The basic idea of human rights is thus embedded in the notion of respect for person. One of the most influential theory of rights to be offered in recent times is that of Ronald Dworkin[29] to which we will very briefly refer now. Dworkin argues that Rawls' theory presupposes the existence of a basic right to equal concern and respect which finds expression in the required unanimity of the choice of the principles of justice in the original position. Like Rawls, Dworkin also holds that individuals have certain rights that are not subject to the calculus of social utility. For Dworkin, anyone who talks about right "seriously" must accept the basic idea of human dignity which consists in the moral requirement that people have a basic right to equal respect and concern when certain laws are made or political decisions are taken by the government. Rights, he says, should be understood as *trumps* over some background justification for political decisions that state the goal for the society as a whole.

Ronald Dworkin, like Rawls, rejects a general right to equal liberty and places great emphasis on equality. He rejects both legal positivism and the classical utilitarianism of Benthamite type and offers a modified form of utilitarianism. He believes that rights have a dimension of *weight* and therefore one cannot talk of rights coming and going with fluctuating calculus of utility. Individual rights cannot be overridden everytime and should be immune from considerations of general welfare. For example, if individuals have a right not to be tortured or be subjected to degrading treatment, these acts cannot be justified on the ground that by imposing some hardship on some individuals general welfare involved in preventing terrorist killings will be achieved. Simply if people have a right to education, to means of livelihood, to a decent living and health care, these rights must not be "traded off" for advancing certain governmental policies like liberalised economy, increase in industrial activity, an efficient transport system, an efficient balance of payment system and so on. If rights can be overridden this way they cannot be genuine rights. A genuine right must have the power to override the considerations of general welfare.

Dworkin should, however, not be misunderstood for advocating a theory of absolute rights. Rights can certainly be restricted on "special grounds" to protect the rights of another person. For example X's right of free speech can be restricted to protect Y's right to the integrity of his reputation. Similarly individual rights can be restricted for genuinely urgent reasons of national security. Dworkin rejects a general right to liberty because such a right would always result in an unrestricted right to the free use of property and would thus encourage a market society.

"The central concept in my argument" says Dworkin "will be the concept not of liberty but equality".[30] He holds that an ideal society is that which is dedicated to equality. He draws a distinction between two senses of equality. One of these is *right to equal treatment* "to an equal distribution of some opportunity or resource or burden", the other is the right to *treatment as an equal*—"to be treated with the same respect and concern as any one else." Furthermore, Dworkin holds that "the right to treatment as an equal is fundamental, and the right to equal treatment is derivative". Right to treatment as an equal is a right in the "strong" sense, according to Dworkin and the government would "do wrong" if someone is denied this right. He says:[31]

> I shall say that an individual has a *right* to a particular political act, within a political theory, if the failure to provide the act, when he calls for it, would be unjustified within that theory even if the goals of the theory, would on the balance, be disserviced by the act.

He elaborates this point thus:[32]

> Government must not only treat people with concern and respect but with equal concern and respect. It must not distribute goods or opportunities unequally on the ground that some citizens are entitled to more because they are worthy of more concern.

How can people retain their self-esteem and dignity if they are treated by others with indifference and neglect? If human rights are violated when someone is subjected to neglect, torture, exploitation and repression, then the whole idea behind the requirement to act with respect for person would be to develop a sense of human duties. Human rights can be truly established if the politicians, officials, private citizens and everybody respects the individual integrity of others. It is too easy to proclaim that every benefit or value is a human right. Declaring something as a right costs nothing. It, at the same time, means nothing if we do not bring about radical changes in human attitudes. Such a change would include a willingness to share with others beyond what one earns, a sense of sympathy for the unfortunate one without charity and a sense of moral obligation to assist others in need. The best life is a life in a society of compassionate and caring individuals. Showing respect to person's dignity is a moral requirement to live with others in love, friendship, society and political involvement. How can one "have" human rights in society where instead of being loved people are exploited by the dominant and powerful?

When a judge rules that right to live with human dignity implied by a right to life includes claims *to* or *for* something he is pointing out the repressive nature of present social structure and the legal system. Judges speak very glibly of launching 'wars' on poverty, disease, hunger, illiteracy, discrimination, exploitation, repression, lawlessness and a horde of other social evils but these "wars" cannot be fought by mere pious declarations or proclamations of "rights" through judicial rhetorics.[33] Realisation of these new rights require a tight regulation over all aspects of individual and social life. Such regulations on the lives of the people can be achieved by allocating limited resources, controlling the uses of income and properties, regulating the distribution of wealth. The dilemma in which we find ourselves is simple. The realisation of human rights to freedom and welfare imposes duties upon the State and members of the society but imposition of these duties is thwarted by the doctrine of individual rights. The only way to escape from this dilemma is that the rights to positive social goods and services should be accepted as *social* goals.

According to the established theory of rights, the only *genuine* rights are the rights to freedom from interference, oppression, arbitrary coercion or torture or other forms of tyrannical uses of power. A concept of right understood in this sense is supported by a coherent theory accompanied by established legal procedures in common land and constitutional principle. The most common view of human right is that politicians, officials as well as private citizens are prohibited from actively doing certain things or letting something happen which outrages the integrity or personal dignity of human beings. The new human rights activism thus seeks to disempower the State and the dominant elements in the community by using rights as a weapon for struggle against domination and abuses of power.

REFERENCES

1. Section 2(d) Protection of Human Rights Act, 1993.
2. Upendra Baxi, *Law and Poverty*: Introduction XII (1988).
3. V.N. Narayanan, "Populism is Not a Dirty Word." *The Hindustan Times*, January 20, 1995, p. 3.
4. Upendra Baxi, "From Human Rights to the Right to be Human" in U. Baxi (ed.). *The Right To Be Human* 185–199 (1987) at 187.
5. D.J. Ravindran, "Indivisity of Human Rights: A Neglected Concept." *Mainstream* October 15, 199, pp. 8–10.
6. Rajni Kothari "Flawed Democracies: Critique of Indian and U.S. Models." *The Times of India*, May 30, 1994.
7. M.N. Buch "Economic Reforms: Myth and Reality," *The Hindustan Times*, January 31, 1995.
8. A.R. Desai "Agrarian Movement." *Seminar* 418, June 1994, pp. 34–36.
9. Bindeshwar Pathak "Social Development: Search For a New Paradigm." *The Hindustan Times*, January 12, 1995.
10. Quoted in V.N. Narayanan *Supra* n. 3.
11. Bhiku Parekh "The Modern Concept of Rights and its Marxist Critique." In U. Baxi supra note 4, 1–23.
12. U. Baxi, "Law and State Regulated Capitalism in India." In *Capitalist Development: Critical Essays* 185–209 (1991).
13. Rajeev Dhavan "Ambedkar's Prophecy: Poverty of Human Rights in India." 36 *J.I.L.I.* 9–30 at 15 (1994).
14. Carl. J. Friedrich, *Constitutional Government And Democracy* 156 (1968).
15. Jeremy Bentham, *Of Laws In General* p. 120.
16. Iredell Jenkins, *Social Order and the Limits of Law: A Theoretical Essay*. 253 (1988).
17. *Ibid.*
18. *Id.*, at 257.

19. *Id.*, at 251.
20. *Ibid.*
21. *Id.*, at 254–255.
22. H.L.A. Hart "Are there Any Natural Rights." 64 *Philosophical Review* 175, 189–91 (1955).
23. Susan Moller Okin "Liberty, and Welfare: Some Issues in Human Rights Theory." In J. Ronald Pennocle and J.W. Chapman (eds.), NOMOS XXIII: *Human Rights* 235 (1985).
24. See Lloyd's *Introduction To Jurisprudence* 143 (1985).
25. (1994) 3 SCC 569.
26. *Francis Carcilie Mullin* v. *Administrator Union Territory of Delhi* (1981) 1 SCC 608, 610–19. (Right to life includes right to live with human dignity and this includes bare necessaries of life such as adequate nutrition, clothing, shelter and food.) *Bandhua Mukti Morcha* v *Union of India* (1984) 3 SCC 161, 183. (Right to live with human dignity includes right to education, health care, decent living.) *Olga Telli's* v *Bombay Municipal Corporation* (1985) 3 SCC 545. (Human dignity includes right to work and means of livelihood.) *State of H.P.* v. *Umed am* (1986) 2 SCC 68, 74–75. (Right to life embraces not only physical existence of life but access to read also.) *M.C. Mehta* v. *Union of India* (1987) 1 SCC 471. (It includes right to clean and hygienic environment.) *Parmanand Katara* v. *Union of India* (1989) 4 SCC 286. (It includes right to medical assistance.) *Buffalo Traders Association* v. *Maneka Gandhi* (1994) Supp. 3 SCC 448. (Right to hygiene in slaughter house.)
27. Neil Mac Cormick, "Rights in Legislature." In P. Hacker and J. Raz (eds.), *Law, Morality and Society* (1977), Neil Mac Cormick, *Legal Rights and Social Democracy* (1982) Ch. 8.
28. Robert Nozick, *Anarchy, State and Utopia* Chaps. 7, 8.
29. Ronald Dworkin, *Taking Rights Seriously* (1978).
30. *Id.*, at 272–279.
31. *Id.*, at 169.
32. *Id.*, at 272–273.
33. See. *D.D. Horticulture Employees' Union* v. *Delhi Administration*, A.I.R., 1992 SC 789 in which the Supreme Court held that right to work and livelihood could not be viewed as a fundamental right because its realisation depended upon the economic capacity and development of the Indian State. In *Olga Tellis* v. *Bombay Municipal Corporation, supra* note 26, the court interpreted Article 21 as covering right to work, shelter and means of livelihood but contradicted itself by holding that these rights could be denied by complying with a fair procedure such as notice or hearing or could be denied when State lacked resources. Then in *Mohin Jain* v. *State of Karnataka*, A.I.R. 1992 S.C. 1858 the court endowed all citizens with a right to education as an aspect of right to life but in *Unnikrishnan* v. *State of A.P.* (1993) 1 SCC 645, the court limited this right only to the level of primary education. For the failure of the courts to satisfy basic human needs through affirmative litigation, see B.B. Pande, 'When They Came to the Court Seeking Basic Needs: Alternatives to the Flawed Response' 31 *J.I.L.I.* 368 (1989).

2

Human Rights in the 21st Century—Rhetoric and Prognostication

*Naorem Sanajaoba**

Futurology

Human right is a universal constant, which is susceptible to the influence of variables including *zeitgeist*, shifting cultural values, level of scientific temper of a civilisation, and the attainment of the political economy. Post World-War-Second human thought centred around the massacre, amputation, disappearance of and wounds inflicted upon millions and millions of men by men themselves; that haunting spectre is the mother of the contemporary global concern over the human rights. When the framework is extended to the space-time *continuum*, the human rights scenario may be perceived with a futurological perspective.

Futuristic studies that have been integrated in the planning process of science and technology as well as research and development including the ongoing globalisation programmes the world over, could be fruitfully applied in the field of structuration, standardisation, enforcement and perspectivisation of human rights theme. Futuristic studies were initiated with an essay written in 1943 by professor Ossip Flechtheim and courses initiated by sociologist Alvin

* Professor Head and Dean Faculty of Law, Gauhati University, Guwahati

Toffler in the late 1960s in the United States. Ministry of Science and Technology, Government of India constituted futurology-panel in 1973 and by now, some of the Indian universities make efforts to respond modestly to the preponderance of futuristic studies. The west and Japan had already exercised this culture with a definite edge. The writer makes a modest effort to make an assessment of human rights in the totality from the futuristic perspective. Nobody has ever witnessed the future, but every one is a part of the present from which the future would be constructed. This linkage of space-time profiles provides for the core-assumption of futurology.

Notwithstanding the polemic about human rights in the recent past, considering the ideological confrontations that occurred during the cold war period, the post-cold war era, more particularly at the fag end of the twentieth century, has evolved a near consensus about the rights.

The ongoing march from the adoption of the Universal Declaration of Human Rights in 1948 to Teheran Conference, 1968 and the World Human Rights conference in Vienna in 1993 has provided certain markers that indicate watersheds in the movement. Most of the legal and political systems have, in varying degrees, responded to the prerogatives of the first generation of human rights by way of internalising civil and political rights within their domestic jurisdiction, despite adverse reports of occasional infringements. The reference points and standards have, however, been set and countries are now judged by their degree of deviation from these standards. This is no mean achievement of the global order in this century. Unlike the first generation of human rights which are prohibitive to the states, the second generation of human rights empowers the state towards achieving the basic socio-economic rights of its citizens. The states largely fail in this second front. How far the states can succeed in providing for the second generation of human rights in the twenty-first century depends on some other considerations, which are largely political and on the system of economic or trade order in the context of the World Trade Organisation—a progeny of the GATT. Connected herewith is the input of the new physics, new biology and other developmental sciences to the domain of knowledge, wealth and power of the nations. The twenty-first century envisages the dominance of economic super powers like Japan, Germany and European Union, the United States and the emergence of Asia-Pacific rim, represented by China, five Asian tigers and India, some of which stake claim to the top economic power-bracket of the next century. Second generation of human rights is directly interlinked with the level of the economic order that is being speculated upon and sought for and wealth-creating power of the new sciences, as mentioned. The first generation of human rights would not be safe without making grounds for a healthy, viable, equitous and a just set of the second generation of human rights. Rhetoric and formalism could not substitute these basic *sine qua non* of the human rights set.

The trend of human rights perceptions has turned into another direction following the Rio Earth Summit, 1992 and the Copenhagen World Summit on Social Development, held in 1995. Group or collective rights are drawing increasing attention of the world opinion—leaders and decision makers. The third generation of human rights, inspite of contradicting the earlier two generations, has all the more strengthened the legitimacy of the two generations. In terms of chronology, the third generation has taken firm political and ideological roots in the 1960s, when decolonisation process has been initiated by the UN. The next century will be equally concerned with the third generation rights.

The methodology to be adopted for ascertaining the futurology of the human rights in the twenty-first century cannot be based upon Kelsenian purist conceptualisation nor on the dogmatic adherence to the *Volkgeist* doctrine of communalisation of laws. An opportunity is given to the world citizens on their right choice of values, considering the fact that they are strolling in an unprecedented information super highway, a new terrain of Cyberspace and using new intellectual tools which are made out to meet the demands of the next century. Human rights research and decisions are a vital component of these quantum jumps and adventures, the new world order undertakes. The fear of dominance, hegemony and neocolonialism is yet to be totally removed from the role models and structures, we create, be it regional or global.

Human Rights in the New World Order

In the cold war period, human rights remained a subject of the ideological dispute between the two ideologically polarised super-powers. The American foreign policy objectives and humanitarian aid have been based upon American value system and its perception of human rights which are anti-communist, anti-socialist in content. The socialist version of human rights placed the political and civil rights next to the economic freedom of man and Marxian ideology treats economic freedom as the pre-condition for the enjoyment of other set of liberties. American practice of human rights denied a position of equality to the coloured Americans, the Negroes, promoted discrimination in actual life and created indeterminate lumpen-proletariat among the white Americans. Till the other day, American women had been denied adult sufferage and even today, freedom of the citizens to set up communist party is equated with treason. The Soviet experience had its quota of human rights violations like imprisonment of political dissidents and perpetuation of a regimented party life, wherein the party *apparatchiks* behaved not differently from what they called as bourgeoisie. The new world order is either unipolar or multi-polar and the American order enjoys the primacy by default.

In the new world order, the third world perception of human rights centres around the re-conceptualisation of the unfinished agenda about economic emancipation of the third world. The polemic of the cold war period about the primacy question still continues, since the third world considers the physical survival and material self sufficiency to be primary. In this context, the euphoria about globalisation of economy and trade by way of breaking down tariff barriers and promoting equal market access by all the members of the World Trade Organisation and alteration of national patent laws to suit American interest calls for deeper examination. Even economic giants like Japan is threatened, occasionally by the USA. Other countries like China, India, Brazil, among others, are given the indirect signal to behave in tune with the market demands of the USA and other big powers. The second generation of human rights is directly affected by the world economic and trade order. The method of wealth creation and re-distribution of wealth in the new world order is going to determine the status of the second generation of human rights across the world; but as of now, the standard of living as found in developed countries and poor countries varies in the ratio of 1:14. The human economic rights of a Westerner for instance is just fourteen times the standard of living of a poor Indian or Latin American or, Afrikaaner.

The new world order is presently witnessing the emerging science and technology in the west like the new physics of nano-technology, robotics, automation, space sciences, electronics, super conductors, super-computers, polymers accompanied with new forms of smart weapons and also new biology like genetic engineering, cloning, neuro-biology, neurosurgery, IVF, organ transplantation, genome projects, transgenesis, accompanied with unprecedented military capability of altering the molecular biology and structures of the man and machines in enemy countries. Some technology is found to be helpful to human rights promotion, but several areas of the new technology pose direct threat to human survival of mankind. The NPT renewal in 1995 for an indefinite period has empowered the 5 + 3 nuclear weapon powers of the world to bring the apocalypse to every doorstep the world over. In this context, the constructive use of the political and civil liberties till the world is completely disarmed is gaining ground as the human obligation of every citizen. Human rights need not be confined merely to the orthodox domain like the exercise of political and civil liberties, which are also equally important in adverse circumstances.

The status of the third generation of human rights like the Right to environment, Right to development, Right of people to self-determination, Right to common heritage of mankind, among others, as endorsed by the respective bodies of the United Nations in the New world order, is found to be of utmost importance to the third world countries. The third generation has not been fully crystalised and it has to be adequately developed in the twenty-first century. This cannot be achieved without the support of the developed countries.

Human Rights Law and International Humanitarian Law are two viable normative global frameworks within which is constructed, a standard by which the human life, liberty and property should be protected in times of peace and in a situation of armed conflicts. These are two levels of evaluating the human rights standard the world over. Normally, our concern is shown towards the protection of human rights in stable situations; however, the old and new world orders are not devoid of conflict situations. Millions of human lives are lost, millions have been wounded and injured and several lakhs have been missing during the last word war. Post-war world witnesses Somalia, where millions die out of hunger, Rwanda where millions die during the tribal feuds and Bosnia, among others, where millions are lost and killed in the ethnic-cleansing process. Low intensity conflicts like wars of national liberation, proxy wars, terrorism, communal infernos and other similar armed conflicts are still visible. Nobody can justify lack of global or regional concern to these hard realities, because the victims are human beings, children, women, disabled, old age people among others. The safeguards required for the protection of human rights in the situations of armed conflicts are enunciated by the four Geneva Conventions, 1949 and the two additional protocols of 1977. The common Article no. 3 of the Geneva Conventions stipulate that the human lives, property, dignity and the lives of the *horse de combat* have to be protected to the fullest extent. This Article no. 3 is *Jus Cogens* and non derogable.

Till the world is relieved of wars, International Humanitarian Laws have to be strengthened, since man and war can not alienate from each other, save in pious and non-real political statements about the eradication of all wars from the human civilisation. Human rights transcend rhetoric and diplomatic manoeuvres. The theme is connected with the super-eminent principle of justice, without whose integration with law, law remains mere official formalism and a bureaucratic norm.

A new development worthy of mention in the field of International Humanitarian Law is the creation of international criminal jurisdiction viz., Yugoslav Tribunal and Rwanda Tribunal by the United Nations. For the first time in the post war history, the United Nations has created these war crime tribunals in the spirit of the Nurenberg and Tokyo tribunals. The war lords would be held personally liable and accountable for the transgression of human rights and crimes against mankind in these two jurisdictions. However, the United Nations is yet to install a standing UN international criminal jurisdiction under its aegis.

Domestic and UN Jurisdictions on Human Rights

National jurisdictions over human rights are constituted on a large scale under the aegis and encouragement of the UN machineries at the fag end of this century. The United States of America which till the other day refrained itself from accepting international human rights instrumentalities like ICCPR, 1966 has started accepting these global human rights obligations, while countries like Pakistan etc. keep themselves away from signing the human rights covenants of the UN, 1966. World Conference on Human Rights held in Vienna in June, 1993 has strongly urged upon all the member states of the UN to sign and ratify all the international human rights instrumentalities invariably. In this context, the Republic of India is equally obliged to sign and ratify, the Optional Protocol to the International Covenant on Civil and Political Rights, 1966, among others. The union government of India has committed itself in early 1995 to sign and accede to the Anti Torture Convention, 1984.

The twenty-first century envisages that each and every country of the world should arrange its national and domestic jurisdictions so as to match literally with the global standard, set by the world community through the medium of the UN and other regional bodies. The Asian region, unlike Africa, the Americas or the Arab nations or the European Union, has not yet done spadeworks so as to mould Asian consciousness of human rights into a consensus and install Asian Human Rights Commission and Asian Human Rights Court.

The Asian statesmen, being engaged more in conflicts and disharmonies largely of their own making, are yet to apply their mind towards appreciating these structural requirements of human rights. Asian unity itself is a positive structure beneficial to the region and its promotion of Asian concepts of human rights. This paper strongly urges upon the leaders and decision makers to pay heed to this legitimate human rights structure which is long overdue. It is also true that several hitches and nitty-gritty have to be sorted out first at the political and economical levels, as Asia lacks a Jean Monnet.

The periodic reporting obligation of the member states under Article 40 of the ICCPR, 1966 to the UN Human Rights Committee is by and large inefficient and casual. The reporting obligation may be tightened up and in the process, the national governments would use the national NGOs in finalising the national reports. Transparency and fairness has been found missing in this aspect.

The national human rights institutions are most likely to be strengthened with popular support and participation in the next century. In case of India, the National Human Rights Commission, is installed under a national Act in 1994. The performance level of the NHRC of India could be fairly assessed in the 2,000 or 2010 AD, considering the fact that the institution is not even in the teething stage. The judicial activism of the Supreme Court of India in the protection of human rights has been appreciated elsewhere also. Technicalities and frivolous procedural constraints did not prevent the Supreme Court from doing justice in class and affirmative actions.

In the last few years, the Supreme Court has re-enunciated state liability in torts thereby gradually eroding the age-old British concept of sovereign immunity and along with this activism, it has also evolved the norms of payment of compensation to citizens, whose fundamental rights have been infringed upon by the state machinery in terms of unlawful detention or custodial death, among others. However, the trend is not fully established since the Supreme Court has not yet universalised this compensatory doctrine for violation of fundamental rights, as it qualifies the relief in 'appropriate cases'. However, the trend is emerging. While the Supreme Court is pro-activist, Indian bureaucracy, executive and the law enforcement machinery by and large, are institutionally apathetic to the human rights protection. Even under TADA, 1985 as amended in 1993 and which culminates on May 23, 1995, nearly eighty thousand farmers, minorities and political opponents of the ruling party had been dumped along with just a few hundred or, dozens of terrorists. The state is apologetic about this blunder, but it does not come out *suo motu* for providing compensatory relief to these seventy thousands of improperly and wrongfully arrested citizens.

On the legislative front, some of the draconian and emergency laws, which are sentimentally espoused by emotionalists, like the Armed Forces Special Powers Act, 1958 invoked in the North Eastern States of India deviate visibly from the universal human rights standard, as enunciated by the ICPPR, 1966 and as accepted under treaty obligations by the Union Government of India. Sections 4, 5 and 6 of the above mentioned Act, 1958 are not only found incompatible with the relevant provisions of the ICCPR, 1966 by the UN Human Rights Committee in 1991, but are also criticised widely by global and national NGOs, because these sections legalise extra judicial murder and immunity of the those who committed extra judicial murders in the name of emergency laws. Similarly, Sections 3, 4, 5, 15, 16, 19 and 21, among others of the TADA, 1985 as amended in 1993 have been found to be in blatant violation of the established norms of criminal and constitutional laws. It reminds us of Jennings, who said once that English parliament has the prerogative to make laws to declare male to be female so on and so forth, but it smacks of insanity of the collective wisdom i.e. cannibalisation of the human conscience in the name of misconceived positivist legalism. Established natural law and procedure contradict these aberrations as untenable.

The domestic national jurisdictions on human rights protection can not and should not be overstretched on the basis of the medieval political theory of absolute sovereignty, as the sovereignty concept is shrinking all the more in the twenty-first century and with the progressive political devolution of powers, global economic integration is gaining momentum. In this context, the far-fetched assumption of the absolutist concept of sovereignty and trade protectionism could be treated blasphemous in the next century. When the domestic laws including patent laws have to be re-drafted in order to match with the WTO prerogatives, the wildest dream of enacting patent laws independent of the global consensus could be ridiculous and pernicious as well. This anachronistic attitude is a direct threat to the growing global interdependence and it cannot claim to be an accepted standard. This mind set of isolationism will drag the states to the scaffold of the medieval age island, hostile states. The meaning of peace and security in the world is re-interpreted in terms of active co-operation, and not in terms of absence of hostilities in their exclusivity.

An important UN Human Rights machinery is the UN High Commissioner on Human Rights, which has been installed in 1994. Some Asian countries objected to the proposal for the installation of the Human Rights Commissioner due to an inbuilt fear that their ongoing human rights violations would be brought under international jurisdiction, but the international opinion prevailed upon this feeble opposition. The office of the Commissioner and its institutional achievements are yet to be examined, as it has no track record so far for evaluative purposes. This institution would flourish in the next century, considering the growing global thrust on human rights standard setting. *Firstly,* the jurisdictions of the theme mechanisms and human rights rapporteurs should not overlap with the Commissioner's jurisdiction. They have to be complimentary to each other. *Secondly*, the Commissioner has to carve out a place of its own by opening up dialogues with governments and coordinating all the human rights agencies under the UN and elsewhere.

International Politics and Human Rights

The locus of human rights in the intersecting coordinates of the global power equations is yet to be ascertained with precision. The difficulty arises out of certain apparent contradictions like the sacrosanctity of human rights within the proximity of politics, which has been conceived as the best art of the possibilities. Human rights cannot remain as a distinct entity, completely isolated from political *apartheid*. The post cold war unipolarity or multipolarity as well as the balance of power and equilibrium of power-centres affects the standard and materialisation of the human rights. The correlation of power and justice also varies in two ways viz., justice of power or, power of justice. The ideal aspect of human rights lies in the powers of justice, but *realpolitik* shifts its locus within the justice of power.

Looking back into the human rights of the Mileans of Milos with respect to the aggressive and hegemonistic Athenians in the period before Christ, the Mileans refused both the options offered to them by the Athenians—surrender to the superior Athenian power and live happily or, vanish yourselves completely. Milos vanished, but its spirit is survived for good. Power can vanish human rights and can retain them also. The contemporary power has not changed much either and it is not going to change substantially in the twenty-first century. Power equations at macro and micro levels may change.

Power relationship considers basic parameters of the contemporary civilisation like population explosion, technology, information explosion, hunger, disease, war, low intensity conflicts, border and territorial disputes. These variables influence the response of power to the standards of human rights, accepted as such within its jurisdiction. The next century will not at all rule out conflicts and power disequilibrium and the perception about human rights would be altered accordingly. The UN outlaws 'war', but war is a reality and demolition of human rights on a massive scale in war is also another concomitant reality.

The United Nations is committed by the provisions of the Charter to secure peace and security on earth, the goals which are always evasive. Terrorism of all kinds including private or state terrorism is branded the world over as crime against mankind. Even a universally accepted definition of terrorism cannot be laid down by the intelligentsia and legislators of the world, because there are many gray areas like political violence and wars of national liberation, which have been consistently approved and legitimised by International Law and all the organs of the United Nations including the General Assembly, Security Council, Human Rights Committee and Commission, the International Court of Justice, specially after endorsing the decolonisation movements by the UN in the 1960s. Interestingly, terrorism is a crime against mankind, while National Liberation Movements are subjects of

International Law and while exercising the right of people to self-determination, the people can lawfully exercise force, but the force applied by the terrorists are unlawful and reprehensible. Herein lies the significance of justice of power and power of justice on the other hand. The dichotomy is not country-specific or culture- or region-specific, but it is universal. The situation of human rights in an unstable situation or conflict-torn geography has to be assessed with this perception.

Another interesting dimension of politicalised human rights is the politics of foreign aids. The USA evaluates the human rights standards of any aid recipient country at the time of granting American aid to other countries. The evaluation of the standards is done by using American values and yardsticks. How far American or European strategic interest has not been considered within the bounds of its hidden agenda is a question, which constitutes the vital component of power-politics. In this sense, all the nations do play the same game and human rights are not completely dissociated from these exercises. This perception, however, would not degrade the universally accepted standards of human rights to the political function of expediency and convenience; we may accept the situation as permissible level of pollution so long as the pollution does not render the environment hazardous. Once we venture a statement that India is the sole exception, it would be an absurdity *prima facie*. Politics and power equations have their own space in the domain of human rights, but human right by itself is not politics, since it is the unalienable essence of man. The UN system, regional power structures, member states of the United Nations and organised bodies including the NGOs have increasing global responsibility to set the standard, enforcement pattern of and for constant monitoring of human rights. The ultimate beneficiary of this responsibility is none other than 'man'.

3

The Asian Perspective on Human Rights

*Yash Ghai**

The title of my paper notwithstanding, there is not one but many Asian perspectives on human rights. It is easy to believe that there is a distinct Asian approach to human rights, because some government leaders speak as if they represent the whole continent when they make their pronouncements on human rights. This view is reinforced because they claim that their views are based on perspectives which emerge from the Asian culture of Asian realities. The gist of their position is that human rights as propounded in the west are founded on individualism and therefore have no relevance to Asia, whose culture is based on the primacy of the community. It is also sometimes argued that economic underdevelopment renders most of the political and civil rights (emphasised in the west) irrelevant to Asia. Indeed, it is sometimes alleged that such rights are dangerous in view of fragmented nationalism and fragile statehood.

It would be surprising if there were indeed one Asian perspective, since neither Asian culture nor Asian realities are homogenous throughout the continent. All the world's major religions are represented in Asia and are in one place or another state religions (or enjoy a comparable status: Christianity in the Philippines, Islam in Malaysia, Hinduism in Nepal and Buddhism in Sri Lanka and Thailand). To this

* Faculty of Law, University of Hong Kong.

list we may add political ideologies like socialism, democracy or feudalism which animate peoples and governments of the region.

Even apart from religious differences, there are other factors which have produced a rich diversity of cultures. A culture moreover, is not static and many accounts given of Asian culture are probably true of an age long ago. Nor are the economic circumstances of all the Asian countries similar. Japan, Singapore and Hong Kong are among the world's most prosperous countries, while there is grinding poverty in Bangladesh, India and the Philippines. The economic and political system in Asia likewise show a remarkable diversity, ranging from semifeudal kingdoms in Kuwait and Saudi Arabia, through military dictatorships in Burma and Cambodia, effective one party regimes in Singapore and Indonesia, communist regimes in China and Vietnam, ambiguous democracies in Malaysia and Sri Lanka, to well established democracies like India. There are similarly differences in their economic systems, ranging from tribal subsistence economies in parts of Indonesia through highly developed market economies of Singapore, Hong Kong and Taiwan and the mixed economy model of India to the planned economies of China and Vietnam. Perceptions of human rights are undoubtedly reflective of these conditions, and suggest that they would vary from country to country.

Perceptions of human rights are also reflective of social and class positions in society. What conveys an apparent picture of a uniform Asian perspective on human rights is that it is the perspective of a particular group, that of the ruling elites. What unites them is their notion of governance and the expediency of their rule. For the most part the political systems they represent are not open or democratic, and their publicly expressed views on human rights are an emanation of these systems, of the need to justify authoritarianism and repression. It is their views which are given wide publicity domestically and internationally.

There are other Asian voices as well. There are admittedly somewhat muted or censored, the voices of the oppressed and the marginalised. There are the passionate voices of the indigenous peoples whose cultures are destroyed by governments which claim to be the custodians of Asian cultures; they speak in a language which finds few resonances even in the west (because their language is threatening to the system of the market). There is the voice, rising in intensity, of the middle classes, with a stake in affluence whose new-found prosperity and economic enterprise shows to them the virtues of the legal protection of property and the rule of law. There are the strident voices of ethnic minorities who seek collective autonomies which challenge governments' claims of political monopoly and state sovereignty. There are the well modulated voices of the non-government organisations, which provide the most consistent and coherent alternative view of human rights to that of governments.

The unity of governments is more apparent than real. Some of the governments which joined in a Bangkok communique in the Asian regional preparatory meeting for the Vienna World Conference on human rights did themselves a disservice, for the domestic record, and their commitment to human rights, are better than one might think from their adherence to the communique. India is one example. Along with some other states, it is committed to human rights by its constitutional instruments, has a strong and independent judiciary, and despite problems and setbacks tries hard to maintain human rights. The reason for presenting a united front is not unconnected with a perceived North-South confrontation. Asian governments feel that since the end of the cold war, the west has focused its attention on what it perceives to be the "undemocratic" nature of third world polities. In Africa and Latin America the western concern for human rights is seen to be an instrument for the establishment or strengthening of the market, in an attempt to restrict the interventions of the state in economic relations. In Asia, however, the key economies are heavily market oriented, and for the most part are successful. Even China is now turning to the market, which is widely credited for its economic success. So the emphasis on human rights is not necessary as a spur to the market (and indeed, as I explore later the relationship between the market and human rights is problematic).

Some Asian governments consider that the western pressure on them for an improvement in human rights is connected with the project of western global hegemony. This is to be achieved partly through the universalisation of western values and aspirations and partly through the disorientation of Asian state and political systems (and the consequent negative effect on their burgeoning economies). They have fashioned their response accordingly. There is some danger in this internationalisation of the Asian debate on human rights. It shifts the focus away from the practices of Asian governments and the restrictions on human rights. It enables the governments to attack, as western stooges, indigenous supporters of human rights. It leads to spurious stereotypes, of "orientalism" and "occidentalism", with either defensive eastern counterparts of western universalism or aggressive retreat into an imagined past or culture. It politicises the question of human rights in an unproductive way.

I turn first to "official" views of human rights of a number of influential Asian countries (Singapore, China, Malaysia, Indonesia). These views have developed primarily in response to two contingencies: the imperatives of control, and confrontation with western pretensions. They are therefore formulated somewhat defensively. It also means, that since they are an engagement and a debate with the west, they are formulated in universalistic terms in the usual discourse of human rights. Several ingredients constitute the official view I am discussing. One which flows directly from both the contingencies is the assertion of "domestic jurisdiction" over human right. Human rights are encapsulated within state sovereignty: the national treatment of human right is no concern of other states or the international community to intervene in domestic situations to redress violations. In its "White Paper," *Human Rights in China* (1991), the Chinese government states that "Despite its international aspect, the issue of human rights falls by and large within the sovereignty of each state". The Chinese delegation to the UN Commission on Human Rights at its meeting in February 1993 urged that the World Conference in Vienna should "reiterate the principle of state sovereignty contained in the UN Charter and international law which is basis for the realisation of human rights. Only when the state sovereignty is fully respected can the implementation of human rights be really ensured." This is also pre-eminently the position of the other countries mentioned above.

Another element in the official view is the relativity of rights, determined by the economic and political circumstances of each country. The Chinese White Paper states that "the evolution of the situation with regard to human rights is circumscribed by the historical, social, economic and cultural conditions of various nations, and involves a process of historical development. Owing to tremendous differences in historical background, social system, cultural tradition and economic development, countries differ in their understanding and practice of human rights." Other countries too have used the state of national economic development as explanations for the failure fully to guarantee the complete range of human rights. There are two major implications of this relativist position on human rights. The first relates to conditionalities of political stability; and the other to the primacy of economic development. The first of these represents restriction on civil and political rights. The Chinese use this framework to establish the priority of social and economic rights in their country, and much of the Paper is taken up with an account of the ending of pre-Communist regime practices of feudalism and other forms of human exploitation and the steady progress in nutrition, education, health, the position of women and the disabled (to eat their fill and dress warmly were the fundamental demands of the Chinese people who had long suffered cold and hunger).

A forthright statement of this position is to be found in pronouncements of the Singapore Government following the detention of various social workers and activists in May 1987. I quote here from one such statement (dated 24 June 1987 and addressed by the Minister of Home Affairs to US Congressmen who had written to complain about the detentions). It compared the "resilience and cohesiveness" and shared values of the US nation (which presumably makes possible the tolerance of human rights) to the fragility and heterogeneity of Singapore. "We are vulnerable to powerful centrifugal forces and volatile emotional tides. Like many other developing countries, Singapore's major problem of nationhood is simply to stay united as one viable nation . . . . In our short history, Singapore has repeatedly encountered subversive threats from within and without . . . . To combat these threats to the nation, the usual procedures of court trials, which apply in Singapore to most criminal cases, have proved totally inadequate. The very secrecy of covert operations precludes garnering evidence to meet the standards of the criminal law for conviction. In many cases of racial agitation, the process of trial itself will provide further opportunity for inflammatory rabble rousing . . . . Singapore cannot be ruled in any other way . . . . Preventive detention is not a blemish marring our record; it is a necessary power underpinning our freedom." (Another aspect of the Singapore by-passing the formal legal system, with its guarantees of fairness, not discussed in the minister's statement, is the taped and doctored "confessions" extracted from the detainees under some coercion, and then shown on the national television as proof of guilt and calculated to destroy their credibility and dignity.)

These remarks were directed at a justification of administrative powers of detention without any kind of trial, but similar arguments have been used to justify other curtailments of civil rights, like the right to associate and assemble, of peaceful marches, of speech and expression. The Chinese Paper says that the people's right to subsistence will be threatened in the event of social turmoil or other disasters, and that it is the fundamental wish and demand of the Chinese government to maintain national stability and concentrate their efforts on developing productive forces.

The economic backwardness of Asia has been used to establish the primacy of economic development over human rights. The argument is, in part, that civil and political rights are neither meaningful nor feasible in conditions of want or poverty. Therefore the first priority of state policy must be to promote economic development. It is implied that economic development may well require restriction on human rights, both to provide a secure political framework in which it can be pursued and to remove obstacles in its way (e.g. through forced movement of people from lands required for "development"). The opposition of human rights and development is assumed rather than proved by argument and illustration. It is also used to establish the priority as between different kinds of rights, in which civil and political rights occupy a lowly position (in part a response to an argument that human rights are indivisible and all of them enjoy an equal status).

The emphasis these governments purportedly place on economic development has led them to support the right, is a matter of considerable contention internationally, with developing countries arraigned on the side supporting it, and most developed countries united in their opposition to it. It certainly does not have the quality of other kinds of rights, which inhere in individuals or groups and for the most part are entitlements against the state. Nevertheless the General Assembly of the United Nations adopted, in face of abstentions by most western states, a Declaration on the Right to Development on 4 December 1986. The Declaration ties the realisation of human rights in the developing countries to international economic aid for them and gives to "people" (presumably meaning "states") the right to "participate in, contribute to, and enjoy economic, social, cultural and political development, in which all human rights and fundamental freedoms can be fully realised." In return for these several concessions are made in emphasising the indivisibility of rights and the claims of individuals of full participation in development and in the fair distribution of the benefits resulting from it.

The Declaration is a fuzzy document, trying to be all things to all persons. So while there are sections of it which can be used to advance the (more traditional) cause of human rights, the gist of it is an attempt to establish reasons for the failure of the realisation of human rights in the international economic and political systems (including encroachments on the principle and practice of self-determination), while affirming that the primary responsibility for human rights is vested in states as part of their sovereignty. In other words, the rich countries must provide economic assistance to the poor countries, but must not question their human rights situation. (The Western riposte to the Declaration has been a massive imposition of political conditionalities on economic assistance and indeed, in the case of China on economic relations and co-operation.) The Declaration is also an attempt to provide an alternative framework for the international discourse on human rights. It shifts the focus from domestic arenas (where most violations of human rights take place) to the international, and takes attention away from specific rights, for example, speech, assembly, social welfare to an ambiguous portmanteau right of development, for which in the nature of third world affairs, the state must take the responsibility in defining and implementing it. Through the Declaration, Asian governments seek to promote the ideology of developmentalism, which justifies the repression at home and the evasion of responsibility abroad.

Another Asian initiative in changing the framework for the discourse on human rights is even more fundamental. The approaches discussed so far have taken the western discourse as the main framework and have advanced qualifications to it or provided justifications for derogation from its values. Some governments have put forward the argument that the cultural matrix within which relations between individuals and the State are embedded are fundamentally different in Asia from that in the west. This matrix governs the nature and salience of human rights. This approach has been taken up aggressively in Singapore and Malaysia (less so in China, where the government's residual loyalty to Marxist thought is inconsistent with the adoption of this cultural approach, especially since so much of it is based on semi-feudal thought in Asia).

I take, as the basis of my discussion of this point, an official statement of the Government of Singapore, *Shared Values* (1991). The context of this White Paper is concern of the government that the cultural values of its people are under attack from foreign ideas and values. It poses the rhetorical question, "Can we build a nation of Singaporeans, in Southeast Asia, on the basis of values and concepts native to other peoples, living in other environments?" It goes on, "If we are not to lose our bearings we should preserve the cultural heritage of each of our communities, and uphold certain common values which capture the essence of being a Singaporean". It then finds certain perceptions and values which are common to the different ethnic communities of Singapore and which also distinguish them from society in the west. The key section of the Paper is devoted to a discussion of the relationship between the individual and society. Disputing the proposition that values are universal and common to all mankind, it states that there is a major difference between Asian and Western values in the balance each strikes between the individual and the community; Asian societies emphasise the interests of the community, while western societies stress the rights of the individual. The Singapore society has always weighted group interests more heavily than individual ones. "This balance has strengthened social cohesion, and enabled Singaporeans to pull together to surmount difficult challenges collectively, more successfully than other societies. An emphasis on the community has been a key survival value for Singapore."

The core values of Asian society are identified as placing society above self, upholding the family as the building block of society, and resolving major issues through consensus instead of contention. There is a strong element of Confucianism in this elaboration, although the government denies that the values it propagates are purely Confucian. It however, picks up an element of Confucian teaching as particularly relevant to Singapore. "The concept of government by honourable men (*iunzi*), who have a duty to do right for the people, and who have the trust and respect of the population, fits us better than the Western idea that a government should be given as limited powers as possible, and should always be treated with suspicion unless proven otherwise."

The supremacy of political authorities is emphasised by the first of the Shared Values, "Nation before Community". Another aspect of Asian values, implicit though not explicit in the Paper, is the importance of duty as a counterpoint to right. The cohesion of society as well as the fulfillment of the individual is secured through a chain and hierarchy of duties.

The individual does not disappear altogether as a bearer of rights in the Singapore Paper. However, characteristically the concern with the individual is expressed more in terms of the obligations of the community to look after its less advantaged members. (In Singapore there is a twist to this, in that the 'community' in question is the ethnic community of the individual, not the 'state' to avoid the dependent mentality and severe social problems of a welfare state as experienced in many developed states, laying the foundations of a kind of community corporatism in the wake of declining popularity of the ruling party, showing how much these questions are viewed in that country from the perspectives of governance and management.)

Cultural "embeddedness" is not the only justification for this view of the relationship between the individual and the community and the interposition of the family. It is also said to be rooted in more pragmatic considerations. The White Paper hints at this, but it has been developed elsewhere. In at least Southeast Asia, there is a strongly held view that an authoritarian political system is the secret of its economic success (a point I have already mentioned earlier), and the frequent Singaporean mocking of the democratic efforts of the Philippines (with a rather inefficient economy) is advanced as proof of it (forgetting that under the authoritarianism of Marcos that economy fared little better). But there is also the belief that it is not the individual but the family (tied into a network of clan associations and relationships) which has been at the forefront of the phenomenal economic success of the region. It appears to be the view of a significant number of people (primarily but not only among the business community as is well evidenced in the debates in Hong Kong) that this combination of authoritarian rule and family and kinship networks lies at the root of economic success. This model is seen as threatened by democracy and human rights (in a neat reversal of western perceptions of the positive link between the market and human rights). Hence democracy and human rights are not high on many people's agenda.

Before I turn to other Asian voices, I offer a brief critique of my own of some aspects of the official perspectives I have outlined above (although, as I discuss later, these views are not entirely devoid of merit). The "communitarian" argument suffers from at least two weaknesses. First, it overstates the "individualism" of western society and traditions of thought. Even within western liberalism, there are strands of analysis which assert claims of the community (for example Rousseau); and most western human rights instruments allow limitations on and derogations from human rights in the public interest, or for reasons of state. Western courts regularly engage in the task of balancing the respective interests of the individual and the community. Furthermore, liberalism does not exhaust western political thought or practice. There is social democracy, which emphasises collective and economic rights, and Marxism, which elevates the community to a high moral order, is also reflective of an important school of western thought. There is much celebration in western political thought of "civil society".

Secondly, Asian governments (notwithstanding the attempt in the Singapore Paper to distinguish the "nation" and the community) fall into the easy but wrong assumption that they or the state are the "community." (A similar conflation occurs in the African Charter of Human and Peoples' Rights). Nothing can be more destructive of the community than this conflation. The community and state are different institutions, and to some extent in a contrary juxtaposition. It is the tension between them which has underpinned human rights. In the name of the community, most Asian governments have stifled social and political initiatives of private groups. Most of them have draconian legislation like the British colonially inspired Societies Act which gives the government pervasive control over civil society. Similarly rights to assemble and march peacefully have been mortgaged to the government. Governments have destroyed many communities in the name of development or state stability, and the consistent refusal of most of them to recognise that there are indigenous peoples among their population (who have a right to preserve their traditional culture, economy and beliefs) is but one demonstration of their lack of commitment to the real community. The vitality of the community comes from the exercise of the rights to organise, meet, debate and protest, dismissed as "liberal" rights by these governments. It is ironic that the "community" is much more lively and significant in the supposedly individualistically oriented western states than in Asian states which are in the custody of governments which pay lip service to the primacy of the community (even to the extent, as in Singapore, of defining values for the community!). (Nor is the tight regulation of society as in Singapore and Malaysia particularly Confucian.)

Another attack on the community comes from the economic policies of the governments. As I have mentioned, for the most part these are market policies. Although Asian capitalism appears to rely on the family and clan associations, there is little doubt that it weakens the community and its cohesion. The organising matrix, seeking new resources, has been particularly disruptive of communities which have managed to preserve intact a great deal of their culture and organisation during the colonial and post-colonial periods. Market policies have relied greatly on multi-national capital and corporations, which have brought new values and tastes, and are increasingly integrating their economies and elites into a global economy and culture. Indeed it is these very considerations which prompted the Singapore White Paper, but the contradictions of official policies largely escaped its authors. It totally ignored the impact, indeed the onslaught, of modern technologies on traditional communities.

A final point is the contradiction between claims of a consensus and harmonious society and the extensive arming of the state apparatus. The pervasive use of draconian legislation like administrative detention, disestablishment of societies, press censorship, sedition, etc., belies claims to respect alternative views, promote a dialogue, and seek consensus. The contemporary state intolerance of opposition is inconsistent with traditional communal values and processes. I fear that the contemporary state processes in Asia are worse than the much derided adversarial processes of the west, which at least ensure that all parties get a fair hearing.

Non-official voices are many. For reasons of space, I concentrate on the views of the non-governmental organisations (NGOs). But there are other voices that must be taken into account. The views on human rights of the most oppressed are not articulated, or when articulated, are not heard. They are the worst victims of the denial of human rights, and in desperation they turn to violence or other dramatic challenges to authority. An important and articulate group are intellectuals who are alienated from the state, and for the most part are not apologists for the regime. Intellectuals respond to and engage in international debates; and like the NGOs they form networks with their counterparts in other parts of the world.

Like the NGOs they have a commitment to human rights and democracy (even in China there is a growing and vibrant academic community with a keen interest in human rights and constitutionalism). They are less ready to accept western conceptions in totality, and attempt to relate questions of human rights to specific national conditions.

An authoritative statement of the position of Asian NGOs was issued on 17 March, 1993 on the occasion of the Asian intergovernmental conference on human rights preceding the Vienna World Conference. It endorsed its commitment to the view that human rights are universal, and are equally rooted in different cultures. While it supported cultural pluralism, it condemned those cultural practices which derogate from universally accepted human rights. Since in its view human rights are of universal concern and universal value, it does not regard the advocacy of human rights as an encroachment upon national sovereignty. Indeed it recommends international co-operation and solidarity for the promotion of human rights, as a refutation of claims of national sovereignty over human rights issues. The NGO signatories of the statement support the principle of the indivisibility and interdependence of human rights.

If in these perspectives the views of the NGOs are at variance with those of governments, there is some common ground on other points. The NGOs attribute the poor state of human rights to the international economic order, whose reform through structural changes as well as the adoption of a Convention on the Right to Development, they urge. Unlike the governments, they see a much closer connection with domestic oppression and international exploitation, in the collaboration of local economic and political elites with multinational corporations and aid agencies. Unlike the governments, they are critical of the consequences of the market system. They share with governments the desire to establish a broad framework for the analysis of human rights, but their framework (unlike that of governments which is informed by a statist view of development) is suffused with notions of social justice, eradication of poverty through equitable distribution of resources and the empowerment of people, especially of women and other disadvantaged communities.

The NGOs also part company with governments in their assessment of the state of human rights, which they find marked by massive and terrible violations of these rights and pervasive lawlessness on the part of state authorities. They deplore the militarisation of their governments and societies which is a primary cause of these violations. Their prescription for the ills of their countries is through going democracy and an unambiguous recognition and enforcement of human rights.

It is clear that it is no longer possible for Asian governments, NGOs or scholars to ignore the international discourse of human rights. Nor have they chosen to do so. Even China has engaged vigorously in this discourse, refusing to accept a purely defensive position even in the face of criticisms about the massacre in Tiananmen Square, arbitrary detention, extensive use of capital punishment, and prison labour. It has instead opted to establish the legitimacy of a distinctive approach to human rights. Other countries have also tried to establish a distinctive Asian approach. This is surely a proper position for the context of human rights is delineated by the social and economic conditions of the place and the time. So-called universal human rights of the west have evolved over a long period of European history, responding to the changing configurations of power and the tasks of each epoch of history.

Nor is the process complete. Social welfare rights were acknowledged only in this century, and the appalling degradation of the environment has now set the stage for a new conception of rights and responsibilities, in which the community will have to be accorded a key position as a bearer of rights as well as duties. There is no reason why contemporary concerns and fads in the west should define the parameters of international discourse in and aspirations of human rights.

If human rights have to be located in their social and economic contexts, what are the appropriate features that constitute the context for them in Asia? We should first perhaps abandon the search for a set of features that explain the whole Asian context, since there is such a marked diversity among Asian countries. There appears to be no common context between the small, urbanised, economically prosperous Singapore and the vast, impoverished, largely rural India. I have already indicated that the attempt to establish a common context through the invocation of a common and distinctive culture is spurious. I do not argue that culture is irrelevant, but that the implications drawn from it by governments are disingenuous.

If one may generalise (despite my preceding remarks), the following specifics of the Asian situation stand out. The first point is that the function of human rights (and discourse on them) in Asia is quite different from that in the west. Human rights in the west have responded to the configurations of power and economic relationships as they have evolved over a long period. They are consequently consistent with the patterns and structures of authority, and people's aspirations as well as expectations. There are no serious competing paradigms of political organisation. The role of human rights is to fine tune the administrative and judicial system and fortify rights and freedoms that are largely uncontroversial. In Asia, on the other hand, human rights have a transformative potential. They are a constant challenge to vested interests and authority in societies riven by enormous disparities of wealth and power, with traditions of authoritarianism and the helplessness of disadvantaged communities, of militarisation and the conjunction of corrupt politicians and predatory domestic and international capital. Human rights are therefore a terrain for struggle for power and the conceptions of good society. It is for this precise reason that Asian governments have engaged in the debate with the west which I outline above; the real audience is, of course, their own people.

The second point is that there are massive violations of human rights in Asia; of women and children, of lower castes and otherwise disadvantaged communities, of ethnic minorities, of workers. Violations range over whole conspectus of human rights; civil and political rights, as well as cultural, social and economic; there are mass killings and widespread disappearances; torture; wide displacements of communities from their traditional abode; arbitrary detentions and extensive censorship of thought and expression. The state is a major culprit, brutalising whole populations, but massive violations also take place in and through civil society, sometimes with the connivance of the state, and frequently reflecting feudalistic and patriarchal dimensions of culture. Social conflicts, particularly those stemming from ethnic differences, have politicised and militarised civil society in many states.

The third point is that despite these violations, human rights consciousness is low. Explanations for this paradox may lie in the weight of oppression over centuries, a fatalistic acceptance of one's miseries, obstacles placed in the way of those who would seek to make explicit to the downtrodden the causes of their oppression. It certainly lies in the ethnic divisions of societies; ethnic consciousness can dull human rights consciousness, for the oppression of others is frequently viewed as their just rewards. A major challenge to human rights workers is undoubtedly this ethnic consciousness which compels a perception of outsiders as less than human. Another cause of low human rights consciousness may be widespread poverty. Poverty is a great cause of denial of human rights. The international system refuses to accept this reality—for largely political reasons. It refuses to acknowledge that poverty destroys human dignity; and without human dignity there can be no human rights; or indeed the capacity to challenge the system of oppression.

Thus economic development is undoubtedly important. But not just any kind of economic development. Economic growth must be accompanied by a wide measure of egalitarianism, the protection of the rights of workers, particularly migrant workers, and democratic practices at work places. Nor must economic growth be undertaken at the expense of land, customs and autonomy of long settled communities. Unless these and other community concerns are safeguarded in the process of economic growth, development is perverse and add to the violations of human rights and dignity.

A further point about human rights in Asia is that challenges to their violations are not individual based but group or class based. This is particularly the case in multi-ethnic states. The protection of human rights is therefore pursued through the group. This fact, and that the state is a major violator of human rights, suggests strategies that are different from the traditional western approaches, which are legalistic and court centred. Asian strategies cannot realistically be court centred, however favourably the judiciaries may be disposed towards human rights (and for the most part they are not). Human rights conscientisation and mobilisation based on connections between them and their oppression are a fundamental starting point (connections which neither local governments or the west are anxious should be made).

Nor must the terrain of struggle be purely domestic. Despite the resistance of governments, the realisation of human rights in each country is intimately tied to wider global forces. Even today many governments in the third world are surrogates for external economic and political interest, and it is necessary to take the battle to the homelands of these interest, just as it is necessary to recruit foreign interests to put pressure on domestic governments which deny their people the right to participate in decisions affecting their own destiny. Fruitful Asian perspectives on human rights must therefore transcend obfuscation of culturalism, locate human rights in the contingencies of their political economy, and urge struggle domestically as well as globally since no economies now are purely national.

4

Human Rights in Developing Countries: A Perspective

*Jawahar L. Kaul**

The subject of human rights[1] is of seminal interest to humankind. Much has been written on the subject and it shall not cease to be discussed. The idea of human rights is a major theme in the development of the modern world. The subject has been discussed more or less on a universalistic basis keeping into view the developments taking place in the West. Of course these developments have in any case formed a part of every thinking on human rights. However, what should essentially be stressed is the fact that the stream of thought conditioning the evolution of human rights in a particular country is reflective of the particular socio-economic conditions operative at the relevant time. This thought may in no case correspond to the one existing in other countries. For comparisons are dubious and may result in either romanticism or at worst distortions.

The subject of human rights in developing countries should then be approached keeping in view their special socio-economic circumstances. This will help one to substantiate the theory and practice guiding the protection of human rights in developing countries. One must appreciate that these countries

* Reader, Department of Law, Maharshi Dayanand University, Rohtak-124 001

share some common characteristics, which help to make generalised comments on human rights in these countries. The present paper purports to analyse the subject of human rights in developing countries. Section II traces the evolution of human rights. Section III shows how protection of human rights has been universalised. Section IV analyses the human rights in developing countries. Section V is the concluding one giving an account of policy and legal considerations.

Evolution of Human Rights

A study down the memory lane of human rights reveals two parallel trends having evolved over the years, particularly in the European context. The first and foremost is the liberalist tradition advocated by philosophers like Locke and Bentham.[2] Both of them advocated their philosophies as a reaction to the existing socio-political conditions, in which the individual human beings were subjected to extreme conditions of supression by the state whoever it was. They damned their predecessors who advocated extreme powers for the State, which was most often than not utilized against the individuals. Both Bentham and Locke advocated liberty and freedom for individuals. This school of thought was much more popularly reflected in American and French Revolutions. Indeed these revolutions were largely successful in highlighting and protecting liberty and freedom of individuals. This individualistic approach to human rights resulted in a hierarchy of civil and political rights for individuals which has carried the day.[3]

Another significant consideration towards sustenance of individualistic approach to human rights in the West was the evolution of the economic system based on free enterprise and free competition. The legal system advocated in this connection was the one to provide a body of predictable and ascertainable standards of behaviour allowing each economic factor to maintain a set of relatively safe expectations as to the conduct of other social factors. Such a legal system was necessary being a convenient device for permitting economic activities and consolidating and protecting the fruits of such action.[4]

A further consideration is that a large section of law in the West was the fruit of political struggles between contending groups. The first 'Bill of Rights' resulted from a continued bitterness between the kings and his barons for the former's arbitrary behaviour. The continued struggle between these competing forces resulted into constitutions, placing restraints on the powers of aristocracy and its feudal privileges. The evolution of human rights in such a circumstance became quite essential for social progress and equilibrium.[5]

Thirdly with the gradual secularisation of religion, mainly Christianity, there occurred a gradual erosion of the metaphysical components of religious tenets and their absorption into daily life as general moral precepts. Resting on religious or ethical principles, legal rules acquired an extra-legal dimensions which strongly enhanced their value.[6]

Such a kind of theory was instrumental in evolution of a legal system and law which showed its commitment to uphold the dictates of individual rights based on the economic necessities of a *leisezz-faire* system. Indeed the States showed a greater resilience towards human enhancement by minimalist interventions in the domain of individual rights. As J.R. Strayer puts it,

"the fact that there was a strong emphasis on law at the very beginning of West European States was to have a profound influence on their future development. The State was based on law and existed to enforce the law. The ruler was bound morally (and often politically) by law. In no other political system was law so important, in no other society were lawyers to play such an important role. European states did not attain their ideal of being primarily law states, but that this was their ideal was an important factor in gaining the loyalty and support of their subjects."[7]

In contradiction to the above school, Marxian concept about human rights puts emphasis on group (social) rights rather than individual rights. Dominated by the writings of Marx and the Fabian club particularly Laski, the argument runs that full realisation of an individual's self is possible only within the context of a society. In as much as an individual should be concerned with his development, the society has an interest in facilitating the advancement of individuals. Because of the overwhelming responsibility of the state towards its subject, it is but natural that economic and social rights should have predominance over the individual ones. As Pollis puts it,

"Such a conceptualisation of the nature of society precludes the existence of individual rights rooted in the state of nature which are prior to the state. Only legal rights exist, which are granted by the state and whose exercise is contingent on the fulfillment of obligations to society and to the state. Furthermore, since capitalism is exploitative, and individual rights, is inclusive of right to property, are bourgeoisie rights, social rights which satisfy the basic needs of survival and security, constitute the substance of human rights."[8] This school of thought has been over the years carried to its logical ends by the States pursuing welfare economics in which State carried on its shoulders the vast responsibilities of pursuing the goals of social development. Even if they had written constitutions, still they were biased towards the social rights. The legal system and the law thus enacted has had to be in the light of the economic/social philosophy writ large in these societies.[9]

In addition to above a brief account of the Modern rights theory must also be given. These theories have been developed either as a reaction to the earlier ones or as the refinements to the existing jurisprudence on human rights. Among them must be mentioned Rawls, Radbruch, Robert Nozik, Mcdougal and Dworkin. These theorists display a number of common characteristics. First, they, are eclectic, benefiting from each other's insights so that it is imprecise to characterise their theories as simply utilitarian, natural rights, intuitive, behavioural, etc. Secondly modern theorists recognise and try to address, using various approaches, the tension between liberty and equality. Some do so through theories of resolution which try to show that these goals are reconcilable and achievable within the same social order. Some find the tension irreconcilable and seek to resolve the dilemma by ranking goals hierarchically. Others evolve refining theories which accept a relationship between liberty and equality characterised by shifting readjustments. Thirdly, most theorists acknowledge the need to construct an entire system of rights.[10]

Universalisation of Human Rights

After the second world war, many changes occurred on the world scenario. Amongst them are the emergence of a large number of countries as independent nations, which were colonial domains of the West. Secondly the emergence on the world scene of a large number of international organisations including primarily the United Nations and other allied organisations. Although the basic objective of the U.N. was to pursue the models of activities maintaining international peace and security. But over the years it undertook diverse activities in fulfillment of the objectives of an interdependent world. United Nations and its allied organisations have shown a remarkable interest in pursuing, though in a modest way the goal of protection of human rights at universal levels.[11]

The worst kind of brutalisation of human rights in the first and second world war was the main motivating factor in pursuing the goals of protection of human rights in the post war period. Although the relationship between the individual and the states was deemed to be the sole domain of the state, yet the international protection of individuals was either in the form of individual treaties as happened after Ist world war or through humanitarian intervention.[12] Nevertheless the main plank of allied powers included wider questions involving guarantee of human rights. It was, therefore, deemed necessary that protection of human rights became one of the purposes of UN (Art. 1) and the Charter has imposed obligations upon the member states to this end. (Art. 55–65)

Art. 55 and 56 of the Charter imposes upon the United Nations and its member legal obligation to "promote" respect for and "observance" of human rights. The action taken by UN in this pursuit has taken several forms. A large number of declarations and treaties have been adopted mostly as a result of the work of UN Commission on Human Rights. The extent to which such declarations and treaties have had or will have impact upon general protection of human rights in national countries is less clear. The United Nations acting mainly through the General Assembly and the Security Council, has sometimes acted to protect human rights by means other than the adoption of treaties and other documents.[13]

In pursuance of the implementation of the principle of 'respect for human rights and fundamental freedoms', the Human Rights Commission considered a preliminary draft of an international Bill of Rights prepared by a drafting committee in 1947. Because of difference of opinions as to its contents, the commission decided to draw up simultaneously a draft declaration, a draft convention and implementation. In the process Universal Declaration of Human Rights (1948), Covenant on Civil and Political Rights (1966) and Covenant on Economic, Social and Cultural Rights (1967) were adopted. They together would form what is referred as 'International Bill of Human Rights.'[14]

The international standards of human rights as delineated in the above documents have not been incorporated by many countries, thus restricting the universal application of human rights. However, with growing interdependence, the States particularly the developing ones would have to cater to these international standards.[15]

Human Rights in Developing Countries

The diverse socio-cultural matrix of developing countries does not permit them to approach the promotion and protection of human rights in a thorough and unified way. Nor can they be guided by the Western style ideology and thinking on protection of human rights. This is because of three reasons. The first being that incorporation of Western theories of human rights shall be a continuation of the Colonial heritage. Secondly these countries being in a flux, the human rights as determined and evolved by West shall be either inappropriate or too rigid for these countries to adopt changing priorities. Thirdly, the politics of human rights practised by the ruling elites in these countries. They are united in their notion of governance and expediency of their rules which is often taken as a justification for derogation and violation of human rights. It is indeed these views which are highly publicised at national and international levels.[16]

As a matter of fact developing countries show a remarkable difference of cultures and socio-economic realities *inter-se* and *intra-se*. They also represent world's major religions and political ideologies like socialism, democracy or feudalism. At the same time they are faced with tremendous problems of state building, economic reconstruction and recurrent regional, sub-regional and ethnic conflicts. These conflicts have grown to the extent so much so that even the foundation of the States as such is threatened. There remains a sharp disagreement on the exact scope and nature of basic human rights, on the treatment of substantive human rights, economic issues and the methodology of protection of these human rights in these countries. More often than not the conflict between liberty, equality and other values is easily discernible and is prone to many distortions, sometimes even hostility. This is again because of three reasons.[17] Firstly the primary aim is to strengthen the authority of the State and do not favour centrifugal tendencies which could benefit full recognition of the rights and freedoms of individuals. Secondly after decolonisation, for purposes of economic development a strong government was needed for reconstruction and development. The restriction on certain rights and liberties seemed inevitable. The economic and social rights had to be promoted at the expense of civil and political rights. Thirdly because of peculiar social structures in these countries the governments had to exercise undisputed powers. The freedom-authority dialectic operative in Western European tradition is alien to the cultures operating in developing countries.

However, over the years three distinct legal systems have evolved in the group of developing countries.[18] The first may be described as an absolutely autocratic state, which does not show any regard towards the promotion and protection of human rights. Being based on the traditions of ruler-ruled relationship, the ruler is deemed to be above law. In the process of amalgamation and furtherance of his rule, nothing stops him even if it would mean brutalisation of certain minimum rights. This is particularly true in some Asian and African countries. The second category comprises of those countries with progressive regimes 'aiming at total or near total mobilisation for rapid economic and social transformation and with *de jure* or *de facto* one party rule.' In these countries one should find greater emphasis on social and economic transformation at such a pace that civil and political rights are 'qualified' by the exigencies of social and economic development. These countries have developed a highly mobilised social and political system geared to rapid economic and social system. It is true that these countries have made immense strides in economic and social transformation. But over the years these countries have faced graver problems in terms of the challenge to the one party authority from groups and sub-groups, representing various shades of opinion and ideologies thus forcing the governments for tougher measures against these groups, sometimes even nationalities at the expense of human rights. Thus human right violations have occurred because of threat to the social cohesion and economic progress.[19] The third group of countries constitute the countries having democratic rules and institutions with two or multi party systems including India. Possessed with written constitutions and instruments of democracies, and a judiciary these countries are purportedly adherents to the theory of promotion and protection of human rights as enshrined in their constitutions. Of course, the written constitutions guarantee individual liberty, equality and freedom, yet the working of these countries have not shown praise-worthy results. Of course this is because of the fact that reality of socioeconomic backwardness of huge populace is in their minds which puts a premium on the protection of human rights. Being plurastic and having deeper social stratification of classes, there are no ideal solutions to the problem of promotion and protection of human rights. Being also faced with demands of large groups and subgroups, a homogeneous approach to protection of human rights is neither tried nor can perhaps be achieved. Consequently very often in meeting such demands it is either the basic law which is violated or leads to other unmanageable problems.[20]

Some Legal and Policy Considerations

On any discourse on human rights, it is too often hurrying to consecrate a common standard of mankind for human rights. Althroughout the world at all stages of history there seems to have been difficulties for evolving a concrete and particular theory and model for human rights. This is true for the developed West and shall be true for developing countries. Of course the course of events in developed West has been too favourable for promotion and protection of human rights.[21] Nonetheless the developing countries are in chaos concerning the protection and implementation of human rights. Notwithstanding the core concern shown by international declarations and principles upon protection of human rights, it is difficult if not impossible, to arrive at a concept of human rights in developing countries, which is unanimously acceptable, nor is there a common framework of action. It often happens that at any international action the developing countries are quick either to enter reservations or even if accepted are silently violating it. The disrespect shown to some of the international covenants on human rights is a growing recognition of the overestimation of the role of State and a positive threat to human rights.[22]

Faced with immense under-development combined with long periods of colonial exploitation, poverty and illiteracy the human rights are illusory to a large populace of these countries. In the process of pursuing socio-economic goals, the developing countries show a second rate respect to civil and political rights. Of course it is true that present international economic system is largely responsible for under-developed conditions of poorer nations.[23] In this connection it is instructive to refer to the efforts undertaken by developing countries and UNCTAD to modify and change the conditions of international economic relations to the advantage of developing countries. It was presumed that equity in international relations could also percolate in the economies of developing countries. However, contrary to the expectations of developing countries, not only did the call for New International Order fail, but over the years new forms of economic dependency has been thrust upon developing countries by IMF, World Bank Sponsored structural adjustment programmes. These programmes have forced developing countries to change their economic policies. These policies have deeper implications for developing countries particularly for their marginalised sections of populations. The net result of it is that potential for upliftment of human rights should be in danger. Needless to say that an unjust international order would be reflected in these States.[24]

The tendencies of dehumanising the human rights is large in developing countries. Whether in economic reorganisation schemes/programmes or in a bourgeoise administrative and institutional set up, the misery of human rights has further been accentuated. The criminalisation of politics and the lack of accountability has become the order of the day. The brutalisation of the state power is reflected in the increase in number of state crimes, with little or slight comfort from judiciary in terms of payment of compensation. The elites are becoming powerful enough to obstruct the ordinary course of rule of law. Rule of law is confined only to academics. A situation of no return has reached in the politics of governance in developing countries. Apart from occasional outbursts from the judiciary, press, human rights activists, non governmental organisations, there is no meaningful attempt to formulate a clear cut methodology for protection of human rights. An overall rethinking in this context is not only desirable but necessary also.[25]

It should be reemphasised that the recognition of guarantee and effective protection of human rights of individuals and groups is of prime importance in maintaining the stability and cohesion in any society including developing countries. No economic or social progress can be reached at the cost of violation of human rights, whatever they are. The promulgation and protection of human rights have to be consistent with the patterns and structures of authority, and people's aspirations as well as expectations. The role of human rights is to tune the administrative and judicial system and fortify rights and freedoms.

In any country with low level of literacy and under-development, a massive input is required for removing them. Of course it is for the State to consider the required means and ways which should go a long way in reinforcing the importance of human rights. But along with it a massive effort is required to educate vast majority of people about the exact role of State and the incorporation of human rights in all models of human existence. This is an effort which has to be carried at all levels. This would help to lessen the overestimated role and authority of the State in developing countries.[26]

Secondly, if the human rights have to be successfully implemented in a developing country, a free and independent judiciary to protect the rights is necessary. In India e.g. the judiciary particularly the higher judiciary has served the cause of human rights. However, there should be every effort to maintain and uphold the Rule of law in all its aspects. Moreover, the peoples movement for successful and judicious working of the institutions of democracy has to be strengthened with more stress on the accountability of these institutions. That would indeed serve the cause of human rights in every society including the developing country.[27]

Thirdly, there is every justification for more and more protection to 'marginalised persons' in developing countries. Because over the years these 'marginalised persons' have been forced into an element of depravity, dehumanisation and brutalisation. If developing countries have to progress and prosper they cannot do so with an open disregard to the necessities of these people. The governments have to be conscious of the plight of these classes. Any economic rejuvenation plan must have an element of egalitarianism and protection of weaker sections at all levels. Because market can act as factor for allocation but cannot act as benefactor of the marginalised and deprived segments of populations of developing countries.[28]

Lastly, it must be added that any developing country has its own difficulty in arriving at a consolidated thinking on the promotion and protection of human rights. This is because of very special kind of considerations in which a country is in. However, these difficulties must not be advocated as justification for abrogation of human rights. On the contrary there should be an examination into them while building a course on human rights.[29]

REFERENCES

1. Human rights may be said to be rights that are inherent in people by virtue of being human beings, the rights that are absolutely essential for full and complete development of human personality. Generally two generation category of human rights are recognised namely civil and political rights, and economic, cultural and social rights. However, a third generation of human rights has also come up but has as yet not been fully

established. That includes right to development, right to common heritage of mankind etc. These rights have been forcefully advocated by developing countries. Secretary General Boutrous Gali has highlighted the importance of these in meeting the needs of international human development.
See *The Times of India*, Feb. 18, 1995.
See also Theodor Meron (ed.), *Human Rights in International Law* (1985).

2. See generally McDougal et al., *Human Rights and World Public Order* (1986).
3. See H. Gros Espiell, "Evolving Concept of Human Rights" in B.G. Ramacharan (ed.), *Human Rights: Thirty years after the Universal Declaration* (1979) 41–67.
4. See Antonio Cassese, *International Law in a Divided World* (1986), 287–315.
5. *Ibid.*
6. See generally J. Shestack, "The Jurisprudence of Human Rights" in Meron *supra* note 1, 69–101.
7. J.R. Strayer, "On the Madieval Origin of Modern State" (1970) 23–4.
8. Quoted in Shestack, *supra* note 6, 82.
9. *Ibid.*
10. *Id.*
11. See generally Moses Moskowitz, *International Concern with Human Rights*. (1976).
12. See generally Harris, *Cases and Material on International Law* (Third Edition).
13. *Id.*, Also *supra* note 4.
14. Besides these there are other conventions on Genocide Racial, Discrimination, Refugees, Rights of Women, Torture, Degrading Treatment etc. See *supra* note 12.
15. See generally A. Cassese. Human Rights in a Changing World (1992).
16. See Yash Ghai, *The Asian Perspective on Human Rights* (1992) Mimeo 1–10.
17. *Id.*
18. *Supra* note 2
19. *Id.*
20. See generally Tahir Mahmood, (ed.) *Pressing Issues Facing the Nation* (1992).
21. *Supra* note 4.
22. See T.O. Tripathi, "Human Rights and TADA" *Kanpur Law Journal* 8 (1992–93) 13–22.
23. Gros Espiell, *supra* note 3.
24. See generally J.L. Kaul, "Globalisation, Social Justice and New Economic Policies" in K.L. Bhatia (ed.). *Social Justice and Indian Constitution* (1994) 146–60.
25. Ghai *supra* note 16.
26. *Supra* note 4.
27. *Supra* note 16.
28. *Supra* note 24.
29. *Supra* note 20.

5

International Protection of Human Rights

*Geeta Madhavan**

The ravages of Second Word War caused great concern in humanity and resulted in the positive development of a new concept in international law. All over the world people demanded a change in the treatment accorded to their fellow human beings, particularly when the treatment falls far below the minimum standards of universal behaviour. Human rights had no existence in traditional international law. Oppenheim the leading authority on international law at the beginning of this century, held the opinion that the (rights of man) cannot enjoy any protection under international law because international law concerns itself exclusively with relations between States and cannot confer rights on individuals. Many governments still seek to shelter behind this view of international law and justify themselves by claiming national sovereignty. However, in recent times there has been tremendous development in the number and scope of international human rights instruments. Several judicial and non-judicial supervisory organs and procedures have also come into existence with the express intention of securing respect for human rights. Decision makers, media and the public at large have become involved in this issue.

* Advocate Madras High Court. Formerly Lecturer, Department of Legal Studies, University of Madras, Madras.

The concept of human rights has its origins in the Promulgations of Cyrus the Great almost 2000 years ago, and later in the liberal democratic tradition of Western Europe which is inspired by Greek Philosophy, Roman Law and Judae—Christian tradition. Formulation of this philosophy is found in the French Declaration of Rights of Man and the Citizen of 1789. This political philosophy was inherited by the colonists in North America. Thomas Jefferson asserted that Americans were a "free people claiming their rights as derived from the laws of nature and not as the gift of their Chief Magistrate" and enshrined this concept in the Declaration of Rights.

The Charter of United Nations contains a number of references to the promotion and protection of human rights. The Preamble itself reads:

> We the peoples of the United Nations, determined . . . to reaffirm faith in fundamental human rights, in the dignity and worth of the human person, in the equal rights of men and women and of nations large and small . . . have resolved to combine efforts to accomplish these aims.

The most important provisions are set out in Articles 55 and 56 of the Charter. Article 55 provides that the United Nations shall promote 'universal respect for, and observance of human rights and fundamental freedoms for all without distinction as to race, sex, language or religion.' Article 56 states 'all members pledge themselves to take joint and separate action in co-operation with the organisation for the achievement of the purposes set forth in Article 55.

On 12th February, 1946, the General Assembly of the United Nations approved the recommendation made by the Preparatory Commission and the Economic and Social Council acted on it four days later. The Commission of Human Rights was constituted with a nucleus of 9 members. In 1962, the membership was twenty one and in 1966, it increased to thirty two. By May 1990, fifty States of the 91 States which had ratified the International Covenant on Civil and Political Rights had also accepted the competence of the Human Rights Committee in respect of individual communications to the Committee. The Committee forms a significant part of the system of accountability in human rights, that is to say, the zone in which objective assessment overrides assertion and propaganda.

The first regular session of the Commission opened in January 1947, and its first task was the drafting of the International Bill of Rights. A drafting Committee of eight members was appointed: the representatives of Australia, Chile, China, France, Lebanon, the United Kingdom, the United States and the Soviet Union. The Universal Declaration was adopted by Resolution 217 (III) of the General Assembly. It was not intended to impose legal obligations on the States, rather to establish goals for States to work towards. Since 1948, the Universal Declaration has acquired a greatly reinforced status not only as 'a common standard of achievement for all peoples and all nations' but also as a statement of principles which all States should observe. Besides this, it has also inspired many State constitutions and led to regional human rights treaties in Europe, Africa and the America. The constant and widespread recognition of the Universal Declaration means that many of the principles have acquired the status of customary law. For eighteen years discussion, drafting and negotiations were carried on. The proposal of several States were considered including Australian suggestion for an International Court of Human Rights, Uruguay's proposal for the establishment of a United Nations High Commissioner for Human Rights and a French suggestion for an International Investigation Commission. India suggested that alleged violations should be brought to the notice of the Security Council which should investigate them and enforce redress. The United Kingdom and the United States proposed that Human Rights Committee should be set up only for inter-state disputes. The USSR opposed all suggestions on the ground that they would interfere with the internal affairs of States. Finally, the Commission decided in favour of establishment of a permanent Human Rights Committee to consider complaints of violations of human rights on an inter-state basis. Until 1945, how States treated its nationals was a question within its jurisdiction and competence in which no other State had a right to concern itself. That legal position has now changed and other States have legitimate interest in seeing that human rights are respected.

The Draft Covenants prepared by the Commission on Human Rights were received by the General Assembly's Third Committee and after they were revised, were finally approved unanimously by the General Assembly in December 1966. Individual Petitions or Communications to the Human Rights Committee was incorporated in a separate 'Optional Protocol' to the Covenant, applicable only to States which by a separate act had ratified the Protocol. By 1988, ninety one countries had ratified the covenant on Economic, Social and Cultural Rights, eighty seven, the Covenant on Civil and Political Rights and thirty nine, the Optional Protocol.

As of 27 July, 1990 fifty of the ninety two States which had ratified or acceded to the International Covenant on Civil and Political Rights have accepted the competence of the Human Rights Commission to deal with individual communications by ratifying or acceding to the Option Protocol. These States are Algeria, Argentina, Austria, Barbados, Bolivia, Cameroon, Canada, Central African Republic, Colombia, Congo, Costa Rica, Denmark, Dominican Republic, Ecuador, Equatorial Guinea, Finland, France, Gambia, Hungary, Iceland, Ireland, Italy, Jamaica, Libyan Arab Jamahiriya, Luxembourg, Madagascar, Mauritius, Netherlands, New Zealand, Nicaragua, Niger, Norway, Panama, Peru, Philippines, Portugal, Republic of Korea, Saint Vincent and the Grenadines, San Morino, Senegal, Somalia, Spain, Surinam, Sweden, Togo, Trinidad and Tobago, Uruguay, Venezuela, Zaire and Zambia. Among the countries of the East European block, Hungary is a member. A small number of African states are parties. As the United States has not ratified the International Covenant on Civil and Political Rights, it is precluded from ratifying the Option Protocol. The Option Protocol sought to remedy, the classic concept under international law that a citizen's interests are supposed to be protected by the State of which he is a national, and he has no *locus standi* before international tribunals or international organisations. In 1970, by Resolution 1503, the Economic and Social Council authorised the Commission to examine 'communications, together with replies of governments if any, which appear to reveal a consistent pattern of gross violation of human rights.' The Optional Protocol is now included separately in the list of United Nations treaties, and ratifications are published. The Optional Protocol provides that any State party to the Covenant which ratifies the Protocol thereby recognises the competence of the Committee to receive and consider communication for individuals subject to its jurisdiction, who claim to be victims of a violation by that State party of any of the rights set forth in the Covenant. Article 2 and 3 of the Protocol introduce the rule of exhaustion of domestic remedies and provide that communication shall be considered not admissible if they are anonymous, abusive or incompatible with the provisions of the Covenant. Article 5, Para 2 excludes communications which relate to a matter which is being examined under another procedure of international investigation or settlement.

In 1979, the Human Rights Committee made public its first 'decision' on private communication under the Protocol. The 'communication' was from an Uruguayan citizen alleging mistreatment of herself and 3 members of her family. The Committee brought this to the attention of the Uruguayan Government, which objected to its admissibility on the ground that domestic remedies had not been exhausted and the complaint had occurred before the Covenant entered into force for Uruguay. After 6 months when no satisfactory explanation was given by the Uruguayan Government, the Committee expressed the view that facts disclosed several violations of the Covenant including torture and detention and that the Government of Uruguay was obliged to "take immediate steps to ensure strict observance of the provisions of the Covenant and to provide effective remedies to the victims."[1] In the Cubas Simones case[2] a thirty seven year old Uruguayan woman complained that she was arrested without a warrant at her family's home, held incommunicado at an unknown place for three months, then charged before a military court with subversion and aiding a conspiracy to violate the law. She was tried in camera without being present. The Human Rights Committee found the communication admissible and decided that there had been violations of Article 10(1) (right to be treated with humanity), Article 14(1) (the right to fair and public hearing), Article 14(3)(B) (the right to adequate defence) and Article 14(3) (d) (the right to be tried in one's presence) of the civil and Political Covenant.

In the Conteris case,[3] the victim was a former Methodist pastor, journalist and university professor who was arrested by the security police of Uruguay for previous connections with the Tupamoros movement and held incommunicado for three months in various military establishments where he was subjected to severe forms of torture. After signing a confession he was sentenced by a military court to 15 years in prison. The communication was submitted by the victim's sister and declared admissible in 1984. Based on the evidence submitted and since no information was forthcoming from the Government, the Committee concluded that many Articles of the Civil & Political Covenant had been violated *viz.* Article 7 (Prohibition of torture), Article 9(1) prohibition of arbitrary arrest, Article 9(4) *habeas corpus* and Article 14(a) and 14(3).

In 1985, the Committee decided the Wight case[4] which involved Madagascar. A South African Pilot, enroute from Mauritius made an emergency landing in Madagascar. He was sentenced to 5 years' imprisonment for overflying the country without prior permission, he escaped and was recaptured and kept incommunicado and in solitary confinement for a period of three and a half months and then spent the remainder of his two years' sentence in prison. The Human Rights Committee decided on facts that Articles 7, 10 and 14 of the Covenant had been violated.

In 1982, a case involving Colombia was the Suarez de Guerrero case.[5] It concerned the application of a law providing members of the Colombian police force with a defence to certain criminal charges. The police had shot dead at point blank range, and mostly in the back, seven people who had arrived at a house suspected to be a kidnapper's hideout. Criminal proceedings were commenced against the police men but all were acquitted on the ground that law provided a defence where the act which was the subject of a criminal charge was committed in the course of operations to prevent kidnapping. The communication was by the wife of one of the victims. She alleged that Articles 6(1) (right to life) had been violated. The Committee while agreeing, pointed out that the emergency which according to the Colombian Government required special measures necessary, could not justify a derogation from the right to life.

A case which concerned the States obligation under Article 18(4) to have respect for the liberty of parents—to ensure the religious and moral education of their children in conformity with their own convictions, is the Hartikainen case.[6] The author of this communication was a school teacher in Finland who complained that children who did not receive formal religious instructions were required to enrol in a course on the history of religion and ethics, which was biased towards Christianity and violated the rights of parents under the Covenant. The Committee decided that the law requiring the alternative course was not in compatible with the covenant, provided 'such alterative course of instruction is given in a neutral and objective way and respects the convictions of parents and guardians who do not believe in any religion.' Noting that even the alternative course was not obligatory in all circumstances, and that the State was taking steps to deal with difficulties which had arisen over its implementation, the Committee decided that in all the circumstances there was nothing incompatible with Article 18(4).

Article 17(1) and discrimination on the ground of sex, contrary to Articles 2(1), 3 and 26 were alleged in the Aumeeruddy–Cziffra case,[7] brought by a number of Mauritian women married to foreigners. They complained that their husbands' rights to residency and citizenship were subject to review. Since the same was not applicable to foreign wives, they alleged violations of human rights. The Committee upheld the complaint and two years later in the light of this decision, the Mauritian Government amended the legislation removing sexual discrimination.

The Lovelace case[8] raised an issue under Article 27 of the Covenant concerning minorities. The Petitioner, a Canadian Indian woman married a non-Indian and lost her status under Canadian law. After her marriage ended, she returned to the Indian reserve where she was not accepted. Indian men who marry non-Indians, however, do not lose their status. The allegation was made that this violated the Covenant. The Human Rights Committee decided that the Covenant guarantees the members of a minority access to native culture and language, and the Canadian Government following the decision amended the legislation. However, leaders of the reserve opposed this on the ground that sex-based discrimination was necessary to maintain their social structure. This case, therefore, demonstrates how complex the issues are and how different Articles of the Covenant can come into direct conflict.

There are several United Nations instruments and procedures that cover different facets of the human rights issue. The area of human rights that they deal with are evident from their titles. They include the Convention on the Prevention and Punishment of the Crime of Genocide of 1948; the Supplementary Convention on the Abolition of Slavery and Slave Trade of 1956; three Conventions on Nationality and Statelessness, which deal with the Nationality of Married Women (1957), the Reduction of Statelessness (1961) and the Status of Stateless Persons (1954); the Convention on the Status of Refugees (1951) and its Protocol (1966); the Convention on the Political Rights of Women (1952); the Convention on the Non-applicability of Statutory Limitations to War, Crimes and Crimes against Humanity (1968) and the Conventions against Torture (1984). United Nations has been particularly concerned with discrimination and the concern is obvious from the 1965 International Convention on the Elimination of All Forms of Discrimination and the 1979 Convention on Elimination of All Forms of Discrimination Against Women, the International Convention on the Suppression and Punishment of the Crime of Apartheid of 1973 and the 1981 Declaration on the Elimination of All Forms of Intolerance and Discrimination based on Religion or Belief.

With the increase of membership in the United Nations by the entry of Afro-Asian Nations and the increase of membership of the Commission of Human Rights, with the intention of encouraging the new members particularly those agitated by the problems of racial discrimination, apartheid, colonisation and underdevelopment; the General Assembly in 1966 by a Resolution called the Economic and Social Council and the Commission of Human Rights to 'give urgent consideration to ways and means of improving the capacity of the United Nations to put a stop to violation of human rights wherever they might occur.' This resulted in 'The Resolution 1503 Procedure'—a procedure by which the commission would be permitted to examine 'communications, together with replies of Governments, if any, which appear to reveal a consistent pattern of gross violations of human rights. The aim of the procedure is to communicate to the Government the matter at hand and to make it realise that if there is no improvement the case will continue, whereas cooperation will be appreciated. The object of the procedure is to maintain political pressure and induce the Government to co-operate.

M.J. Bossuyt in "The Development of Special Procedure of the United Nations Commission of Human Rights", Human Rights Journal VI 1985 at pp 183–4 states:

> ". . . human rights friends overlook the point that there is no real solution to the problem at the end of the procedure. The succession of steps comprising the procedure is more influential than the actual step itself."

The Resolution 1503 procedure brings the abuse of human rights to the attention of international bodies and when the complaints of abuse of human rights which are taken up for consideration are numerous and serious, they are not likely to be ignored.

The Economic and Social Council by adopting Resolution 1235 in June 1967, allows a member State or group of States or the Sub-Commission on the Prevention of Discrimination and the Protection of Minorities, to initiate procedures. If a thorough study of the situation at hand is required, the Commission may appoint a working group or a Special Rapporteur to study and report. A resolution considering a situation may also be notified. In 1967, the Commission appointed the Ad Hoc Working Group of Experts to investigate and report on the torture and ill-treatment of prisoners and people arrested by the police in South Africa. This included Namibia, and until they became independent, the Portuguese Colonies of Angola, Mozambique and Guinea Bissau and Southern Rhodesia. Although the Ad Hoc Working Group of Experts were not allowed entry, by visiting neighbouring countries and hearing over 100 witnesses on the situation, the resolution and recommendations of these bodies were communicated to all organs of the United Nations concerned with the situation in South Africa and was given a lot of publicity. A Special Committee was created by the General Assembly in December, 1968 to investigate Israeli practice in the territories occupied by Israel after the War of 1967. Another Ad Hoc Working Group investigated the situation of human rights in Chile. Permission which was first granted was later cancelled by the Chilean Government but by collecting information by other methods, the Group submitted several reports to the General Assembly and the Human Rights Commission in which they pointed out the obvious violations of human rights in Chile. Several investigations were later taken up in Equatorial Guinea, Bolivia, El Salvador and Guatemala. Later investigations were carried on by Special Rapporteur in 1984 in Iran and Afghanistan.

In December 1975, The General Assembly adopted the Declaration on the Protection of All Inhuman or Degrading Treatment and Punishment and in 1984 the Convention against Torture and other cruel, Inhuman or Degrading Treatment or Punishment was adopted by the General Assembly. Collection of information on violation of human rights is the only mean of keeping human rights in constant international focus and pressurising the Governments to change their policies.

The sincerity of United Nations in acquiring respect for human rights has led to this tremendous development. However, it is an indisputable fact that human rights is the aim for which member States pledge to work and not a condition for membership to the UN. Such a condition would be indeed incongruous for an organisation with more than 150 members, half of which do not observe the rule of law and the fundamental principles of democracy.

A natural reaction to the rise of Nazism and Fascism regimes was that after their downfall there was a reaction all over Europe for the protection of human rights. The flagrant violation of human rights was not incidental under these two regimes but was in fact a deliberate policy and a method of ascendancy and consolidation of power. Therefore, the Consultative Assembly of Council of Europe in September, 1949 devised an organised system to ensure collective guarantee of human rights and a Convention was signed in Rome by the Foreign Ministers in November, 1950. The twenty one contracting parties were Austria, Belgium, Cyprus, Denmark,

France, Federal Republic of Germany, Iceland, Ireland, Italy, Liechtenstein, Luxembourg, Malta, the Netherlands, Norway, Portugal, Spain, Sweden, Switzerland, Turkey and the United Kingdom. In 1988, San Marino became the twenty second member. They established the European Commission of Human Rights and the European Court of Human Rights. Every year Protocols are passed, giving wider scope and adding further rights. A case may be referred to the Human Rights Court only if the respondent Government has accepted its jurisdiction either in general terms or on an ad hoc basis. Nearly all the Governments which have accepted the right of individual petition have also accepted the compulsory jurisdiction of the Court. In its consideration of the Lawless case[9] decided in 1961 which concerned the detention without trial in Ireland of a suspected members of the IRA under the Offences against the State Act, the Court held that the derogation was justified and there was no violation as the case involved emergency situation. Cases which resulted in the Federal Republic of Germany and Austria amending their law on detention before trial, were Wemhoff and Matznetter[10] and those of Neumester, Stogmuller and Ringeisen.[11] The Court decided on facts that there was no violation as regards Wemhoff and Matznetter but there was violation in the other cases and awarded Neumester his costs and Ringeiseon a substantial sum as compensation.

In the Golder case[12] the applicant serving a sentence of imprisonment in the UK prison wished to see a lawyer for a civil action and was refused permission. The Court found a violation of the right to a fair trial in a civil action as the applicant was refused permission. The Court found it a violation of the right to a fair trial in the Convention. As a result a change of prison rules was introduced to comply with the judgement.

The right to respect for private and family life were upheld by the decision of the Court in Klass case[13] and the Marckx case.[14] In the Klass case clandestine control of correspondence and private life had taken place and it was held by the Court not to be violative, in the interest of safeguarding national security and preventing crime. However, in Marckx case, the provision of Belgian law that put children born out of wedlock at a disadvantage regarding inheritance, the Court held that it was violative of the Convention. The Court in Marckx case did not adhere to the narrow principles of the Convention but went on to interpret it in a modern social context. In cases dealing with freedom of expression where the freedom of expression has been infringed or limited, the Court has often assessed individual rights against the background of general interest. The Court has applied this concept called the 'margin of appreciation' in many other areas.

The Conference on Security and Co-operation in Europe opened in Helsinki on 3 July, 1973 and ended with the signing of the Final Act on 1 August 1975. The Final Act of the Conference was a declaration of intentions. It set out political and moral obligations of the States and is concerned with their international relations and security. The Final Act which had the ratification of the East European States was an acceptance by them of their obligations in international law to respect human rights. This led to the development of political consciousness, and individuals looked to their governments for greater freedoms. For example, about 500 intellectuals and other in Czechoslovakia subscribed to a human rights manifesto called "Charter 77". Similar movements occurred in East Germany, Yugoslavia, Poland and Romania. Since 1985, there developed in the Soviet Union, too, a greater awareness of human rights. Other regional co-operation on human rights are the permanent Arab Commission on Human Rights and the African Charter on Human and People's Rights.

The Inter-American Court of Human Rights came into existence in 1979, but it did not receive its first contested case until 1986, and it issued its first ruling in 1988. Until 1988, no Court had held a country liable for the forced disappearance of one of its citizens. The case was concerning a student activist and a labour activist who had disappeared in Honduras. The ruling represented a tremendous doctrinal advance followed by a very practical step forward in that the Court awarded several hundred thousand dollars in damages to the widows and children of the two disappeared victims.

After the review of various instruments and procedures and organisations dealing with human rights, it will now be pertinent to examine the present state of human rights. The dramatic development of human rights in international law is apparent. The European Convention of 1950, the two Covenants of 1966, the American Convention of 1969 and the African Charter of 1981 are significant landmarks in the evolution of human rights.

The touchstone of legal process is not the number of new agreements but the ratification of human rights treaties. Human rights treaties are now rarely concluded without a form of supervisory machinery, thereby stressing the fact that implementation is an essential element in the growth of human rights law. The bodies that interpret and apply the substantive principles thereby convert the law into action.

Assessing the work done under the Optional Protocol and by the Human Rights Committee calls for consideration of several aspects. The Committee's 5 + 10 decisions on merits each year is an achievement. However, in comparison with the worldwide human rights abuse it seems insignificant. The Committee is set at a disadvantage by the fact that majority of the members of the United Nations have not accepted the Optional Protocol and the States which have not accepted the right to individual petition include areas of worst human rights abuse. Further, in cases involving flagrant violation of human rights the Governments concerned are not helpful, with the result that the Committee is faced with the problem of gathering evidence. The Committee is not an international court but a quasi-judicial body and its reasoned decisions constitute an important body of case-law dealing with fundamental issues of human rights and life.

The effects of decisions of the Human Rights Committee is that the Government which co-operates with the Committee at the stage of investigation is likely to take steps to amend the law or legislate taking into consideration the committee's decision as seen in the Lovelace case of Canada and the Hartikainen case of Finland. However, Governments involved in serious human rights violations obstruct investigation and after the decision of the Human Rights Committee do little in the way of compensation or rectifying the problem. The decision of the Human Rights Committee publicises the abuses and puts political pressure on the State to improve its record. Therefore, the Human Rights Committee has a significant role to play in dealing with the law of human rights. Although the U.N. Charter does not demand an observance of human rights from all its members and while standards are set there is no machinery to enforce it.

The UN Covenants and regional instruments define human rights. Human rights issues are totally political and when a Government subscribes to protection of human rights, it endorses certain political values and seeks to implement it. Therefore ratifying a human rights treaty amounts to a moral gesture asserting certain ideals. This is the reason that negotiation of a human rights treaty takes such political significance. Further, the human rights treaty makes the State accountable to an international body and has major political implications. Many States, therefore, hide behind the concepts of domestic jurisdiction and national sovereignty when faced with human rights issues. The laws and practices of a State come under international scrutiny and States are reluctant to submit themselves to scrutiny by independent bodies. This, too, is considered an invasion of privacy of the State. Highly controversial matters like violation of liberty in the form of control of freedom of speech and expression, control of immigration, detention of suspected terrorists are sensitive and controversial problems faced by States.

The role of theory in retention of human rights law is indispensable. Actions of Governments, Committees, Commission and Courts are shaped by theories held on human rights and therefore decide the development of the law. Action based on such law is its consequence. Theoretical assumption have practical influence on the development of human rights law.

In the 20th century the number of people killed by their own governments under authoritarian regimes is four times the number killed in all this century's wars combined. The years 1993 to 1995 have seen contrasting trends in human rights. The world witnessed the birth of multi-racial democracy in South Africa. In Haiti the brutal dictatorship was removed and President Jean Bertrand Aristide and his democratic government was restored. Creation of international institutions of accountability to bring war criminals from former Yugoslavia and Rwanda to justice has also been mooted. Individuals like Nelson Mandela, Lech Walesa and Vaclav

Havel who were victims of human rights abuse have become heads of states and the fight of Wei Jingsheng, Aung San Suu Kyi and Wole Soyinka have gathered international support.

Unfortunately, these years are also marked by severe setbacks like the horror and violence in Rwanda and the continued genocide in Bosnia. The Chinese government launched a brutal crackdown on dissent and the totalitarian dictatorships in Burma, North Korea, Iran, Iraq, Libya and Sudan boldly violate human rights. The encouraging fact is that the past five years have seen dramatic changes in the former Soviet Union, Eastern Europe, South Africa, Zambia, Cambodia, El Salvador, Chile and Mongolia. The movement for human rights as the 1993 United Nations World Conference on Human Rights in Vienna demonstrated, is a strong growing movement today. The appalling slaughter in Rwanda and "ethnic cleansing" in Yugoslavia has flung new problems in human rights on the world. The violation in countries like China, Yugoslavia, Burma, Korea, Rwanda and others has outlined sharply the need to develop rather urgently international institutions that will hold political leaders accountable to their nations and the international community as a whole, since such movements are motivated by persons seeking to gain political ends through heinous means. Creation of tribunals to deal with such matters removes the illusion that conflicts with ethnic dimensions are complex and impossible to solve. Moreover tribunals are necessary to deter future crimes. Institutions of accountability have in fact contributed to reconciliation and solving of problems in many countries. The Truth Commissions of Nicaragua, El Salvador and Haiti, the United Nations Verification Mission in Guatemala and the National Human Rights Commission established in India and Mexico show the earnestness of nations and the diverse way's in which human rights abusers are made accountable. Newly independent states of Kazakhstan, Kyrgyzstan, Tajikistan and Uzbekistan despite human rights abuse have held elections with various degrees of freedom and fairness.

Armed conflict throughout the world has generated human rights abuse. To prevent Chechenya's secession from Russia in December, 1994, Russian troops crossed into Chechenya and by massive aerial and artillery bombardment in civilian areas created major humanitarian and human rights crisis. The civil war in Angola has left 100,000 dead, mostly civilians and the guerilla violence in Colombia has one of the highest violent death rates in the world. Turkish Governments armed struggle against the Kurdistan Workers Party (PKK) and the arrest and trial of Turkish Parliamentarians and citizens expressing their views has led to widespread human rights abuse by the Turkish Government. Since 1992 Algeria is embroiled in its civil strife with armed Islamic group and human rights abuses abound on both sides. In Sudan, in the intensified civil war, government and insurgents are engaged in massacres and extra-judicial killings.

Systematic abuses of human rights has become a routine in China, Iraq, Iran, Burma, North Korea and Cuba. Nigeria's military regime crackdown on opposition has perpetuated all forms of torture, incommunicado, detention, suppression of ethnic and religious minorities, and discrimination against women.

The Governments of Singapore and of Egypt continue human rights violations. India, too, has come in for sharp criticism from the international community for the human rights abuses committed by the military and security forces in areas of unrest, particularly Kashmir. The UN's Special Rapporteur on Kashmir produced some carefully worded documents about the allegations expressing "serious concerns" and asking for an invitation to investigate them. The Indian Government, however, did appoint in October, 1993 a National Human Rights Commission, an independent body with a brief to investigate brutality but the Commission is not allowed to investigate allegation against the army and the para-military forces. In fact, human rights abuses have resulted in many countries because of the inability of civilian authorities to control armed forces and security services.

There are a few countries where situation has changed. In Argentina, the Senate rejected the promotion of two Navy Commanders because of their admitted role in torture during the years of military rule.

In Guatemala, the Congress held hearings on the killing of a student by security forces during the riots in November. In Sri Lanka, the Government has set up regional commissions to investigate allegation of disappearances.

The year 1994 saw an increased international focus on Women's Human Rights. The International Conference on Population and Development held in Cairo in September, 1994, the World Summit for Social Development in Copenhagen in March, 1995 and the Fourth World Conference on Women to be held in Beijing in September, 1995 draw attention to human rights abuses against women. In early 1995, the UN Human Rights Commission established a Special Rapporteur to examine its causes and consequences. Women in many countries are subjected to discriminatory restrictions of their fundamental freedom regarding voting, marriage, travel, property ownership and inheritance, custody of children, citizenship and court testimony. Women also face sex-based discrimination in access to education, employment, health care, financial services, etc.

Human Rights violation span the globe and the realisation of basic rights has to be an internationally coordinated movement. Non-Government human rights organisations hold the key to the future. They have a unique role to play as they develve in and reflect the unique features of their societies. Grass root groups have taken on new roles globally such as election monitoring, active negotiations in democratic transitions and accountability and reconciliation.

One of the human rights activist turned leader Vaclav Havel powerfully expressed "I am not an optimist because I am not sure that everything ends well. Nor am I a pessimist, because I am not sure everything ends badly. Instead, I am a realist who carries hope, and hope is the belief that freedom and justice have meaning . . . and that liberty is always worth the struggle," while summing up the struggle against the abuse of human rights and the need for establishment of the law of human rights globally.

REFERENCES

1. Report of the Human Rights Committee doc. A/34/40 1979.
2. Comm. No. R 17/70 of 3 May, 1980—Decision 1 April, 1982.
3. Comm. No. R 139/1983 Decision of 17 July, 1985.
4. Comm. No. 115/1982 Decision of 1 April, 1985.

5. Comm. No. R 11/45, Decision of 31 March, 1982.
6. Comm. No. R 9/40 Decision of 9 April, 1981.
7. Comm. No. R 9/35, Decision of 9 April, 1981.
8. Comm. No. R 6/24, Decision of 30 July, 1981.
9. Series A, Nos. 1, 2 and 3 (1960–61).
10. Series A, Nos. 7 (1968) and 10 (1969).
11. Series A, Nos. 8 (1968), 9 (1969) and 13 (1971).
12. Series A, No. 18 (1975).
13. Series A, No. 28 (1978).
14. Series A, No. 31 (1979).

OTHER READINGS

1. Theodor Meron, *Human Rights and Humanitarian Norms as Customary Law* (Clarendon Press, Oxford) 1989.
2. A.H. Robertson and J.G. Merrills, *Human Rights in the World* (Manchester University Press, Manchester) 1989.
3. Legal Perspectives: Documentation File No. 35, Legal Resources for Social Action.
4. Paula R. Newberg (ed) *The Politics of Human Rights* (New York University Press, New York) 1980.
5. Myres S. Mc Dougal, Harold D. Laswell and Lung–Chu Chen, *Human Rights and World Public Order* (Yale University Press) 1980.
6. Human Rights and Democracy in Asia, U.S. Department of State Dispatch July 18, 1994, Vol. 5, No. 29.
7. *The Economist*, February 4th 1995.
8. The Future of Human Rights: An interview with Douglass W. Carrel Jr.: Christian Century, April 13, 1994.
9. *American Political Science Review* Vol. 88, No. 4, December, 1994.
10. M.J. Bossuyt, "The Development of Special Procedure of the United Nations Commission on Human Rights", *Human Rights Law Journal* VI 1985.
11. Thomas B. Jabine and Richard P. Claude (ed.), *Human Rights and Statistics*, (University of Pennsylvania Press) 1992.

6

Islamic Law and Human Rights: A Historical Perspective

*Shahabuddin Ansari**
*K.P.S. Mahalwar***

Introduction

The problem of human rights has recently cropped up due to insurgent activities of secessionist groups and responses of security forces in many parts of the globe such as Kashmir, Sri Lanka, Bosnia, Palestine, Chechniya, Israel, Algeria, Libya and so on. Human beings are terrorising and blaming each other for violating human rights. State terrorism and individual terrorist activities are on rampant. Some people have shown scant respect to basic rights of man. Many people show apathy towards violation and infringement of human rights. Sometimes security forces have been blamed for committing atrocities against innocent citizens and the security forces justified their actions and held that they always retaliated to the brutal acts of secessionists' insurgents. But all are agreed on the point of the sanctity of human rights.

A section of mass media of the world is accusing Islam as a terrorist religion and its followers as intolerant killers show-

* Lecturer, Deptt. of Law, K.G.K. (PG1) College, Moradabad. U.P.
** Reader, Deptt. of Law Maharshi Dayanand University, Rohtak 124001.

ing scant respects to life and property of others. This stimulates a dispassionate researcher to make an impartial and objective study of the Islamic charter of human rights protecting Muslims and non-Muslims alike. In this compendium a humble attempt is being made to study the concept and meaning of human rights as contained in Islamic legal system.

Islamic Law is basically derived from Qur'an and Sunnat or precedents of the Prophet of Islam. The Qu'ran is the main instrument of legislating legal and moral rules. Whatever has been ordained in the Qur'an, muslims are duty-bound to implement it in letter and spirit. Qur'anic injunctions and edicts have been expounded, explained and interpreted by the precepts, practices and judgements of the prophet of Islam. Therefore, it is desirable to study Islamic tenets regarding human right. Rights without remedy are insignificant. It needs to evaluate the effectiveness of implementing agencies and response of judiciary in case of violation of Human rights.

Basic Rights and their Implementation

Here we propose to peruse some basic rights of man as enunciated in Qur'an and Sunnat more than one thousand and four hundred years ago, even much before the well acclaimed Magna Carta of Europe.

Human Dignity and Privacy

Man (using the term in generic sense) is the foundation of human society. All round development of human personality depends on respect to individual provided by the society. All democratic values are destined for the protection of human dignity.[1] Man should be treated as an end in himself. He should not be discriminated and lowered at the point of nadir. A bonded labour without rights, a coloured person persecuted inhumanly in apartheid society, persons suffering due to pollution, and persons suffering due to untouchability cannot be proclaimed to have humanly developed personality. To counter this inhuman concept Islam evolved a value-system which recognises the privacy of human beings as an entity and human dignity as the foundation of that system.[2] It is ordained:

"Certainly we have created man in the godliest fabric."[3]

Qur'an attaches a personality to human being of highest order i.e. *Ashref-ul Makhluqat* (superior among all creatures).

It is strictly prohibited to sarcast, defame or make a fun of fellow human beings. It is revealed:

> "O, ye who believe, let not some man
> amongst you laugh at others, nor defame
> nor be sarcastic to each other, nor speak
> ill of each other behind their backs."[4]

Thus, the practice of insulting each other, sarcasm, libel, defamation and back-biting, all are wholly prohibited in Islam. Privacy is also an attribute of human dignity. Qur'an seems very particular about maintaining the privacy of the individual. It is commanded by holy Qur'an:

> "O believers; enter not houses of others until you have asked for permission."[6]

And further it is propounded

"Spy not each other"[7]

Violation of this right is to be punished. Prophet of Islam went to the extent of saying that a man peeping unlawfully in another person's house could be lawfully rended blind.[8] The implication of this provision is that people be protected against spying, bugging, violating confidential conversations between others, censuring letters of others, maintaining secret files for spoiling and blackmailing others. It is specifically asked not to glance through what was being written for or by others.[9] Another implication of this injunction is that there is no room for intelligence agencies like ISI of Pakistan, RAW of India, CIA of America, K.G.B. of Russia and SAVAK of Raza Shah's Iran, whose functions are to mete out ruthless behaviour to individuals jeopardising the interests of their states and sovereigns. These organisations are also engaged in inciting terrorist activities in adversary countries.

Right to Equality and Equal Protection of Law

The equality of status and opportunity is universally recognised in Islamic legal framework. This principle is enforced by the body-politic every time in letter and spirit. The social divisions into tribes and nations are meant only for their recognition.[10] In his famous "Farewell Sermon" (*Khutba-e-Hajjatul Vida*) the prophet laid down the cardinal principle of social equality of human beings. He addressed the gathering at the occasion of Hajj and proclaimed:

"The Arab is not superior to Ajami or non-Arab, nor an Ajami to the Arab; neither white to the black nor the black to the white; except by the degree of righteousness and piety (*Taqwa*) that he displays in his practice with each other." The prophet specifically hit hard at pre-Islamic practice of discriminating between man and man on the basis of race, colour and financial status. Nobility of descent was totally discarded by him, as he ordained that nobody could claim any specific descent except from Adam—the father of mankind.[11] In Islamic social fabric righteous deeds are only mark of distinction and not birth, colour, caste, race or wealth.

In legal arena all persons are accorded equal protection of Law. No society can claim to be civilized one without practically implementing the rule of equality before law. The prophet is reported to have warned the people against discrimination on the ground of nobility in the matter of enforcement of the legal code. A woman belonging to a high and noble family was arrested in connection with a theft. The case was brought to the prophet and it was recommended by some advisers that she may be spared the punishment of the theft. The prophet replied that early nations were destroyed by God because they punished the common man for their offences and let their dignitaries went unpunished for their crimes.[12] The prophet declared that even if his own most beloved daughter Fatima committed theft he would award her the same punishment as was prescribed for an ordinary thief.[13] The successors of the prophet followed the suit and eliminated all discriminations between the rich and the poor, the white and the black, the ruler and the ruled. The second Caliph Hazrat Umar did not sanction any special position to a syrian feudal, Jabala

Ghassani, even at the cost of his apostasy. Rulers were not above the law in Islamic normative set up. On the occasion of the battle of Badar, the prophet was setting the rows of the soldiers. A soldier was hit by stick and complained of it to the prophet. The prophet immediately said, "I am very sorry, you can revenge by doing the same to me."[14]

During the Caliphate of Hazrat Umar, the son of the Governor of Egypt whipped an Egyptian. The Egyptian went to Madina and lodged his complaint with the Caliph. The Caliph immediately summoned the Governor and his son to Madina. They appeared before him. The Caliph asked the complainant to whip the son of the Governor in his presence. In Islamic body-politic the doctrine of rule of law is the norm equally applicable to the rulers, ruled, Muslims and non-Muslims. This is evidenced by two cases in which Caliph Umar directed the judge that he must not discriminate between him and an ordinary citizen arraigning with him, and Hazrat Ali placed himself before the judge to contest his case on equal footing with Christian against him.

It is a natural corollary of the doctrine of equality that no religious personality enjoys higher status than ordinary man. In Islam there is no priesthood and hence no priestly class. A black slave, Bilal, an African, who was freed, was the Muazzan (caller for prayer) in Masjid Nabavi of Madina. Even non-Muslims were accorded equal protection of laws. In respect of mundane affairs, Islam would never discriminate between Muslims and non-Muslims. The prophet of Islam assured non-Muslims to be complainants on their behalf on the day of judgement against every Muslim who violated the rights of those non-Muslims who were faithful to the state. It is reported that Hazrat Ali asked his bureaucrats not to harm the non-Muslims because "they have accepted our protection only because their lives may be like our lives and their property like our property."[15] In other words, in Islamic parlence the lives and properties of non-Muslims are as sacred as the lives and properties of the Muslims. In this way we see that the honour and property of non-Muslims is very well protected legally and judicially.

Right to Life, Personal Liberty and Security of a Person

Terrorists all over the world are killing innocent persons and the men of security forces in the name of religion, though the religion itself prohibits taking away the life of any one. With reference to Islamic religion human life is as sacred as the most sacrosanct aspects of faith itself. The Holy Qur'an holds:

> "Do not take away life that God has made sacred except when the law so demands."[16]

> The Holy Qur'an further proclaims:

> "If one slayeth another, unless it be a person guilty of manslaughter, or of spreading disorder in the land, shall be as though he had slain all mankind, but he who saveth a life shall be as though he had saved all mankind."[17]

> The Prophet of Islam directed the people:

> "(O people) your lives are wholly forbidden to one another until the day of judgement."[18]

> The Prophet further held:

> "The believer in God is he who is not a danger to the life and property of another."[19]

> Again the Prophet laid down:

> "Your lives, your property and your honour are as sacred as this day (the day of Hajj) is sacred."[20]

The cumulative effect of these principles is that a person is accorded full protection to his life. It is nobody's business to destroy any human life. Even state shall not take away the life of a person except when the law so requires or permits.

The pre-Islamic history of Arabia made it clear that female infanticide was the order of the day. They were killed by the parents themselves. Islam imposed a total ban on this inhuman practice and laid down that female children had the right to live and grow, in the same way as did the male infants.[21]

Islamic history showed that Islam had guaranteed to every individual personal liberty. Illegal detention, wrongful confinement, kidnapping and unlawful arrest were totally prohibited by Islamic law. The right of personal liberty was extended even to the strangers. They could challenge the illegal confinement of their kins. And that was an enforceable right. A tradition of the Prophet makes it clear. In the Prophet's court a person lodged a complaint about wrongful arrest of his neighbour. As he repeated his complaint the Prophet ordered that the detenu be released forthwith. It was because the police officer present in the court offered no explanation about the arrest. The legal principle deduced by this decision of the Prophet is that no one should be detained illegally and without the proof of guilt in an open court. The person should be given opportunity to defend himself against accusation. This legal norm was established by the Prophet himself in his famous decision which was pronounced before the conquest of Makka. One of his companions Haatib bin Abi Baltaa sent a letter to the rulers of Makka informing them about the proposed attack. Somehow the Prophet came to know about this treacherous act. He ordered Hazrat Ali and Hazrat Zubayr to quickly recover that letter and bring it to him. They recovered the letter and brought it to the Prophet. This was a clear case of treachery. It was a serious offence of informing the enemy about a secret of an army and that too at the time of war. This case was to be heard in camera. But the Prophet preferred hearing in open court before hundreds of people. He summoned Haatib and informed him about the charge framed against him and asked him to explain his position, with regard to his letter addressed to the leaders of Quraysh of Makka which had been intercepted on its way. Haatib admitted his crime and explained the circumstances in which he was tempted to write such letter.[22]

The Prophet trained his companions to uphold the basic principles of due process of law. The second Caliph Hazrat Umar laid down the constitutional norm to be observed by the officers of state, viz. "No one can be imprisoned except in pursuance of justice."[23]

The students of Islamic legal history are acquainted with the attitude and activities of the people of Kharji sect in the days of Hazrat Ali. They scolded the Caliph openly, and threatened him with murder. But whenever they were arrested for those offences, Caliph Ali set them free and directed his officers, "As long as they do not actually perpetrate offences against the state, the mere use of abusive language or the threat of use of force are not such offences for which they can be imprisoned."[24] Thus non-violent opposition, though vituperative, is not sufficient ground for imprisonment.

Freedom of Thought, Expression and Conscience

The treatment of other religions and tolerance towards them by Islam are based on fundamental commands of Qur'an and the practices of the Prophet. Islam is against compulsion in religion.

"Let there be no compulsion in religion."[25]

Again Qur'an enunciates:

"Say (O Prophet) O non-Muslims I don't worship them whom you do, Nor you do (want to) worship whom I do . . you adhere to your religion and for me is mine."[26]

The Prophet of Islam himself followed this principle throughout his mission.[27] At Taif when people stoned him he only said, "I can only persuade you to come to truth, if you do not want to hear, leave it". And his successors were not far behind in implementing his precedents. Hazrat Umar had a Christian house-boy, and he remained a Christian all his life. The Caliph did not exercise any undue influence on him for the sake of converting him to Islam. It was in his reign that a Governor in the Syrian region had to quit his post as the penalty for rebuking a non-Muslim on account of ridiculing the form of worship followed by him.[28]

Right to Justice

Below mentioned Qur'anic verses reveal the independent nature of judiciary which must not suffer with hatred, ill-will or prejudices of any kind:

"And when ye judge between persons, judge with justice".[29]

"Do not let your hatred of a people incite you to aggression."[30]

"And do not let ill will towards any folk incite you so that you swerve from dealing justly, be just that is nearest to heedfulness."[31]

These norms are to be followed by the state and its organs particularly its judicial organs. The rulers and judges must be just not only with ordinary human beings but with their opponents and enemies also. The prophet was very particular in protecting the right to justice in its widest possible terms as he proclaimed:

"It is better for a judge to err in acquittal than in conviction."[32]

Freedom of Association

Islam also sanctioned the right to freedom of association and formation of parties or organisations of different shades of opinion propagating virtues and righteousness and should never be used for spreading evil and mischief.

Freedom of Movement

The concept of nation-state, citizenship and domicile have been preferred by western political thinkers. In their names man's freedom of movement is curtailed. These have no place in Islamic socio-political doctrines. Even mosques are not out of reach of non-Muslims. The Prophet's mosque was open for Christians, Jews, Pagans and fire worshippers during his life time. Of course, the state can regulate the movements for safety and protection. In fact, the restrictions on the entry of non-Muslims into Kaaba in Makka and Masjid Nabavi at Madina, that are now in force, are of recent origin and are based on security reasons.

Right to Property and Earnings

Each individual enjoys the right to acquire, hold and dispose of and inherit the property. There is no distinction between man or woman in having property rights. It is an independent right. Therefore, there is no concept of son's share in father's property by birth, joint family property or matrimonial property. Similarly, each individual is entitled to his earnings. The Holy Qur'an lays down:

> "For the man what he has earned, for woman what she has."[34]

Islamic law do not club the earnings of husband, wife or father and son. Every one is entitled to amass the wealth and to utilize it independently.

Right to Work and Prohibition of Slavery

In Islamic politico-legal frame work the dignity of the labour and right to wages are fully protected. No one can be compelled to work for another against his wishes. Everybody must work at his own pleasure. Though there is a provision for alms giving in Islam, yet the Prophet disapproved begging and ordered to work. It is evident from his tradition that the Prophet did not give anything to a beggar, but prepared an axe with his own hand and gave it to the beggar and asked him to do work of cutting the wood for his livelihood. The Prophet is reported to have said:

> "There are three categories of people against whom I shall myself be a plaintiff on the day of judgement. Of these three, one is who hires a labour, take work out of him but denies him his wages."[35]

Again the Prophet issued the command:

> "Pay the wages of the labourer before his perspiration dries up."[35]

He forbade "the forcing of the labourer to enter on his work before setting his wages."[36]

The protection of the labourer and his right to wages is fully provided in Islamic jurisprudence. Similarly Islamic law is against enslaving of any person. It is a fact of history that slavery was an established institution when Islam emerged on the surface of Arabia. In its early days Islam tolerated this inhuman custom but ordered and encouraged to uproot it. The Prophet forbade his followers to enslave anyone and proclaimed to be plaintiff himself against any Muslim on the day of judgement who enslaves a free person, then sells him and eats this money." The Prophet encouraged the freedom of slaves and declared that freeing a slave was the biggest act of piety. He himself freed, Zayd, his slave and practically adopted him as his son (later on adoption was forbidden by divine revelation).

Rights of the Enemy

Pagans of Arabs were so infuriated by the message of the Prophet regarding oneness of God and against idol worship that they compelled Prophet to leave his homeland. And later on the Pagans attacked the Prophet and his people and thus acquired the character of enemy country. Islamic legal theory divided people of the warring state into combatant persons and noncombatant people. Islam accords some basic rights to both these segments.

Right of Non-Combatant Population

The Prophet issues commands to his army to spare innocent population:

> "Do not kill any old person, any child or any women."[38]

He asked not to kill the religious heads of places of worship and the people who took shelter in the place of worship.[39] During a war, the prophet saw the dead body of a woman laying on the ground and observed: "She was not fighting. How then she was killed." From this statement of the Prophet the doctors of Islamic jurisprudence propounded that those who are non-combatants should not be killed during or after the war.

Rights of Combatants

Islam does not permit the torture of anyone with fire. The Prophet is reported to have said, "punishment by fire does not behove anyone except the Master of the Fire". The injunctions deduced by the expounders of law from this order is that the adversaries should not be burnt alive. Similarly, the attack on wounded soldier is prohibited and prisoners of war must not be put to death. The Prophet had prohibited the killing of anyone who is tied or in captivity. The looting and destruction of enemy property was strictly forbidden. The first Caliph Hazrat Abu Bakr Siddique used to instruct the army while sending them to war, "Do not destroy the villages and towns; do not spoil the cultivated fields and gardens and do not slaughter the cattles."[40] The booty (known as Mal-e-ghanimat) of war which was acquired at battle field included the wealth, provisions and equipments captured from the military camps and head quarters of the combatant armies.

Sanctity of the Dead Body of Enemy

The dignity and honour of the corpses of the enemy were maintained even during the fighting in field. The Prophet had prohibited mutilating the dead bodies of the enemies. This order was given when the corpse of his uncle was mutilated by enemy army on the battlefield. That occasion was highly instructive. In the battle of Uhud the enemy soldiers mutilated the bodies of the Muslims who had fallen on the ground. The abdomen of Hazrat Hamza, the uncle of the Prophet, ripped open by the enemy military, his liver was taken out and chewed by Hinda, the wife of Abu Sufiyan, the leader of the enemy army. The Muslim soldiers were enraged by this horrible sight. But the Prophet ordered his followers not to mete out similar treatment to the dead bodies of the enemy soldiers.

Conclusion

These are some basic rights accorded to human beings by Islamic shariat. The shariat not only prescribed these rights but also made adequate arrangement for their enforcement. The judiciary was there to extend full protection to the victims in case of violation of these rights. The western countries were far behind in according these rights to their citizens. The Magna Carta, Bill of Rights were latter developments in the political philosophy of Europe. The much debated renaissance was the outcome of the interaction of Islamic knowledge with that of Greek culture. But this glorified position of Islamic frame work of legal doctrines belong to remote past. The situation is quite different in the contemporary Muslim nation-states. Militancy is taking precedence over the missionary. The militant groups working in some countries have been coloured by western media as fundamentalists. But truly speaking they are far from fundamentals of Islamic shariat. The terms fundamentalism, extremism and terrorism have different connotations. The latter two are opposed to Islamic way of life. The insurgent groups are painting a wrong picture of Islamic tenets. It is a pious duty of fundamentalists to expose them and their sinister designs.

REFERENCES

1. V.A. Syed Mohammed, "Islam and Human Rights," in *Islam at a glance* (New Delhi, 1981), p. 78 (editor) Hakeem Abdul Hameed.
2. *Ibid.*
3. Qur'an, 94: 4.
4. Qur'an, 40: 11, 12.
5. Tahir Mahmood, "Human Rights in Islam," an article presented in a conference on "Christian's presence in Muslim Countries" held in Varanasi (U.P.) on Nov. 26–Dec. 4, 1983.
6. Qur'an, 24: 27.
7. Qur'an, 49: 12.
8. *Supra* note, 5.
9. Abul A'la Maududi, *Human Rights in Islam*, (Delhi, 1982) p. 27. His Urdu work on Human Rights in Islam was rendered into English by Khursheed Ahmed.
10. Qur'an, 49: 13.
11. *Supra* note 6.
12. *Supra* note 9, p. 36.
13. *Supra* note 5.
14. *Supra* note 9, p. 35.
15. *Ibid.*
16. Qur'an, 6: 151.
17. Qur'an, 5: 32.
18. Farewell Sermon of the Prophet; *Sahih Bukhari*, Vol. I (Delhi 1375 A.H.) p. 8.
19. *Fath al-Qadir*, Vol. II, p. 257.
20. *Supra* note 18, p. 21.
21. *Supra* note 5.
22. *Supra* note 9; p. 29.
23. *Id.*, at p. 28.

24. *Id.*, at p. 30.
25. Qur'an, 2: 256.
26. Qur'an, 190: 1–6.
27. Qur'an, 6: 108.
28. *Supra* note 5.
29. Qur'an, 4: 58.
30. Qur'an, 5: 3.
31. Qur'an, 5: 8.
32. *Supra* note 5.
33. *Ibid.*
34. Qur'an, 4: 32
35. *Mishkat*, p. 258.
36. *Supra* note 1.
37. Encouraged by Prophet his wife Hazrat Aisha freed sixty seven slaves; Hazrat Abbas freed seventy slaves; Hazrat Abdullah bin Umar freed one thousand slaves and Hazrat Abdul Rahman purchased thirty thousand slaves and set them free.
38. *Supra* note 9.
39. *Ibid.*
40. *Ibid.*

PART II

WOMEN AND HUMAN RIGHTS

7

Gender Equality: Theory and Practice in India

*S.K. Verma**

Human rights are said to be those fundamental rights which every man or woman inhabiting any part of the world should be entitled to by virtue of having been born a human being. Basic to human rights is the concept of non-discrimination and equality of treatment. The United Nations, since its inception, is working in the direction of achieving this concept. Women, who represent more than half of the world's population and the vast majority of them are engaged in work that contributes vastly to the life and wealth of nations, are subjected to discrimination at work, in their homes, and in every sphere of human activity. In no other area, the disparity between the formal or "proclaimed" equality (under the law) and the reality of discrimination is so great. The national conditions, policies and programmes are so structured as to relegate the women to the level of "passive" participants rather than the "active" ones in all activities.[1] There are either no efforts or half-hearted efforts towards their empowerment, i.e., their placement in decision-making, and sharing power with men on equal terms. At the III UN Conference on Women in Nairobi in 1985, in the "Forward Looking Strategies for the Advancement of Women to the Year 2000", the participating governments resolved for the empowerment of the women in order to realise the concept of equality.[2]

* Professor of Law, University of Delhi-110 007

Women all over the world fare worse than males in the scale of development, which relegates them to a position of inferior status. The only difference between women from the developed and developing countries lies in the nature of gender deprivation and discrimination suffered. In subsistence economies (such as in India), women perform the lion's share of work in and around the home and in the field. Although they contribute substantially towards family income, they are viewed unproductive by government statisticians, economists, development experts and even by their husbands. Gender bias, in its various forms, prevents millions of women from obtaining education, health services, child care and legal status needed to escape poverty. Women comprise 66 per cent of the world's iliterates and 70 per cent of the world's poor. They are constantly subjected to violence and suffer from physical, sexual and psychological abuses.[3] Violence against them is a violation of their human rights. Each year thousands of young brides are harassed because of lack of adequate dowry with them.

Besides rape, trafficking in women and child prostitution, other forms of abuse include female foeticide and infanticide. In India, the Medical Termination of Pregnancy Act, 1971, allows termination of pregnancy: (1) as a health measure—to avoid the risk to life and health of the women; (2) on humanitarian grounds—when pregnancy arises from a sex crime like rape or intercourse with a lunatic, etc.; and (3) on eugenic grounds—where there is a substantial risk that the child, if born, would suffer from deformities and diseases. The Act, unfortunately, has been increasingly used to abort the female fetus, thus making the fact of inequality suffered by a woman even before her birth a blatant reality.

Deeply rooted societal and religious traditions are, to a great extent, responsible for this pathetic situation of women.[4] The sex-based discrimination and deprivation are premised to a large part on the arbitrary division of male and female roles in the society. The social process based on putative qualities of "maleness" and "femaleness" is not conducive for the genuine equality between the sexes.

The United Nations, from the beginning, is concerned with the plight of women. Mere inspection of the basic human rights instruments churned out by the United Nations so far demonstrates that sex-discrimination, apart from racial and religious, is certainly the over-reaching human rights concern of the international community. Apart from the Charter Provisions,[5] in many of the instruments on human rights, sex/gender has been prohibited as a ground for discrimination.[6] There are special conventions adopted for the betterment of the women, viz., the Convention concerning Night Work of Women Employed in Industry, 1948; the Convention concerning Maternity Protection (Revised), 1952; and the Convention on Consent to Marriage, Minimum Age for Marriage and Registration of Marriages. Other conventions of importance, conferring formal and effective power on women are, the Convention on the Political Rights of Women, 1952; the Convention on the Nationality of Married Women, 1957; and the Convention against Discrimination in Education, 1960. But the latest in this battery of instruments is the Convention on the Elimination of All Forms of Discrimination against Women (Discrimination against Women Convention) adopted by the General Assembly on 3 September 1979,[7] which is a comprehensive instrument on women's rights.

In the recently concluded world summit on Social Development held in Copenhagen, Denmark from 6 to 12 March 1995, the draft Declaration ordained the commitments of the nations "to achieve equality and equity between women and men."[8] The Fourth World Conference on Women, to be held from 4 to 15 September, 1995 at Beijing is again going to discuss the plight of women and the discrimination to which they are systematically subjected to.[9]

But in spite of the encouraging record of the United Nations in laying down the standards of human rights and a concerted drive to eradicate sex-based discrimination, gender-equality is quite elusive and discrimination against women is all pervasive. As a matter of fact, these international instruments are merely statement of intent and policy statements, which are to be carried out by the nation-States. It is through the State machinery that these rights reach to the governed, domestic aspect gives shape to these rights. The political will of the State is a *sine qua non* to implement these norms, enshrined in international instruments, and promote the development of women and alter the unequal conditions and structures condemning the women to a low position.

Here a brief account will be taken of the Indian law towards the realisation of the goal of gender-equality as required under the international instruments. The main emphasis here will be on the personal laws as practiced by different communities, viz., Hindus, Muslims, Christians and Parsees. India is a party to the Discrimination against Women Convention, 1979 which it signed on 30 July 1980. At the time of signing of the Convention, the Indian Government appended a unilateral declaration to the Convention that "with regard to Articles 5(a) and 16(1) (Marriage and Family Relations) . . . the Government of India declares that it shall abide by . . . these provisions in conformity with its policy of non-interference in the personal affairs of any community without its initiative and consent."[10] The Convention has since been ratified by the Government of India on 9 July 1993 without reservations, it is therefore obliged to implement the entire Convention, and eliminate all sorts of discrimination against women. This makes it imperative to highlight the main provisions of the Convention.

'Discrimination against Women' Convention

The Convention has been greatly influenced by the 1967 Declaration on the Elimination of Discrimination against Women[11] and the 1966 International Convention on the Elimination of All Forms of Racial Discrimination.[12] Its twin objectives are: to prohibit discrimination and to ensure equality (Arts. 2, 3, 4). The States are obligated to achieve them not merely *de jure* but *de facto* (Art. 4). The scope of the obligations created by the Convention extends to political, economic, social, cultural, legal, familial and personal fields of activity.

The Convention gives an extensive definition of the term "discrimination against women," which is stated to be as "any distinction, exclusion or restriction made on the basis of sex which has the *effect* or purpose of impairing or nullifying the recognition, enjoyment or exercise by women, irrespective of their marital status, on a basis of equality of men and women, of human rights and fundamental freedoms in the political, social, cultural, civil or *any other field*" (emphasis added). Thus, the Convention prohibits discrimination not only in public life but in private life as well, which clearly extends to family relations. The phrases, "effect" and "any other field" together not only prohibit intentional and unintentional discrimination but also regulates private and public actions. The Convention guards against the use of apparently any neutral criteria as a pretext for discrimination, for example, the use of height or weight requirements, with an objective to keep the women out as a group. Again, the "effect" criterion avoids the need of proving the discriminatory motives. In fact, the prohibition of unintentional discrimination is necessary to achieve systematic change, because policies undertaken without discriminatory motive may perpetuate inequalities established by prior acts of purposeful discrimination.[13]

Towards its obligation to eliminate discrimination against women, a State is to pursue all appropriate means by undertaking, among other things, to "embody the principle of equality of men and women in its national constitution"; to "adopt appropriate legislative and other measures, including sanctions" to "establish legal protection of the rights on an equal basis with men . . . through competent national tribunals and other public institutions," and to "take all appropriate measures . . . to modify or abolish existing laws, regulations, customs and practices" constituting discrimination. It also mandates appropriate measures to eliminate discrimination against women by any person, organisation or enterprise (Art. 2). The Convention further requires States-Parties to take "all appropriate measures . . . in all matters relating to marriage and family relations" to ensure gender equality in relation to specified fields, including property ownership, choice of spouse, choice of occupation and profession. They will have the "same rights and responsibilities during marriage and at its dissolution" and as parents as well as to guardianship, wardship and trusteeship (Art. 16). This provision, in its overbreadth covers wide range of inter-personal relations, and may come in conflict with an individual's right to privacy, freedom of opinion and belief, associational rights related to marital and family relations. Beside religious beliefs, the societal attitudes are further hurdles to bring about gender equality in this area. Hence, the State will be confronted with an uphill task to draw a balance to accord equality to women and protecting the unity of the family. In accordance with the Convention, India is mandated to eradicate discrimination against women in all its manifestations. There are many areas, viz., legal, cultural and social fields where necessary action is required by the Government.

Legal Position on Gender Equality in India

The Constitution of India has very eloquently embodied the equality concept in its "Fundamental Rights" chapter. Article 14 ensures equality before the law to all persons within the territory of India. The Article is in the nature of an admonition addressed to the State and the obligation thus imposed on the State is the measure of the fundamental right which every person in the territory of India is to enjoy.[14] Article 15 expressly prohibits discrimination by the State "on grounds only of religion, race, caste, sex, place of birth or any of them." However, clause (3) of Article 15 provides that the State can make "any special provision for women and children." This provision has been used by courts to justify reservation and upholding statutory provisions in favour of women, such as exempting them from punishment for adultery;[15] providing them special rights in respect of bail under Section 497(1) of the Cr. P.C., 1898;[16] authorising service of summons on men only;[17] providing maintenance for women only;[18] reservation of seats for women in local bodies[19] or in educational institutions;[20] or punishing indecent assault only on women.[21]

In addition to these, Article 16 mandates equality of opportunity for all citizens in matters related to employment or appointment to any office under the State. Article 16(2) clarifies that "no citizen shall, on grounds only of religion, race, caste, sex, descent, place of birth, residence or any of them, be ineligible for, or discriminated against in respect of any employment of office under the State." However, the ambit of this provision is confined to employment and appointment under the State and does not include the non-governmental sector where this rule of non-discrimination can be deviated.

In Supreme Court's view, the rule of equality means that "among equals the law should be equal and equally administered and the like should be treated alike."[22] Accordingly, if inequality exists between the parties, the rule has little meaning and special measures are required to bring equality. However, whereas the rule of "equality before law" is a command to the State, to make special provisions for women (Art. 15(3)) is not and the State, in its wisdom, may not adopt any such provision. Hence, the women are at the mercy of the State to enjoy and realise the full potential of the rule of equality.

Article 21 guarantees the protection of life and personal liberty. This right has been widely interpreted by the courts and has been held to include the right of privacy[23] and the right of an individual to live with dignity.

Apart from these fundamental rights which are enforceable in a court of law, there are certain specific provisions related to women in Chapter IV, the "Directive Principles of State Policy." Though they are not enforceable, but are fundamental in the governance of the country. The State is under a duty to apply these principles in making laws. Article 39(a) requires the State to ensure that all the citizens, men and women equally have the right to an adequate means of livelihood. The State is directed to ensure, under Article 39(d), equal pay for equal work for both men and women. In this regard, the Parliament passed the Equal Remuneration Act, 1976 which provides equal pay for equal work to man and woman for doing the same work or work of a similar nature. The Act also provides that there will be no discrimination against woman at the time of recruitment or later at the time of promotion.

Under Article 39(e), the State is required to secure that the health and strength of workers, men and women, and the tender age of children are not abused and citizens are not forced by economic necessity to enter occupations unsuited to their age or strength. The State is under a duty to protect the childhood and youth against exploitation and against moral and material benefit (Art. 39(b)). For this purpose, the Immoral Traffic (Prevention) Act, 1986 has been passed which covers all persons, whether male or female, who are exploited sexually for commercial purposes. Article 42 directs the State to provide just and humane condition of work and maternity relief. The 1961 Maternity Benefits Act was passed to give effect to this provision. The Act was amended in 1976 to cover women who do not fall within the purview of the Employees State Insurance Act, 1948. Other important legislation passed in pursuance of these principles is the Factories (Amendment) Act, 1976, providing for the establishment of creches where 30 or more women are employed. To improve their conditions and to tackle crimes committed against women. the Dowry Prohibition (Amendment) Act, 1986 makes the provision of the Act more stringent and effective than the 1961 Dowry Prohibition Act. The Criminal Law (Amendment) Act, 1983 amended the Indian Penal Code and introduced certain reforms concerning the punishment of rape, the procedure and the rules of evidence. New provisions are added in the Indian Penal Code for the dowry death (Sec. 304 B) and domestic violence committed against woman by husband and his other relatives (Sec. 498 A).

Another important provision is Article 44 which directs the State to "secure for the citizens a uniform civil code throughout the territory of India." It aims at ending the regime of personal laws practiced by different communities.

Personal Laws

Personal laws deal with marriage and divorce, maintenance, guardianship, adoption, inheritance and succession, ownership of property etc. These laws are basically divided along religious lines in India, irrespective of their religious basis.[24] Thus, Hindus are governed by the Hindu Marriage Act, 1955; the Hindu Succession Act, 1956; the Hindu Guardianship and Minority Act, 1956; and the Hindu Adoption and Maintenance Act, 1956. Muslims are governed by the Shari'a Act, 1937; the Muslim Women's Dissolution of Marriage Act, 1939; the Muslim Women's (Protection of Rights on Divorce) Act, 1986; and uncodified Muslim personal laws. Christians are governed by the Christian Marriage Act, 1872; the Indian Divorce Act, 1869; and the Indian Succession Act, 1925. The Parsees are governed by the Parsi Marriage and Divorce Act, 1936.

The main characteristic of all these personal laws is that they are anti-women and blatantly discriminatory. Apart from unequal treatment meted out to them within each community, these laws subject them to varying degrees of discrimination against each other. For example, while a Hindu, Christian and Parsi wife can sue her husband for bigamy, a Muslim woman cannot because Muslim personal law allows a Muslim man to have four wives at a time. Even in those cases where the law is codified, as among Hindus, and accords equality, wide gap exists in legal prescriptions and societal acceptance. The girl's consent to marriage is generally never sought or obtained. In all family matters, she is expected to allow her husband to take all decisions. Even though she has a remunerative job, the choice relating to "matrimonial home" is the prerogative of the husband though there have been new welcome judicial developments in this direction.[25]

In the matter of inheritance, while the Hindu Succession Act maintains the equality of the sexes in general and confers rights of inheritance on female heirs (Section 8), it contains several retrogressive features to the detriment of the women. By virtue of Article 4(2), "laws providing for the prevention of fragmentation of agricultural holding" have been exempted from the application of the Act. This means that in the name of "prevention of fragmentation of agricultural land," a Hindu woman could be deprived of her right to property. Further, a restriction on her right to demand partition is imposed by Section 23, that is, if a Hindu dies intestate, his female heir cannot claim partition of the dwelling house until the male heirs choose to divide their respective shares therein and till then the female heir is entitled to a right of residence only. Where the female heir is a daughter, she has a right of residence in the dwelling house only if she is unmarried or has been deserted by or separated from her husband or is a widow. The Act also provides that if a female Hindu dies intestate without leaving behind children or husband, her property will devolve on her husband's heirs, except the property inherited from her parents, which in the absence of a son or a daughter or their children, will devolve on the heirs of her father.

The Hindu Guardianship and Minority Act also accepts the father as the natural guardian of the child, and only in his absence, the mother can be the natural guardian. The mother can have the custody of the minor child who has not completed the age of five years, a provision which in itself is inhuman and unequal.

The Muslim personal law requires a bit of pruning to make it conform to the concept of equality. The polygamy practice is at variance with other personal laws. Regarding divorce, the Dissolution of Muslim Marriage Act has undoubtedly ameliorated the conditions of Muslim women. However, the retention of the provision of unilateral divorce by pronouncing Talak by the husband under the Muslim law, together with the prevailing practice of polygamy, has undermined severally the dignity and the status of women. After the passing of the Muslim Women's (Protection of Rights on Divorce) Act, 1986 in the wake of *Shah Bano's case*,[26] the Muslim woman's right to seek maintenance from her husband under Sections 125–127 of the Criminal Procedure Code has been severally curtailed in comparison with other Indian women. The Act restricts the right of maintenance only to the *iddat* period (about three months) after divorce and stipulates that thereafter her own family and the Waqf Board would be responsible for her maintenance. In the matter of inheritance, though she has the right to inherit, she is treated unequal to her male counterpart. For instance, a son will take double the share of the daughter and a brother will take double the share of the sister. But this is in accordance with the *Shariat*. There is no provision for adoption under the Muslim law. Earlier attempts to have an Indian Adoption Act failed because of the opposition of the Muslims to such an optional law governing adoption. Any attempt to change the Muslim law is considered to be an interference in the religious matters and contrary to the *Shariat*.

The Christian and the Parsi laws of marriage and divorce do not reveal any major disparity in the status of men and women. But the law is found to be demonstrably inadequate where cruelty alone is not a ground for divorce under the Indian Divorce Act, but is a ground only for judicial separation, unless accompanied by another ground of divorce. This

Act, besides being archaic, obviously is discriminatory against women. The inhuman treatment is meted out to a wife who is subjected to cruel behaviour of the husband and yet cannot get divorce. Divorce by mutual consent is not permissible under the Indian Divorce Act, 1869. The Act recognises only adultery as a ground for divorce for men. Wife can ask for divorce only if the husband has changed his religion (a Christian husband cannot seek divorce on wife's conversion to another religion) and married another woman or has been guilty of adultery along with bigamy or rape, sodomy, bestiality, cruelty, or desertion. Thus, provisions of the Act clearly discriminate against women on the grounds of sex alone.[27] The Parsi Marriage and Divorce Act governs the Parsees. But in the matter of inheritance, the Indian Succession Act accords complete equality among Christians, but under the Parsi law, son gets the share of the daughter.

To overcome the existing disparity in treatment of women from different communities and to give effect to the equality concept under personal laws, the enactment of a uniform civil code, as directed under Article 44 of the Constitution will be a desired step. This is also required to fulfil India's commitment under the Discrimination against Women Convention, 1979 which mandates States to accord complete equality on matters of marriage, divorce, inheritance, ownership etc. But the Government of India has not done anything so far to fulfil its constitutional or treaty obligations, inspite of the judicial eloquence to enact such a code. In the *Shah Bano case*,[28] the Supreme Court expressed its deep regret that Article 44 of the Constitution had remained a dead letter. It observed that "there is no evidence of any official activity for framing a common civil code for the country" and that a beginning has to be made if the Constitution is to have any meaning. Similar views were expressed by Justice Chinnappa Reddy in *Ms. Jordan Diengdeh* v. *S.S. Chopra*.[29] Again, in a recent judgement of 10 May 1995, the Supreme Court once again asked the Government to take a fresh look at Article 44 and has directed it to ask the Law Commission to draft a comprehensive legislation incorporating the "present day concept of human rights for women, in consultation with the Minorities Commission."[30]

The judgement was rendered on the four writ petitions filed by Hindu women deserted by their husbands who remarried after they converted to Islam. The issue before the Court was whether a Hindu married man can enter into another marriage, by embracing Islam, without dissolving his first marriage. The Court ruled such a second marriage as invalid and the apostate husband would be guilty of committing the crime of bigamy under Section 494 of the Indian Penal Code. The Court observed that "religious practices, violative of human rights and dignity and secredotal suffocation of essentially civil and material freedoms are not autonomy but oppression" and, therefore, a unified civil code is imperative "both for the protection of the oppressed and promotion of national unity and solidarity." The Court did not find any justification whatsoever in delaying the formulation of a uniform personal law in the country when "more than 80 per cent of the citizens (Hindus) have already been brought under the codified personal law."[31]

But once again, the Government is dithering over its constitutional duty, and the Prime Minister, P.V. Narasimha Rao has reportedly stated to a Muslim delegation that the Government would not impose any particular system of law on any community without its consent, the opinion of the Court, being of a division bench, is not "obligatory" on the Government.[32]

One of the main arguments advanced against reform of personal law or to have a common civil code has been that it will be violative of the citizen's right of freedom of religion, guaranteed under Article 25 of the Constitution. But this right in Article 25 is subjected to the following provisions:

a. public order, morality and health;
b. to the other provision of Part III of the Constitution, including the right to equality in Article 14, and Article 15.[33]

Further, it clarifies that:

i. the State can regulate any economic, financial, political or other secular activity that may be associated with religious practice;

ii. the State can make any law providing for social welfare and reform.

Article 25, therefore, clearly delineates the parameters within which the right to practice, propagate, and profess religion freely is limited. It may, however, be stated that the laws may not interfere with religious beliefs and opinions, but they may with practices.[34] In its recent judgement, the Supreme Court has stated that Article 44 had sought to "divest religion from social relations and personal laws." The personal laws are to operate under the authority of legislation and not of the religion, and they can be superseded or supplemented by a uniform civil code.[35]

It is also pertinent to note that Article 30(1) of the Constitution grants the right to "establish and administer educational institutions of their choice" by the minorities and the State will not "discriminate against any educational institution on the ground that it is under the management of a minority" (Art. 30(2)).[36] Thus, the minority institutions are allowed to propagate sex-discrimination, deep-rooted in religious practices or beliefs, unless it is against public order, morality and health. This is against the fiat of Article 10 of the Discrimination against Women Convention, which requires a State to eradicate discrimination and women should be provided "the same conditions for career and vocational guidance, for access to studies." The State is required to take steps to eliminate "any stereo-typed concept of the roles of men and women, through education, reduce female drop out rates and organise programmes for females who have left school prematurely." Similar obligations have been imposed by the 1960 Convention against Discrimination in Education to which also India is a party. Thus, the Government has to do the proper balancing between the two conflicting principles: equality between the sexes and freedom of religious belief (and not of practices).

Conclusion

The United Nations from its inception has strived to protect the dignity of women by endowing them with human rights and fundamental freedoms, but they still stand as a deprived lot of the society. Their rights are observed more in violations than in adherence. Their position is particularly pernicious in the economic matters. They have little access to productive resources and control over family income. Sex-discrimination ranges from the exclusion of women from development programmes to wage discrimination and violence against them. Development programmes are premised on the notion that what is good for the men is good for the family. In the domain of family, they are subjected to systematic discrimination.

It may be noted that the real protection of human rights cannot only be the result of a good codification but, above all, would be the result of the concrete action by the governments. In the matter of according identical legal capacity to men and women, majority of the States are abiding by adopting the laws, but in the execution it is missing. Even in the legal aspect, wherever there is a discretion to follow the rule, invariably it is enforced against the women. The status of women in India is no way different. But now the Government has ratified the Discrimination against Women Convention, hence, is obliged to bring gender-equality in all its facets. This requires a lot of pruning of its laws, particularly in the personal laws, where different communities have their own laws, discriminating against women in different degrees. To change the law, in accordance with the concept of gender equality, a uniform legislation is required which should not discriminate women inter-religiously as well as on the basis of religion. Religious and cultural practices cannot become the ploy to deny equality. But this requires a strong political will on the part of the Government. Such a legislation will also automatically take care of the societal attitudes about the pre-determined roles of the women. The Government should adopt the policy and frame the laws which should make the social roles of men and women, with the exception of child-bearing, as nearly interchangeable or equivalent as far as possible.

REFERENCES

1. "Passive" participation is merely a managerial technique, while "active" participation involves empowerment. See, "The Realisation of the Right of Development," UN Doc. HR/PUB/91/2, p. 37 (1991).
2. At the International Conference on Population and Development (ICPD) held in Cairo in September 1994, the nations agreed that empowering women must be at the centre of efforts to address the problems of population and development. Women's equality was considered to be a gateway to population. *UN Newsletter*, Vol. 50 (6 May 1995), p. 4.
3. Cf. *UN Newsletter*, Vol. 50 (4 March 1995), p. 3. It is reported that between January and June 1994, in India, there were 3504 cases of rape, 3700 cases of kidnapping and abduction, 1226 cases of dowry death, 4822 cases of cruelty, 7037 cases of molestation and 3992 cases of eve-teasing. See A.K. Jha, "Women: Saga of Struggle," *Civil Services Chronicle* (April 1995), p. 16 at 18. In 1993, the UN General Assembly adopted a Declaration on the Elimination of Violence against Women, cf. *UN Newsletter*, Vol. 50 (May 27, 1995), p. 3.
4. See, M.C. Dougal, Lasswell and Chen, "Human Rights for Women and World Public Order: The Outlawing of Sex-Based Discrimination," 69 *A.J.I.L.* 497 (1975).
5. Relevant Charter provisions are: The Preamble, Articles 1, 8, 13(1)(b), 55(c), 62(2).
6. See, for example, the Universal Declaration of Human Rights: Arts. 1, 2, 4, 7, 10, 16, 18, 21, 23 and 26; Art. 3 of the International Covenant on Civil and Political Rights; Art. 3 of the International Covenant on Economic, Social and Cultural Rights; Art. 2 of the ILO Convention concerning Equal Remuneration for Men and Women Workers for Work of Equal Value.
7. G.A. Res. 34/180, 18 Dec. 1979, UN Doc. A/34/46 (1979). The Convention entered into force on 3 Sept. 1981. There are 133 States parties to the Convention as of November 1994. *UN Newsletter* (26 Nov. 1994), p. 4.
8. *UN Newsletter*, Vol. 50 (8 April 1995), p. 3.
9. The earlier three conferences were held in Mexico city 1975, Copenhagen 1980, and Nairobi 1985. The issues identified about women for the fourth Conference include: health and education, productive employment, armed conflict, human rights, poverty alleviation, violence, environment and development.
10. Quoted by Anika Rahman, "Religious Rights versus Women's Rights in India, A Test Case for International Human Rights Law," 28 *Col. J. Transnat'l l*, 473 at 486 (1990).
11. A Res. 22/2263, UN Doc. A/6716 (1967).
12. 660 UNTS, p. 195, reprinted in 5 *ILM* 352 (1966).
13. Meron, Theodar, *Human's Rights Law-Making in the United Nations*, p. 60 (1986); Verma, S.K., "Human Rights of Women: The United Nations Approach," *Human Rights Yb* (1993) p. 60, at 66.
14. See, *Kidarnath* v. *State of West Bengal*, AIR 1953 SC 404.
15. *Yusuf Abdul Aziz* v. *State of Bom. and other*, AIR 1954 SC 321, affirmed in *Smt. Soumithri Vishnu* v. *Union of India* (1985) 1 Scale 960. The Court refused to strike down Section 497 of the IPC stating that it is not

violative of Arts. 14 and 15, as it makes a reasonable classification between men and women by punishing a man only for committing the crime of adultery.

16. *Mt. Choki* v. *The State*, AIR 1957 Raj 10 at 11, para 4.
17. *M.I. Shahabad* v. *Mohd. Abdulla and others,* AIR 1967 J&K 120 at 122, para 33.
18. *Thamsi Goundan* v. *Kanni Ammal,* AIR 1952 Mad. 529 at 530.
19. *Dattetreya Motiram More* v. *State of Bom.*, AIR 1953 Bom. 311, at 314, para 7.
20. *P. Sagar and others* v. *State of AP*, AIR 1968 AP 165, at 174, para 28.
21. Sec. 354 IPC was held valid as a reasonable classification in *Girdhar Gopal* v. *State,* AIR 1953, MB 147.
22. *Satish Chandra* v. *Union of India,* AIR 1953 SC 250.
23. In *T. Sareetha* v. *T. Venkata Subbaiah,* AIR 1983 AP 356, the Court held that the remedy of restitution of conjugal rights "violates the right to privacy and human dignity guaranteed by and contained in Article 21 of our Constitution."
24. Singh, Kirti, "Obstacles to Women's Rights in India" in Rebecca J. Cook (ed.), *Human Rights of Women: National and International Perspectives* (1994, University of Pennsylvania Press), p. 375, at 378.
25. *Bharat Heavy Plates and Vessels Ltd.*, AIR 1985 AP 207.
26. *Md. Ahmad Khan* v. *Shah Bano,* AIR 1985 SC 945.
27. The Government is contemplating changes in the Christians' marriage and divorce laws after the Kerala High Court in 1992 asked the Centre to reform Christian law comprehensively, See *The Times of India,* June 6, 1995, p. 11.
28. *Op. cit.,* 26.
29. AIR 1985 SC 935.
30. See, *Smt. Sarla Mudgal, President, Kalyani and others* v. *Union of India,* 1995 (3) *SCALE* 286 at p. 299. Judgement was delivered by Justices Kuldip Singh and R.M. Sahai.
31. *Ibid.,* at p. 288. The Court has directed the Government to report about the steps taken in this direction by August 1996.
32. See, *The Times of India,* June 1, 1995, p. 7.
33. See, *Srinivasa* v. *Saraswati Ammal,* AIR 19532 Mad. 193.
34. See, *Davis* v. *Beason,* 133 US 333 (1890).
35. See, *op. cit.*, 30, at p. 296.
36. See, *St. Stephen College* v. *University of Delhi,* AIR 1992 SC 1630.

8

Gender Justice and Human Rights in India—A Fragile Myth

*Ranbir Singh**

Gender Justice

It would be apt to begin with Lord Denning. He said in 1980:

> A woman feels as keenly, thinks as clearly, as a man. She in her sphere does work as useful as man does in his. She has as much right to her freedom—to develop her personality to the full—as a man. When she marries, she does not become the husband's servant but his equal partner. If his work is more important in the life of the community, her is more important in the life of the family. Neither can do without the other. Neither is above the other or under the other. They are equals.[1]

Sex jurisprudence cannot proceed on the basis of assumed equality of male and female sections of Indian society. For centuries the Indian woman has suffered economic deprivation and social subjugation. The Indian culture has been built on the concept of male superiority and the subordinate status of the woman. This has resulted in her complete extermination from the field of economic independence.[2]

---

* Professor & Dean Faculty of Law, M.D. University, Rohtak-124 001.
Paper presented at 14th Law Asia Biennial Conference, Beijing, August 16–20, 1995.

Almost all the national resources, means of production, industry, trade and business are owned and controlled by men, and even out of the gross national income only a nominal share goes to women. In effect, women comprise the largest deprived section of the society. To combat this ugly situation the Constitution has undertaken to declare India a socialist republic and in Article 39 has provided for equitable utilisation of the country's resources and means of production. It requires the State to abolish monopoly and redistribute, not amongst individuals but on the national scale, the available production resources for the benefit of the entire people. Economic democracy and economic justice for women depends on making available, to men and women alike, the entire wealth of the nation.[3]

There can be no equality amongst unequals. Women cannot obtain economic justice, or even social justice, which ultimately depends on economic justice, unless the male monopoly of the resources and means of production is broken and the entire people become their owners, controllers and masters. The income of women cannot increase so long as they remain in the deprived class of citizens and men continue to hold economic power.[4]

It may be necessary to reorient the entire thinking and educational process in society to make women competent to obtain the better-paid traditionally male-oriented jobs. In the present economic order, women are given the lower jobs meant for unskilled labour.[5]

The Constitution promises social and economic justice to women, but the law has not cared to redeem these promises. Women still remain economically weak and socially handicapped. Exceptions apart, the man is the bread-winner and the woman his dependent. Economic inequality and dependence of women make the promise of economic justice a farce and social justice a pretence.[6]

Even after 47 years of our independence women of India wears a pathetic look. All throughout this period a tale of promises broken-of hopes and aspirations suppressed—a tale of exploitation and oppression and yet we feel the growing struggle—a mighty spirit and strong urge to liberate them from the chains of bondage. In these long years the Government has made laws which glitteringly boast of protecting women's rights but the lack of implementation merely reduces them to paper tags on our statute books. Even the General Assembly of United Nations recognised way back in 1967:

> "Discrimination against women, denying or limiting as it does their equality of rights with men, is fundamentally unjust and constitutes an offence against human dignity."[7]

The United Nations proclaimed the year 1975 as International Year of Women for the abolition of discrimination against women. The resolution endeavours:

> "To strive for equality between men and women; to promote a higher role of women in economic, political, social and cultural life of countries to promote their active participation in the struggle for the development of friendship and cooperation between nations, for peace and social progress."[8]

The Constitution of India guarantees equality of opportunity and status of men and women. It directs that women shall not only have equal rights and privileges with men but also that the State shall make provisions—both general and special for the welfare of women. Despite the above constitutional guarantee, women have been subjected to deprivation, brutality and extortion.

Gender Justice—Constitutional Mandate

To attain these national objectives, the Constitution guarantees certain fundamental rights and freedoms such as freedom of speech, protection of life and personal liberty. While these may be termed positive rights, the negative rights are the prohibition of discrimination or denial of equal protection.[9]

Indian women are the beneficiaries of these rights in the same manner as Indian men. Article 14 ensures 'equality before law' and Article 15 'prohibits any discrimination.' There is only one specific provision in Article 15(3), which empowers the State to make 'any special provision for women and children.' This provision has enabled the State to make special provision for women, particularly in the field of labour legislation like the Factories Act, the Mines Act etc.

Article 16(1) guarantees "equality of opportunity for all citizens in matters relating to employment, or appointment to any office under the State." And Article 16(2) forbids discrimination "in respect of any employment of office under the State" on the grounds only of "religion, race, caste, sex, descent, place of birth, residence or any one of them."

The Directive Principles of State Policy enunciated in Part IV of the Constitution, embody the major policy goals of a welfare state. They concretize, together with the chapter on Fundamental Rights, the constitutional vision of a new Indian socio-political order. The Directive Principles are declared as non-justiciable, but "nevertheless fundamental in the governance of the country," and the State is charged with "a duty—to apply these principles in making laws" (Article 37).

Article 38 in brief directs the State to secure a just social, political and economic order, geared to promote the welfare of the people; Art. 39(b) (c) and (f) provides for distribution of ownership and control of material resources of the community for the common good, prevention of concentration of wealth and means of production to the common detriment, and protection of childhood and youth against exploitation and moral and material abandonment; Art. 40 provides for organisation of village panchayats to promote self-government; Art. 41 provides for right to work, education and public assistance in cases of unemployment, old age, sickness, disablement and other types of underserved wants; Art. 43 enshrines provision of work, a living wage, conditions of work ensuring a decent standard of life and full enjoyment of leisure, of social and cultural opportunities, and the promotion of cottage industries; Art. 44 provides for enunciation of a uniform Civil Code; Art. 45 enjoins the state to provide free and compulsory education for all children up to the age of 14; and Art. 47 provides for raising the level of nutrition and the standard of living of the people and improvement of public health.

Gender Justice and Human Rights

Significant steps towards achieving equality of women with men were made during the United Nations Decade for Women, 1976–1985. As is the case with all ambitious projects, every goal was not achieved, but sufficient advances were made for the sponsors to be satisfied that their investment of efforts and resources were worthwhile and for women to be confident that the goal of equality is achievable. Nevertheless, very much remains to be done, since women in both developed and developing countries of the world remain subjected in legal, cultural, religious and other systems.[10]

The most significant achievements in the field of international law on human rights is the conclusion, and exceptionally rapid adoption by the United Nations (UN) General Assembly and ratification and accession by States of the Convention on the Elimination of All Forms of Discrimination Against Women (The Women's Convention), 1967. The Women's Convention and the Strategies reinforce and amplify obligations in the Universal Declaration of Human Rights that were given effect in two international covenants, that is the International Covenant on Civil and Political Rights (The Political Covenant) and the International Covenant on Economic, Social and Cultural Rights (The Economic Covenant).[11]

These facts indicate the extent and depth of support for the Women's Convention which is heartening not just to women, but to all concerned with human rights and equality. While encouragement can be drawn from such dedicated initiatives, it is clear that formidable obstacles remain in the way to the achievement of the human right to equality.

Apart from the fact that a long leap has been taken in the area of human rights as far as women's rights are concerned by Women's Convention, which clearly mandates many resolutions for the upliftment of women. But the hardships are still there and there are many challenges before the real task of human rights is achieved for women. The formidable challenge is in the following areas:

A) Cultural and religious biases are a basic challenge to the equal rights of women and the concept of equality.

B) A challenge which is faced by activists of human rights at national and international level is the human right to sexual equality because there are cultures which place women at a disadvantage due to their sex. Continuing assertions that women are unfit for political, civil, religious or other offices due to their sex is in itself violative of the human rights of a woman.

C) The inequality that women experience in their very homes is often subtle and is reinforced by traditional practices inherent in the culture itself.

D) The women of all ages disproportionately suffer avoidable premature deaths. Women of all ages disproportionately suffer avoidable sickness. Women of all ages disproportionately suffer disadvantages in educational, economic and social opportunities.

E) Legal obstacles exist to the progress of achievement of justice through elimination of discrimination against women. Flaws in the body of international and municipal law, existing at the levels of both doctrine and practice, often leave the law crippled and impotent to achieve its professed goal of justice.

Inspite of constitutional mandates and the concern for women rights at national and international level one has to still face the ugly truth every day i.e.

> In a country such as ours where a woman is molested every 26 minutes, raped every 52 minutes and falls a victim to dowry death every 102 minutes, would it be enough to ask ourselves whether a woman's identity is to be defined in terms of her sexuality or her gender?[12]

The above scenario has some how been able to emerge and thrive, whereas;

> Women constitute half the world's population, perform nearly two thirds of its work hours, receive one tenth of the world's income and own less than one hundredth of the world's property (United Nations Report, 1980).

In the following pages an attempt has been made to pinpoint some of the major problems faced by the Indian women in the light of Indian socio-legal conditions and attempt has been made to suggest some remedial measures.

India is a land of great diversity, yet various problems are being faced by various sections of society. Women in particular face many problems which deserve immediate solutions if the conditions of Indian women are to be improved. Some of the problems are:

The common Indian rural scene is that a few have a lot and many have very little, whereas most have none. Families with 10 or more hectares of land constitute only 3 per cent of population but own 26.1 per cent of all the cultivable land. Families with 2 hectares or less constitute 72 per cent of population but own only 23.5 per cent of the land. Most of the rural population live below poverty line and women have to do any work, to keep body and soul together. In agriculture, women are not only paid less, but are also subjected to sexual exploitation by the landlords, as most of the women workers come from scheduled castes/scheduled tribes and other deprived sections of the rural population. Their working hours are more; sometimes 12 to 16 hours, and their remunerations meagre. At times of pregnancy or other illness, the first treatment they get is dismissal from their jobs. The landlord moneylender clique in collusion with the police and the administration put them virtually in the category of bonded labour. Landlessness and agricultural unemployment forces the rural families to migrate towards cities and other suburbs in hope of employment, only to face harsher realities[13]. The condition of women in urban industries is no better. Inspite of constitutional guarantee of equality, it is brazenly flouted in non-payment of equal wages for equal work.

Even in the Government owned construction companies, public sector and public works departments, women construction workers are not given regular employment and are left at the mercy of private contractors, thereby subjecting them to victimisation and sexual harassment, besides perpetuation of violation of labour laws. The government fails miserably to act as a model employer.[14]

The sad tale of the Indian woman does not end there. The women, belonging particularly to the scheduled castes and scheduled tribes, are very often made victims of rape and molestation so that the members of the family and the clan to which they belong will be overawed and will not resist their own exploitation. They are forced to remain bonded and to labour without claiming adequate wages.[15]

Gender Justice in India—A Fragile Myth

The law is too inadequate to give protection to the suppressed women of India, and the law enforcing agency is probably not sufficiently concerned and awake to the gravity of the situation.

"Ordinarily, rape is a violation, with violence, of the private person of a woman—an outrage by all canons, a randy molestation which is bad enough in a society where women are often socially weak and sexually victimised.[16]

We hope, at this belated hour, that the central government will defend Indian womanhood by stamping out voluptuous meat markets by the merciless criminal sections. Isolated and occasional rhetoric on the topic of suppression will stultify the law where the vice is widespread and the larger felons are often let loose."[17]

Atrocities against women are not on the decline. The woman is often tortured in her own house, by her own relations. Krishna Iyer views these acts with shock. "Wife-burning—that atrocious species of murder horrendously escalating in some parts of this country—is a shocking crime . . . . The terrible act in this case has taken place in the house, and in the presence of the husband who has been convicted . . . . Gender Justice has a high place in Indian criminal jurisprudence."[18]

Behind all gender justice lies the wail of womanhood for the *karuna* and *samata* of the law, and to alleviate this poignant cry the social justice jurisprudence evolves gender justice to ensure that masculine injustice may not crucify the weaker sex.[19]

It is not that there are not enough laws in India for the protection of women. Most of the laws are in a State of suspended animation. The laws are observed more in breach than in observance. In reality the picture is not as rosy as is sometime painted. Despite fundamental rights and directive principles of state policy, even after 47 years of independence, women are discriminated against—socially, economically and politically.

Women and the Law

One of the main characteristic of modern society is a heavy reliance on law to bring about social change. It is therefore necessary not only to legislate but to see that it is implemented. In the following paras, an effort has been made to point out the areas where the law is failing to achieve the goals enshrined in the Constitution for the emancipation of women in India. The areas where the law is lagging behind to solve the problems of women are:

a) Full equality of sexes can hardly be possible in a legal system which permits polygamy and a social system which tolerates it. (The only personal law, which has remained impervious to the changing trend from polygamy to monogamy is Muslim Law.) There should be no compromise on the basic policy of monogamy. Monogamy should be strictly enforced for all communities. Any compromise in this regard will only perpetuate the existing disparity in the status of women. Inspite of the fact that monogamy has been introduced for Hindus, bigamous marriages are still prevalent among them.
b) Child marriages: Child marriage is another harsh reality of the Indian society where thousands of child marriages are performed every year. The policy of law which do not render illegal a child marriage and rather permits such marriage of a girl before she is physically and mentally mature is open to serious question.
c) Registration of marriages: Due to non registration of marriages, no check can be put on child and bigamous marriages. In view of the fact that such registration is recommended by the United Nations, as it facilitates the proof of marriage, registration of all marriages should be made compulsory in India too.
d) Dowry: Dowry is another teething problem without any solution. Inspite of the Dowry Provision Act 1961 and the subsequent amendments to the Act, though the Act is

made very harsh and punishments are very severe but dowry deaths cases are alarmingly increasing defying all solutions.

e) Divorce: The increase in the rate of divorce in the cities and even in villages is another cause of concern for the country. Of course marriages which have failed beyond repair should break. However in modern times a new approach developing against divorce is the welfare of the child. A child needs a father as well as a mother for proper development. Before pronouncing the decree of divorce the courts need to ensure the secret welfare of the children. Divorce law also needs to be properly streamlined for the Muslims.

f) Maintenance: The provision for maintenance in various laws has been a subject of sharp controversies . . . . At the same time there is a need to evolve a proper legal system which can take care of the maintenance of the wife and also of the divorced wife.
Inheritance and succession are the areas where women are greatly discriminated. Inspite of the fact that there are so many laws on the statues book, the reality remains that women are largely denied these rights.

g) In the area of criminal law, the problems like rape, adultery, bigamy, and other crimes against women are on the increase, causing great concern to the law makers. The indecent representation of women in films and other modes of media are a matter of shame for every body. Prostitution in the society and the ever increasing instances of child prostitutes is a grave problem faced by the Indian society.

The above problems highlight some of the areas where there is a need to do lot of things and make improvement for the betterment of women in India.

Conclusions and Suggestions

Women remain very separate and very unequal in many parts of the world. As we move into the next decade, as a prelude to the next century, every opportunity must be taken to insist that the situation changes in favour of equality for women and men. As long as inequality persists, development will mean increased denial of rights for women and increased distance from the condition in which women exercise rights equally with men. A precondition to exerting moral and legal leadership in observance of human rights by a country, is that it ratifies the human rights conventions in as much as it expects other members of the international community to observe.

There is a strong need today as never before to make Indian women aware of their rights. They have to launch a relentless battle for their emancipation. And it is not their responsibility alone. Workers, youth and students in particular and the Indian people in general have to fight and win this battle. If half the population remains deprived, ignorant, down-trodden and discriminated against, the country cannot usher in an era of prosperity. It is high time for the rulers of independent India to respect the aspirations of crores of working women, so that they may live up to their role of nation-building effectively. Here it is apt to quote Krishna Iyer, J:

> "The fight is not for woman's status but for human worth. The claim is not to end inequality of women but to restore universal justice. The bid is not for loaves and fishes for the forsaken gender but for cosmic harmony which never comes till woman comes."[20]

So in the light of the above, let us fight the truth that is:

"Women's exploitation is a reality and Gender Justice a fragile myth."

REFERENCES

1. Lord Denning, *The Due Process of Law*, 194–195 (Butterworths-London) 1980.
2. Hari Swarup, *For whom the Law is Made* p. 221–222 (Veena Publishers) 1981.
3. *Ibid.*, p. 221.
4. *Ibid.*, p. 222.
5. *Ibid.*, p. 222.

6. *Ibid.*, p. 222.
7. Article 1 of Declaration on the Elimination of Discrimination Against Women proclaimed by the General Assembly of the United Nations on November 7, 1967.
8. Quoted in S. Shams (ed.) *Women Law and Social Change* p. 10 (Ashish Publishing House, New Delhi) 1991.
9. D.D. Basu. *Constitution of India* (3rd edition) p. 69.
10. Rebecca Cook "The International Human Right to Sexual Non-discrimination", *The Lawyers* February–March 1988, p. 15.
11. *Ibid.*
12. *The Tribune* (Chandigarh) August 28, 1994, p. 1, col. 3.
13. *Popular Jurist* Nov.–Dec. 1986, p. 18
14. *Ibid.*, p. 20.
15. *Supra* note 2 p. 230.
16. *Ibid.*, p. 230.
17. *Ibid.*, p. 231.
18. *Ibid.*, p. 231.
19. *Ibid.*, p. 231.
20. Krishna Iyer, *Of Law and Life* (Vikas Publishing House) 1979, p. 31.

9

Women, Human Rights and Environment

*Jill Cottrell**

I began this paper with very little idea of where it would lead me to. One underlying reason for embarking upon it was a gut feeling that economic policies would probably benefit women—if they benefit anyone—less than men, and that if they were disadvantageous they would probably be even more so for women than for men. It is a version of sod's law.[1]

Human Rights and Women

On the whole, constitutional provisions tend to stop at requiring equality. An exception is the rather feminist Constitution of Namibia. All persons shall be equal before the law, and no one may be discriminated against on the grounds of sex . . . (Article 10). It goes into much more detail than most constitutions: positive discrimination may be exercised in view of the fact that women have traditionally suffered special discriminaiton (Article 23), and there is non-justiciable obligation upon the state to enact legislation to ensure equality of opportunity for women, "to enable them to participate fully in all spheres of Namibian society" (Article 95).

The International Convention on the Elimination of All Forms of Discrimination Against Women, not unnaturally,

---

* Faculty of Law, University of Hong Kong.

goes into more detail. For reasons which will become apparent, most relevant for our purposes is particularly Article 14 on Rural Women. This includes:

"States Parties shall take into account the particular problems faced by rural women and the significant role which women play in the economic survival of their families, including their work in the non-monetised sectors of the economy, . . ."

"Specifically, parties should ensure that women have the right

— to participate in elaboration and implementation of development planning,
— of access to adequate health care,
— to benefit from social security programmes,
— to obtain all types of training and education,
— to organise self-help groups and cooperatives,
— to participate in all community activities of access to agricultural credit and loans, and
— to adequate living conditions."

Women and Environment

To turn from law to fact, I begin with a proposition that I think the literature clearly establishes:

Environmental issues very often affect women to a greater extent than, or in different ways from, how they affect men.

Ecological disasters like Bhopal may affect women differently because of physiological factors.[2] But more important (because there is more that can be done about it) is the fact that rural women are differently and disproportionately affected by environmental degradation. Such an assertion implies that women play a different role in economy and society from men. These differences are not those which would tend to come to mind in some societies. In Africa especially, women are to a far greater extent than men the hewers of wood and the drawers of water, they are also very often the farmers. In Africa it is estimated that 60 per cent of the farming is done by women. (Graphic presentation on page 125.)[3]

Not only in Africa, indeed "women perform the lion's share of work in subsistence economies, toiling longer hours and

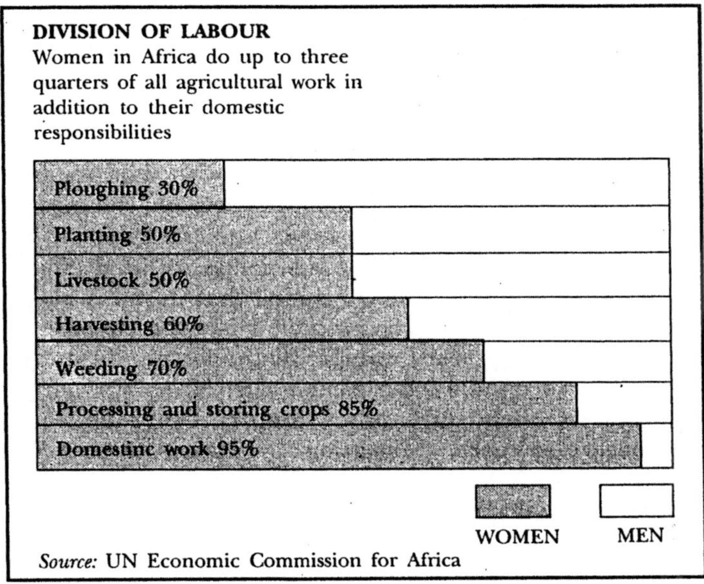

Source: UN Economic Commission for Africa

contributing more to family income than men do."[4] Although most of this paper concentrates upon the position of women in developing countries, it is interesting to note that evidence suggests that in every country in the world except Australia, Canada and the USA, women on an average work longer hours than men.[5]

As striking as the dimensions of women's role is the lack of hard information about it. The role of women has been invisible[6].

There are those who attack the whole notion of "growth" arguing that it is environmentally damaging, and beneficial only to a minority.[7] There is large and familiar literature on the impacts of large development projects, to the point that even agencies like the World Bank have recognised the problems. Again, impacts may be sexually different. Commercial logging and clearance for irrigation projects, which may benefit some. But they reduce the common resources available to the poor. Even land redistribution policies ostensibly intended to benefit the poor may have a similar effect. Bina Agarwal suggests that in parts of Rajasthan land policies have meant giving village commons to the already land-owning. This leaves the poor even poorer, and the impact on women as those who make the greatest use of the commons, the greatest.[8]

Even if one counted the Green Revolution as "success"—as Vandana Shiva does not[9]—side effects for women may be different than for men. "Thousands of rural women who make their living by basket and mat making, with wild reeds and grasses, are also losing their livelihoods because the increased use of herbicides is killing the reeds and the grasses."[10]

Bina Agarwal has looked at the gender-related effects of the 1943 Bengal famine and concluded that in many respects the impact upon women was greater. Disproportionate numbers of the destitute were women, disproportionate numbers of the young to middle aged women die. Many women were abandoned by their husbands.[11] Similar consequences are experienced elsewhere. "Migration . . . appears to be a polite word for desertion. It is a male survival strategy rather than a female survival strategy."[12]

In ways other than their work contribution, also, women's lives may differ from men's with the result that their experience of environmental events is different too. In Bangladesh, it has been suggested, the requirements of purdah, coupled with beliefs that there is a polluting quality to women which requires their contact with the environment to be restricted, mean that their experience of the country's recurrent floods is very different from that of men. But the end of the tale may be familiar. "In addition to women's work being confined and undervalued by men, wives in poor homes are perceived as a burden and finally deserted by their husbands during the severe impoverishment which is the long-term consequence of flood disasters for the very poor."[13]

A chart from the FAO summarises the position (see page 127).

It seems that when things get "better" for society generally, they may get worse for women—and when things get worse generally they may get even worse for women! A very negative view of men emerges from some of the literature, and it should surely be taken with some pinches of salt: when the men get money they spend it on drink and gadgets—and when things get tough the drink is not given up.[14] And when environmental degradation means the reduction of forests it means the women's hours of work increase, for they must

LINKAGES BETWEEN THE FOREST, FUELWOOD, WOMEN'S LABOUR AND HOUSEHOLD NUTRITION

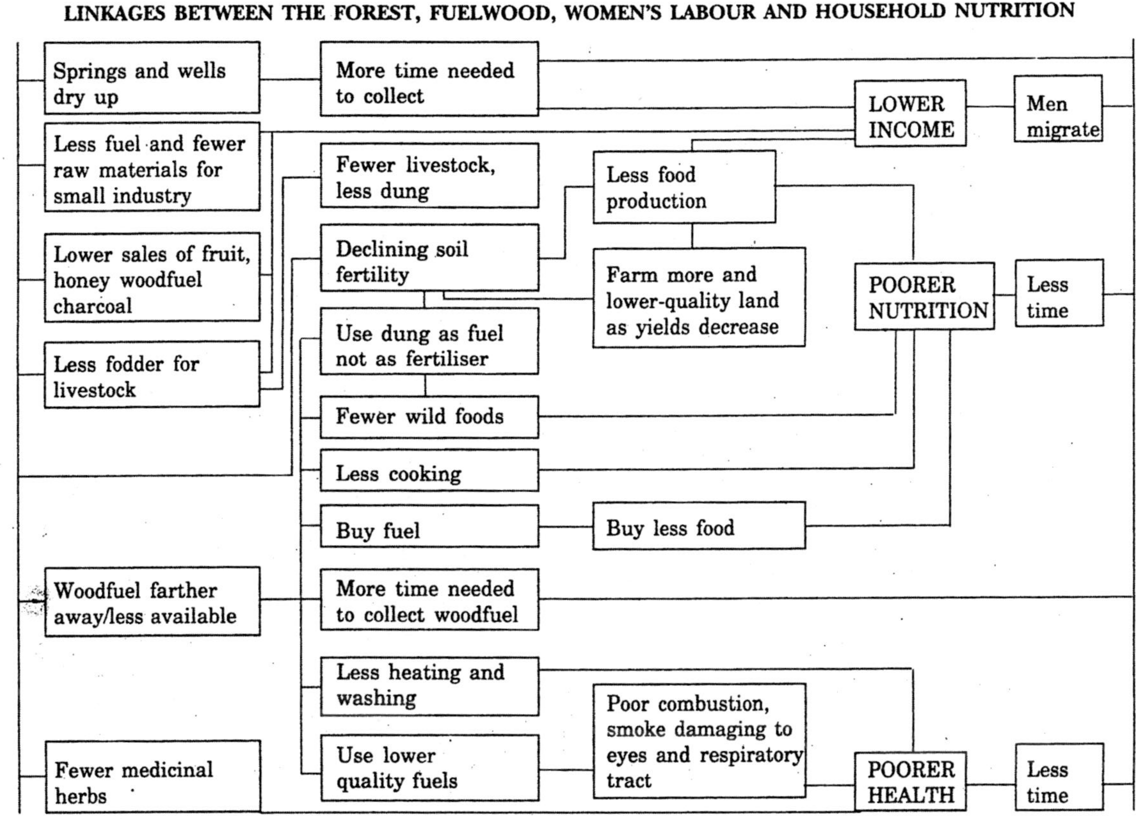

travel further to collect fuelwood, and when it means the drying up of rivers, those hours increase because women must walk further to find water.

Structural Adjustment, Environment and Women

Structural adjustment policies have been required by the IMF since the eighties as a condition for new loans, and are intended (by the IMF and other aid givers and bankers) as a remedy for what were perceived to be the economic ills caused by governmental policies of the previous two decades or so. The remedies have not been identical for every country, nor have they necessarily been forced upon the countries by the lending agencies. Adjustments which have been made in many countries, include: substantial cuts in public expenditure, privatisation of state enterprise, devaluation of currency, lifting of taxes including those on exports, reduction or abolition of agricultural subsidies, abolition of food price subsidies, removal of price controls, and of exchange controls. Essentially what is involved is the introduction of all or some of the elements of a market economy. But it would be wrong, I think, not to recognise a political aspect to this as well. These changes spell the end of socialism; they could not be introduced and leave intact regimes which supported the then Soviet block. The views of the World Bank and the IMF are not autonomous; they reflect the views of the dominant classes of the West (or North), and those classes must have believed that these economic policies would demonstrate the virtues of the western way of life and political system.

SAPs were never, therefore, designed as environmental instruments. Much of the criticism has been directed at the tendency of SAPs to hurt the poor.[15] But there are also specific critiques, of both their environmental impact and their impact on women. A recent study which looked at Ivory Coast, Mexico and Thailand suggested that environmental impacts of structural adjustment were not all one way. Some changes were neutral, some positively beneficial and others harmful. It did suggest that environmental considerations were not built into economic policies as they ought and might. "In all three cases, it is clear that the economic growth that has been achieved could have been realised with less environmental damage had better environmental and economic policies been followed."[16]

This study implies, rather than stating explicitly, that women have suffered especially from adjustment processes that have harmed the environment. Others have looked in more detail at the impact of structural adjustment on women. A Commonwealth study of women and structural adjustment found overall that:

> "the economic crises of the 1980s, and the types of stabilisation and adjustment measures taken in response to it, have halted and even reversed the progress in health, nutrition, education and incomes which women had enjoyed in developing countries during the previous three decades. In the 1980s, despite greater national and international commitment towards gender issues, most women have suffered disproportionately during the widespread economic and social disruption that has occurred in much of the developing world."[17]

Looking specifically at the most environment-related sphere of female activities—farming—the report suggests that incentives for farmers have been of relatively little value for women, since women typically grow subsistence crops but incentives are often greater for cash crops; women farmers have less access to credit; small farms (women usually being 'smaller' farmers) suffered more when fertilizer subsidies were removed and import prices increased; and mechanisation has often meant shorter hours for men but longer hours for women, who do the unmechanised aspects of work on a family farm.[18]

So ?...

What does all this have to do with law, or more specifically with human rights?

Priority must be given to poverty—alleviating economic strategies with a particular focus on stabilizing and strengthening the agricultural sector.... It must give particular attention to strengthening the role of women in the development process.[19]

Greater control by women over their economic and social roles is a pre-requisite to improving their situation. Key elements of this process will be:

— the empowerment and organisation of women themselves,
— affirmative action to incorporate women into the decision-making processes . . . .[20]

It is . . . important to recognize that since floods are constituted as environmental disasters by poverty and, additionally for women, by ideas of female pollution, they can be radically ameliorated by attacking poverty and empowering women.[21]

Women's equal participation in an ecological approach to poverty and development is a human right.[22]

Participation and empowerment are the key words, one might almost say the buzz words, of the literature on women and the environment. They are also notions which may have legal implications and certainly have human rights aspects.

What do Women Want?

I must apologise to women! This question sounds like the sort of thing which men stereotypically lament about women: they don't know what they want. If you look at one book or article you tend to emerge with a feeling that what is required for an approach to environmental issues which takes due account of women is straightforward. Indeed, the buzz words will tend to be the same. No one will say that they are not in favour of participation and empowerment. They wouldn't be writing about women's issues at all if they took that view! But what I am wondering is what even those words mean. It seems to me that there are a number of different strands in the literature.

Women have contributions of a practical nature to make to the environment which tend to be overlooked.

A corollary of the role of women as farmers is that they have a knowledge of farming techniques which may be valuable but which tends to be overlooked, especially by decision-making processes dominated by men. As users of the forests they have unique knowledge of forest products, and they have knowledge of water resources which is also often overlooked.

"Nature herself is the experiment and women, as sylviculturalists, agriculturists and water resource managers, the traditional natural scientists."[23]

It is true that development specialists have very often undervalued the contribution of subsistence farmers who are male, believing that such farmers are primitive and ignorant. But if the farmers are women their expertise is even less likely to be harnessed.

"Women are overlooked when it comes to training and agricultural extension work."

The other side of the coin is that women will be ignored in educational programmes for farmers. Sometimes even indigenous people will be unaware of the importance of women in the agricultural process, or they will assume that women are unimportant as decision makers. In Tanzania, it has been said:

> "The prevailing folk wisdom—particularly male folk wisdom—has it that women are not particularly bright, not capable of learning modern agriculture."[24]

Also

Women are often by-passed when it comes to access to new technologies or training. This is particularly true in water technologies related to economic production, notably those in irrigation, fisheries and industry. Much more needs to be done in these sectors to change the stereotype of women as non-producers and to involve them more fully in decision-making about types and uses of technologies.[25]

Ecofeminism

It is sometimes argued that women have an intrinsically deeper feeling for the Earth than men. Some manifestations can best be described as celebrations of femaleness.[26] Men may be accused: "the male-dominated power structures . . . which for 500 years have recklessly exploited Africa's natural resources."[27] The literature is western but in traditional society women may perceive themselves to have a greater commitment to environmental value than men.

We worked together to gather stones
We made a dam
All the men who travelled to Mecca say they gathered stones to throw at the evil tombs of the unbelievers
Like them, we gather stones
But we are going to build a dam, a future for our children, our village and all of Africa.[28]

The Female Chauvinist

Some feminist writers have contrasted male and female view of life, the environment and everything on the following lines:

Men	Women
Life	
Life is a problem! Physical life is uncontrollable, threatening. Continuation is uncertain.	Life is part of the eternal cycle of birth, maturation, and death.
Eternal life—true life—transcendental—spiritual scientific life	Life is delivered and nurtured by woman and then disappears back into the womb of Mother Earth.
Nature	
Nature is a constant challenge to the desire to control and rule, to be a 'Master'.	Nature is manifestation and sustenance of life.
A constant fight to conquer, exploit and mould nature.	Mutual nurturance [sic] and utilisation.
To leave one's mark behind!	Nothing to fear, suppress or fight against.

I have to confess to finding this type of dualist thinking somewhat repulsive, believing that it does less than justice to men, and romanticises women, and in fact I am not sure that the "ecofeminist"[29] from whose work I took this table adheres to this view. She does, however, say that she believes "women are the largest alternative movement in the world, a hidden subversive counterculture to the overt masterculture of our time which has brought us to the brink of disaster. Feminine culture could bring an untapped source of traditions, values, skills and insights to the service of humanity to reconstruct a sustainable way of live and economy for the future."[30]

However, "not all feminists are convinced of the unity of interest between the ecology and women's movements. Some deplore the connection and see it as a regression which is bound to reinforce sex-role stereotyping."[31]

One may argue about *how* different female perspectives are, but the fact is that traditionally they have been ignored. The assumption has been that a woman's perspective is either a reflection of some man's, or is not worthy of consideration.

Women Can Do

A major theme in the literature is the importance of women organising. No work on women and the environment is complete without a reference to the Chipko movement, described by one writer as "a kind of feminist movement to protect nature from the greed of men"[32] and very often to Kenya's Green Belt movement and there are many less publicised campaigns and committees.[23] And this is a theme of Agenda 21 of the UN Conference of Environment and Development.[34]

It is possible that this is overdone; not perhaps for its potential, but as to its achievement. Everyone writes about Chipko. Could this possibly be because there are not too many other examples of any size to write about? Or is this just another manifestation of the invisibility of women's efforts? It has been suggested that to view the Chipko movement as essentially a movement of hill women is to romanticise it, and that 'women work only as the limbs of the movement not as its brains.'[35] And Diane Elson says of many organisations: "Most of these self-help schemes seem to be women helping one another to meet their practical gender needs. They formalize the informal female support networks that women everywhere construct, but they perpetuate the idea that unpaid labour for the benefit of others is "women's work" and they construct women's role in community organising as an extension of the domestic role."[36]

Women's Work, it is Often Said, Does Not Get "Counted"

UNCED recommended that national accounts should include women's work. US foundations have estimated that household labour represents 33 per cent of the country's GNP. In countries where women do much of the farming, that contribution is often ignored or understated. As subsistence farming it seems to be treated as an extension of domestic work.[37]

Women's work must be given proper economic value, which seems in danger of slipping into: happiness is in earning money. It is ironic that we lament that one of the results of capitalism is the commodification of everything. Yet one of the themes of the women's movement is that women's work must be valued in financial terms. It has even been suggested that a woman might be happy if she works for a full day as a "housewife" and then for most of the night for money. On the other hand, it is clear that there is inequality if men's work is measured in money and women's work is not. And there is justice in Diane Elson's comment, quoted above, about assumptions that women, but not men, will work for nothing.

Women's Place in Traditional Economy and Society

In some societies the agricultural roles of men and women are intricately tied up with social relationships between men and women, and between women. In Sierra Leone "within the upland farm, male and female tasks are different but complementary and mutually dependent, making food production necessarily a joint venture, central to the cultural construction of gender."[38] The reason that women have the traditional lore about crops, trees and water is precisely because of their place in traditional society. One might say that the general trend in some of the literature is towards strengthening the traditional roles of women. The reference in the Agenda 21 recommendation to the maintenance and promotion of "environmentally sound indigenous technologies that may have been neglected or displaced, in particular in developing countries, paying particular attention to their priority needs and taking into account the complementary roles of men and women (34.14(c))"[39] has somewhat the same ring.

The hand that rocks the cradle rules the world and inculcates environmental values.[40] This seems to have gone seriously wrong somewhere! This whole notion surely encapsulates the dilemma of feminism—or one of them ? Women suffer more than men from environmental crises precisely because they are expected to bear the burden of bringing up children as well as working on the land. To place the burden of educating children in environmental values may reflect reality, but it does not seem to assume any fundamental change in existing power structures. When will the men start to inculcate those values (or any values) in the next generation?

What is Development?

Women's literature reflects precisely the same divisions and controversies as development literature generally. There are perhaps more "anti-developmentalists". Vandana Shiva talks about "mal-development". The objection is not to the change and to the improvement of the condition of women, but to the first world, growth-oriented conceptions of development.

Events like UNCED and their outcome, attended by governments, tend to be oriented towards governments. The recommendations of Agenda 21 are all phrased in terms of Governments should do this and that. However, there is a constant reiteration of the necessity to strengthen people's organisations. The importance of initiatives from grassroots organisations in effective environmental action is a prominent feature of the literature.[41]

Sustainable Development

The new buzz phrase. The great environment compromise which suggests that the planet, or at least humanity, can eat its cake and have it, too. The Brundlandt report argued that we could have development, but that this should not be the price of diminishing the world's resources, and that one generation should pass on to the next as much as it received.[42]

The lack of emphasis on the role of the women in the report has often been remarked on (and, I have to say, one looks in vain in the indexes of many books on environment and development, and even on sustainable development, for any reference to women). Later discussions have, however, suggested that sustainable development is something which women are particularly equipped to promote. "There is a major convergence of interest between environmentally sound and sustainable development and the development of women."[43]

The process reached its apotheosis at UNCED. The Rio Declaration states: Women have a vital role in environmental management and development. Their full participation is therefore essential to achieving sustainable development (Principle 20).

More specifically Agenda 21 refers to:

the necessity for a holistic view of development including improvement of the status and income of women (5.16),

population programmes fully recognising women's right (5.17),

planning should ensure that the views of women and men on needs, perspective and constraints are equally well reflected (5.45),

women and men should have equal right to decide on the spacing of their children (5.50),

women's traditional roles should not be marginalised as a result of the introduction of new management systems (8.5(d)),

Governments . . . should review and refocus existing measures to achieve wider access to land, water and forest resources and ensure equal rights of women . . . (14.18(b)),

Empowerment of women is essential and should be assured through education, training and policies to accord and improve women's rights and access to assets, human and civil rights, labour-saving measures, job opportunities and participation in decision-making (5.48).

There are references to the necessity for access to credit, to aid for women's groups, the involvement of women in management teams, research on the impact of hazardous waste, and the role of women in waste management (especially household waste!). The themes of empowerment, participation, organisation, literacy, education and the necessity to take proper account of women's work recur throughout the document.

Rights

The emphasis on rights recurs throughout the literature as it does in Agenda 21. It is heartening to see such enthusiasm for law! A clear violation of equal protection of the law is the almost universal difference between legal rights to land as between men and women. The necessity for women to have rights to the land which they work crops up constantly in the literature.[44] Not all women suffer the same disadvantages. In Zambia, for example, adult women can acquire and hold property, even after marriage, and this is true of land also, although it is not entirely clear what her customary law rights are over payment for formal work.[45] The position in Zimbabwe is very different.[46] A suitable topic for research ? If the law makes a difference then women in relation to their environment ought to be better off in Zambia.

Women or Human Being?

In other words: are there special rights which ought to be sought for women, or ought it to be enough to ensure for women the same rights as men? It has been suggested that programmes which are on the face of them gender neutral are in reality male-biased.[47] In order for women to benefit as they are intended to it is necessary to take special steps. However, this is not the same thing as having special rights, just what is necessary to achieve the same rights. It is argued that aid projects ought not to operate on the assumption that women all have the same interests. That the concept of "women's projects" is itself misguided, and that it accepts or reinforces traditional roles. What is needed is for aid donors to tackle issues of human rights as such, applying universal standards.[48]

Global Sisters[49]

"For women there are no developed countries" suggests one writer, referring to the fact that almost everywhere women work harder. (I am not sure that is not insensitive, if not down-right insulting to third world women.) There is an assumption that globally the interests of women are similar. On the other hand, it is also argued that first world women, as consumers have a responsibility to cut down their consumption[50]—which does suggest opposing rather than unity of interests.

An implication of reduced public expenditure, which is an important aspect of so many SAPs, was identified by one of the preparatory meetings for UNCED: "We call for the rejection of structural adjustment policies which shift the responsibilities of [sc. for] basic social services from governments to women without compensation or assistance."[51]

Women in many Third World countries would comment: "We should be so lucky: our governments have never accepted this responsibility."

Conclusions

Or not conclusions really, but at least nearing the end of this paper. I am not suggesting that one must select one approach only; quite the opposite in fact, for it is clear that women's position in different societies differs, and it is necessary to conceptualise the problem before providing any sort of answer. So an approach to women and the environment requires a diversity of strategies.

But variety of philosophies is a different matter. I do think that there are a wide variety of different assumptions, beliefs and ideologies in the literature, some of which may be incompatible with each other. Perhaps the issues are most concisely expressed in a series of questions:

> When can women draw upon traditional knowledge, especially that which is intricately tied up with their place in society, without remaining subject to the traditional dominance of men?

Can women be given new knowledge and power without destroying society?

Can women be given new roles without simply adding to already excessive burdens?

Is it that women already know what is needed, or do they need to be taught? And the related: does salvation lie in women's own hands or elsewhere, and if elsewhere, where: with the local community, the state, the international community.

Is it necessary to assert some sort of special relationship between women and nature, which tends to exclude men?

If women have some special relationship with nature, does not that detract from the shared struggle of humankind?

What has western women's green consumerism got to do with the environmental role of the third world rural woman? Is it possible that assumptions of global sisterhood actually obscure reality?

Western women are inclined to feel that legal changes have made relatively little difference to the position of women. Feminist writers urge that the third world women be given rights; who is deceiving whom?

Is it possible to embrace the woman and nature link and attack causes of poverty such as the existing world economic order (or is the latter not a female consideration)?

Is it really clear what "empowerment" and "participation" mean, and if not how can we know what we want the law to do, if it can do anything?

REFERENCES

1. Crudely (it is a crude 'law'): things always work out for the worst.
2. See Irene Dankelman & Joan Davidson, *Women and Environment in the Third World: Alliance for the Future*, London, Earthscan, 1988, p. 98, based on Sathyamala. "Lest we Forget the Women of Bhopal" *Women's Voice* No. 14, June 1987.
3. Taken from Annabel Rodda, *Women and the Environment*, London, Zed Books, 1991, p. 59 (*For editorial reasons, display drawings in the original graph are removed*).

4. Jacobsen. "Closing the Gender Gap in Development" in Lester Brown, (ed.), *State of the World 1993*, Worldwatch Institute, pp. 61–62.
5. UNDIESA, The World's Women cited in Jodi Jacobson, "*Closing the Gender Gap in Development*" in Lester Brown, (ed.), *State of the World 1993*, Worldwatch Institute.
6. See the comment from the *UN World Survey on the Role of Women in Development* UN Doc. A/CONF. 116/4 Rev. 1, 1986, p. 15, "The paucity of statistical data on women's participation in agriculture is striking . . . ." Quoted in Keterina Tomasevski, *Development Aid and Human Rights,* London, Pinter, 1989, 198, n. 32.
7. For a recent example of the 'anti-growth' literature see Richard Douthwaite, *The Growth Illusion,* Beideford, Green Books, 1992.
8. Op cit.
9. *The Violence of the Green Revolution,* London/Penang, Zed Press/Third World Network, 1991.
10. *Ibid.*, p. 206.
11. "Gender Relations and Food Security: Coping with Seasonality, Drought and Famine in South Asia" in Lourdes Benaria and Shelley Feldmm *Unequal Burden: Economic Crises, Persistent Poverty and Women's Work*, Boulder, Westview, 1992, 181.
12. Diane Elson, "From Survival Strategies to Transformation Strategies: Women's Needs and Structural Adjustment" in *ibid.*, 26, 41.
13. "Nature, culture and disasters: Floods and Gender in Bangladesh" in Croll & Parkin, pp. 201, 210.
14. As Diane Elson suggests in response to proposals to tax alcohol and cigarettes provide services for women, "men may simply reduce the amount of money they transfer to their wives so as to be able to maintain their preexisting level of alcohol and tobacco consumption" op. cit., p. 44.
15. I have just received notification of a book: National Campaign for Housing Rights, *Sapping India—Sapping the Indian Poor: The Impact of the IMF Structural Adjustment Package on Housing and Living Conditions in India* (1992).
16. David Reed (ed.), *Structural Adjustment and the Environment,* London, Erthscan, 1992, p. 187.
17. Commonwealth Expert Group on Women and Structural Adjustment for the 1990s, London, Commonwealth Secretariat, 1989, p. l.
18. op. cit., 60–1.
19. Reed, op. cit., pp. 163–164.
20. op. cit., n. 17, p. 126.
21. Shiva, op. cit., p. 215.
22. Soon-Young Yoon, "Water for Life" prepared for the UNCED/UNICEF/UNFPA, Pre-EARTH Summit Symposium on Women and Children First, Geneva 27–30, May 1991, p. 18.
23. Vandan Shiva, *Staying Alive,* quote in Rodda, op cit., p. 47.
24. Louise Fortmann, "Women's Work in Communal Setting: The Tanzanian Policy of *Ujamaa,* in Bay, (ed.), *Women and Work in Africa*, Boulder, Westview 1982, p. 191.

   See also Kathleen A. Staudt, "Women Farmers and Inequities in Agricultural Services" in *ibid.* p. 207, "Women are perhaps perceived as traditional, conservative, poverty-stricken and unwilling or unable to adopt innovation that are promoted by the agricultural administration".

25. Soon-Young Yoon op. cit., at p. 14. See also Rosemary Jommo, "African Women's Indigenous Knowledge in the Management of Natural Resources" prepared for the same symposium.
26. I know this word doesn't exist, but feminity conjures up quite the wrong image. For example, see Judith Plant (ed.), *Healing the Wounds: The Promise of Ecofeminism,* Philadelphia, New Society Publishers, 1989.
27. Rosemary Jommo, "African Women's Indigenous Knowledge in the Management of Natural Resources" UNCED Research Paper No. 18, p. 19.
28. The song of Minata, a Mossi Women in Burkina Fasso, quoted in Soon-Young Yoon, op. cit., at pp. 18–19.
29. Actually she is unhappy about this term believing that "matured" feminism must be ecological.
30. Hikka Peitila The Daughters of the Earth: Women's Culture as a Basis for Sustainable Development in Engel & Engel (eds.) *Ethics of Environment and Development*, London, Belhaven Press, 1990.
31. Michael Redclift, *Development and the Environmental Crisis: Red or Green Alternatives*?, London, Methuen, 1984, p. 125.
32. O.P. Dwivedi, "Satyagraha for conservation: Awakening the spirit of Hinduism" in Engel & Engel, (eds.), *Ethics of Environment and Development op. cit. pp. 201, 209.*
33. E.g. see Margaret Mwangola, "*Ensuring Access to Clean Water by Children in Rural Kenya*" Research Paper No. 49 for UNCED, Feb. 1992.
34. See below.
35. Thomas Weber, *Hugging the Trees: The Story of the Chipko Movement,* Indian ed., New Delhi Penguin 1989, p. 96, quoting G. Joshi [who is a woman], 'Bare Himalaya: A Himalayan Problem,' (1980) 20 *Gandhi Marg* at p. 463.
36. Op. cit., at p. 40.
37. Ariel Salleh, "Living with Nature: Reciprocity or Control?" in Engel & Engel, op. cit., p. 245, at 246–7 discusses "Women as invisible workers".
38. Leach, "Women's crops in Women's spaces" in Croll & Parkin, *Bush Base, Forest Farm: Culture Environment and Development* pp. 77, 83.
39. I have taken my quotations from the summary produced by UNIFEM "An Easy Reference to the Specific Recommendations on Women."
40. E.g. Dankelman & Davidson, p. 174.
41. See e.g. Dharam Ghai and Jessica Vivian (eds.), *Grassroots Environmental Action: People's Participation in Environmental Development*, London, Rlutledge, 1992.
42. *Our Common Future.*
43. See fn. 2, p. 174.
44. E.g. Dankelman & Davidson, p. 177, Barry Munslow, *The Fuelwood Trap: A Study of the SADCC Region*, London, Earthscan, 1988, p. 89 (on Zimbabwe).
45. C. N. Himonga, K.A. Turner and C.S. Beyani, "An Outline of the Legal Status of Women in Zambia" in Julie Stewart & Alica Armstrong (eds.), *The Legal Situation of Women in Southern Africa*, Harare, University of Zimbabwe, 1990, pp. 156–7.

46. J. Stewart, W. Ncube, N. Maboreke and A. Armstrong, in *ibid.*, p. 176.
47. See Diane Elson, op. cit.
48. See the discussion in Tomasevki, op. cit. Chap. 10 "Non-discrimination as the central issue: women in development aid."
49. The expression is used by Petral Kelly in her foreword to *Plant Healing the Wounds.*
50. See, for example Maria Mies, "*Consumption Patterns of the North—the Cause of Environmental Destruction and Poverty in the South*" UNCED Research Paper No. 21, July 1991.
51. World Women's Congress for a Health Planet, International Policy Action Committee/Women's Environment and Development Organisation, Miami, Florida, 8–2, November 1991, printed in Robinson (ed.), *Agenda 21 and the UNCED Proceedings* Vol. 2, New York, Oceana, 1992, pp. 1023, 1024.

10

Human Rights and Muslim Women in India

*P.C. Juneja**

Woman, the source of love and compassion, the birth giver of man, has always been exploited by man. Howsoever advancement a society may claim, it cannot boast of equality between men and women. The advanced societies proclaim equality but practise inequality and discrimination against women. The position is worse in under-developed societies. During primitive societies, the woman was treated as chattel and a saleable commodity. Even now when the world is heading towards twenty first century, the existence of prostitution system points to degrading position of women and the callous attitude of male dominated society. It depicts the attitude of men towards women and the place the man has given to a woman.

Women are prone to criminal advancements. Rape, molestation, sexual exploitation of poor women or women under custody, dowry deaths, domestic violence, father raping the daughter,[1] brother raping the sister, eveteasing in buses or on the roads, just shows how much the male dominated society cares for women. The recent tandoor murder case in which political high ups appear to be involved, shows how cruel a man can be against women.[2] Howsoever we may brag about our development and constitutional protection to women and their rising to high positions in police, executive, minis-

---

* Professor of Law, Maharshi Dayanand University, Rohtak-124 001.

tries, and business, the fact remains that women remain subordinate to men.

Let us look into a family where both the male and female are working. Both go out for earning a contribution to the family budget but the household affairs are the responsibility of the women. Howsoever, higher the position of the woman may be, at home she is subordinate to her husband. The word 'husband' itself depicts the dominating position of man. Whatever may be the Declaration of Human Rights or the constitutional guarantees, the women remain subordinate and this subordination of women is not recognised as violation of human rights neither by international lawyers nor by municipal lawyers. Even the educated men do not hesitate in thrashing their wives if they do not agree to their point of view. Difference of opinion is treated by men as revolt by wives and the result is violence. Women are mostly the victims of domestic violence.

Mahatma Gandhi wrote about the position of Indian Women at the time of independence that "Today the sole occupation of a woman amongst us is supposed to bear children, to look after her husband and otherwise drudge for the household. Not only is the woman condemned to domestic slavery but when she goes out as a labourer to earn wages, though she works harder than man, she is paid less wages."[3] Mahatma Gandhi was of the view that women were not only in the position of slaves but were also taught to regard themselves as slaves of men.[4] The position has not changed much even after forty eight years of independence in India. In the traditional legal environment of many societies, women lacked legal capacity themselves and received entitlements according to the disposition of men. Women's interests were subordinated to men's acquisitive, protective and self serving dispositions and to men's perception of the right balance among men's duties of altruism, protection of family integrity and promotion of public moral order.[5] The subordination and indignities of women go unseen, in part, because masculine frames of reference can blind society to women's experience. When suffering is seen, it still may go unrecognised as a human right violation because of conceptual biases in law.[5a]

Even in present day India, the cruel attitude of male dominated society towards women is clear from the report of Home Ministry which has stated that (1) at every 54 minutes a woman is raped (2) at every 26 minutes a girl or a lady is molested (3) at every one hour there is a dowry death (4) at every 51 minutes there is eve-teasing and (5) at every 33 minutes there is some offence towards women.[6] Similar is the position of women in other countries and they are struggling for getting recognition.

But the position of a Muslim women is worst. It may be due to the religion or otherwise, she is subordinated more than the women of other religions and cultures. Let us take the example of a married Muslim woman. Though marriage is a contract under Muslim law, this is a one sided contract. To enter into the marriage bond, both the parties have to consent, but to break it, male is in the.dominant position. He has not to specify any reason, he has not go to the court. He has simply to say *Talaq* thrice and the marriage is gone. But this right is not given to a woman. If she wants *talaq* she has to go to the court on specified grounds and on the condition to surrender the claim for *mehr* and if she has already received the same, to return the same. She does not enjoy the same amount of freedom as the husband does. The husband may divorce her without any reason, simply on whims, simply because she no more attracts him. The sentiments of a Muslim woman have no value. Though marriage is a contract, this contract is between unequal partners, with unequal rights. The municipal law can not help the Muslim women because marriage comes under personal law which is supported by religion and the state is forbidden from interfering with the religion of any person.[7]

Muslim Women's Protection Act 1986 is an another nail in the rights of Muslim women. Though the Act purports to protect the rights of Muslim women, in fact it protects the rights of Muslim husbands. There is a uniform law under Sec. 125 of Cr. P.C. for providing maintenance to divorced wife, if she is unable to maintain herself. This right is given to every divorced wife irrespective of her religion. Same right was given to a Muslim wife also and it was confirmed by Supreme Court in Shah Bano's case. But Muslim males took it as interference in their religion and agitated for amendment of Sec. 125 Cr. P.C. so far as Muslims were concerned. The party in power without caring for the rights of Muslim women to equality, withdrew the protection of Sec. 125 Cr. P.C. to Muslim women and passed a new law i.e. Muslim Women's Protection Act 1986, which provides that a divorced wife can claim maintenance from her husband during her *iddat* period and after that she should knock at the doors of those relatives who will inherit her property on her death. And if the relatives are not able to maintain her, she should look towards *Waqf* board for maintenance.[8]

Since the husband has absolute right to divorce without any reason, the new Act envisages that when the Muslim women looses her charm, she may loose her husband and also the maintenance. She also looses the dignity when she goes to beg the maintenance from her relatives or *Waqf* board. The dominant Muslim male society has deprived her of every right over the divorcee husband, thus making her more and more dependent and subordinate. Now, howsoever cruel a husband may be, she has to remain obedient, subservient and not to interfere with his arbitrariness otherwise she may loose every thing. The Act has put her in such a position that even if the husband is an idiot, she has to obey her and act according to his whims. Now the question arises, can the State not protect its citizens from the high handedness of their religion. If the religion is cruel to the man, is he bound to suffer that cruelty and there is no remedy? Has the State no responsibility towards its citizens? Will she allow its citizens to suffer the violation of their human rights at the hands of their religion? Are Muslim women not entitled to the constitutional rights and freedom as other women are? The State instead of helping her, has withdrawn the protection given to her by Sec. 125 Cr. P.C. Has the State acted with responsibility? No, the State itself under the pressure of Muslim males, has discriminated against Muslim women and violated their right to equality and dignity.

Before the passing of the Muslim Women Protection Act, the judiciary tried to help the Muslim women and bring them at par with other women, at least in case of maintenance from the husband. It was held in many cases that divorced

Muslim woman was entitled to maintenance under Sec. 125 of Cr. P.C. as any other divorced women, may be Hindu, Christian or Parsee.[9] But this Act puts the Muslim women in more subordinate position as compared to men. Or we can say that through this Act the Indian parliament approved the subordination of Muslim women and as a corollary, of all the women and did not treat this subordination as violation of human rights.

There are many consequences of this approval of subordination. Muslim husband has been left absolutely unbridled. He can now divorce his wife without any fear of loosing any thing. After the divorce, he has no liability towards the divorced wife (except for maintenance during *Iddat* period) He has the despotic right of divorcing his wife by simply pronouncing 'talaq' thrice without any justifiable reason. He has not to explain or justify his action. He is answerable to none. The little pop gun of maintenance provided by Sec. 125 of Cr. P.C. has also been snatched by the Muslim Women Protection Act. Look at the unfortunate situation of Muslim women that the Act which deprives the Muslim women of the protection given to their counterparts in other religions is purported to be protecting the rights of Muslim women, as the name of the Act implies, "Muslim Women Protection Act" 1986. Of course the Act protects their right to remain subordinate.

Despite the "Declaration on the Elimination of Discrimination against Women," proclaimed by the General Assembly of the United Nations on 7th November 1967 in resolution No. 2263 (XXII) and despite Article 7 of Declaration of Human Rights crying hoarse that "All are equal before the law and are entitled without any discrimination to equal protection of the law. All are entitled to equal protection against any discrimination in violation of this Declaration and against any incitement to such discrimination," the Muslim women have been discriminated by the parliament itself.

The same Declaration of Human Rights echoes in Art. 14 of our Constitution i.e. "The State shall not deny to any person equality before the law or the equal protection of laws within the territory of India." The unfortunate situation is that instead of guaranteeing equality before law, the State through Muslim Women Protection Act has withdrawn that equality from Muslim women. Art. 15 prohibits discrimination on the ground of sex and clause 3 of the Article allows the State to make special provisions for the welfare of women and children. Just look at the special provision made for Muslim women. It is the State which has violated the human rights of Muslim women. When someone violates our human rights we look towards the State for help. When the State itself is violator of human rights whom shall we look to?

Many jurists, women's organisations and intellectuals cried hoarse against the Muslim Women Protection Bill but the government under the pressure of fundamentalists and the greed for votes of minorities went ahead with the bill, of course, with the ridiculous amendment that the divorced Muslim wife can avail of the benefits of Sec. 125 of Cr. P.C. if the husband agrees for the same.[10] Why should he agree? When he has not to pay any maintenance under the Act except for *iddat* period.

It is a general rule that nobody will help us unless we help ourselves. So, the NGO's should start a legal literacy movement to make the Muslim women aware of their human rights and make them stand on their own feet to fight for their rights. If they become aware of their rights none on earth can snatch the same from them. Unfortunately the Muslim women (and so are other women) are taught at home that they have to obey their husbands and remain subordinate to them. Even the educated Muslim ladies are not ready to come forward and fight for their rights. They can at least fight against those discriminations which are not ordained by religion. They should also fight for changes in religious provisions which discriminate against women because religion proclaimed by Allah cannot be discriminatory.

REFERENCES

1. Ariti Jagirdar, "No Papa No." *Hindustan Times,* Sunday Magazine 7.5.95.
2. A Women Naina Sahni was killed, cut into pieces and thrown into tandoor. The murderer is alleged to be an office bearer of a political party, *Hindustan Times* July 12, 1995.

3. Cf. Lotika Sarkar, "Status of Woman & Law as Instrument of Social Change" *JILI*, 1983, Vol. 25 p. 262.
4. *Ibid.*
5. Rebecca J Cook, "State Responsibility for violation of Human Rights of Women," *Harvard Human Rights Journal*, 1994, Vol. 7, p. 131.

5(a) *Ibid.*, p. 128

6. *Nav Bharat Times*, February 20, 1995 p. 8.
7. Art. 25 Constitution of India.
8. Sec. 4, Muslim Women's Protection Act, 1986.
9. *Bai Tahira's case*, AIR 1979 Sc. 362.
   Fuzlunbi v. *K. Khader Vali* AIR 1980 Sc. 1730.
   Zohra Khatton v. *Mohd. Ibrahim* AIR 1981 Sec. 1243.
   Mohammed Yamin v. *Shamina Bano* 1984 Cr. L.J. 1297 (All.).
10. Sec. 5 of Muslim Women Protection Act 1986.

11

Agricultural Labour and Human Rights in India

*Neena Vashist**

The agrarian structure in India reflects mass poverty among agricultural labourers which is the result of feudal relations of productions and hybrid bourgeois property rights on land. Two thirds of India's total population is dependent solely on agriculture for livelihood, one third of which consists of agricultural labour. The class of agricultural labour is the most exploited and deprived section of the society. Hunger, malnutrition, abject poverty and unemployment are the main maladies from which the agricultural labour suffers. The Indian agricultural labour is not unique in its sufferings as this abysmal poverty grips the lives of no less than one billion men, women and children who constitute the poorest group of people all over the world.

The gravity and awareness of problems of agricultural labour has increased considerably and is drawing attention of the whole world. In the words of J.F. Kennedy, "If free society cannot serve many who are poor, it cannot serve the few who are rich." At the institutional levels the promulgation of equal and inalienable rights of man and women has continued unabated. Article(s) 22 to 25 of the (1948) Universal Declaration of Human Rights lay down in unambiguous words some basic rights which combine together to fructify the dignity

* Lecturer in Economics, Faculty of Law, Maharshi Dayanand University, Rohtak.

and development of both men and women. Art. 22 provides, that "Everyone as a member of the society has the right to social security. . . ."

Art. 23 provides, that "everyone has the right to work, . . . to just and favourable conditions of work, . . . the right to equal pay for equal work. . . ." Art. 24 provides, that "Everyone has . . . reasonable limitation of working hours and periodic holidays with pay". Art. 25 provides, that "Everyone has the right to adequate standard of living . . . , right to security in the event of unemployment, sickness disability, widowhood, old age or other lack of livelihood in circumstances beyond his control . . . ".

It also states, "Motherhood and childhood are entitled to special care and assistance." These rights have been reinforced by the (1966) Covenant on Economic and Social Rights. The above mentioned rights are the most basic rights which have acquired international recognition and application over the years. It is in the background of these universalized rights that the milieu of agricultural labour in India should be examined. . . . ," Further Article 25 states, "Everyone has the right to security in the event of unemployment, sickness, disability, widowhood, old age or other lack of livelihood in circumstance beyond his control." It also states, "Motherhood and childhood are entitled to special care and assistance."

To begin with, it would be necessary to see, how agricultural labour has been defined. Agricultural labour according to international standard classification includes cultivation of land, rearing and maintenance of livestocks, forest operations, fishing and hunting, however, it does not include fruit growing or plantations. Whereas in India Agricultural Labour Enquiry (1950–51) defines agricultural labourers as those who are engaged in raising crops on payment of wages. The second Agricultural Labour enquiry (1956–57) enlarged the category of agricultural workers to include also those who are engaged in allied occupations like animal husbandry, dairy, poultry etc.[1] The National Commission on Labour regards agricultural labourer as one who is basically unskilled and unorganized and has nothing but physical labour to exist upon. National Commission on Labour 1969 expressed the opinion that agricultural labour constitutes an overwhelmingly major section of rural labour.[2]

Rural Labour Enquiry, 1974–75, treats a person as an agricultural labour if he followed one or more of the following occupations in the capacity of labourers on hire or exchange whether in kind or partly in cash and partly in kind; (a) farming, including the cultivation and tillage of soil etc; (b) dairy farming; (c) raising of livestock, bee-keeping or poultry; (d) production, cultivation, growing and harvesting; (e) any practice performed on a farm as incidental to or in conjunction with the farm operations (including any forestry and timbering operations and the preparation for market and delivery to storage or to market or to carriage for transportation of farm products.[3]

The existing poverty of agricultural population is a question mark to the economic development in almost all the countries in general and developing countries like India in particular. The preamble of our Constitution, in consonance with the Constitution of ILO declares; "Justice, Social, Economic and Political, as the first among other objectives of constituting India into a sovereign, socialist, secular and democratic republic." The Directive Principles of State Policy also promise everyone, "the right to an adequate means of livelihood, living wage and a decent standard of life."

Though efforts have been made after independence to improve economic conditions of people engaged in agriculture but the condition of this class has deteriorated with time. Among them the poorest and weakest i.e. agricultural labour has suffered the most. The benefits have been hogged by a tiny minority among the agricultural population.[4]

In the present context it becomes necessary to think seriously about protecting the human rights of agricultural labourers. A great hue and cry is being raised at national and international levels about the violation of civil and political rights, but no attention is being paid to the worst sufferers whose basic rights of means of livelihood i.e. food and shelter are violated everywhere, every day. From time to time various declarations have been made by various international organisations affirming their faith in protection of human rights. The Paris Declaration of November 21, 1990 signed by all European and North American nations seeks to afford protection when it says:

> "Human rights and fundamental freedoms are the birth right of all human beings, are inalienable and are guaranteed by law. Their protection and promotion is the first responsibility of the Govt."

The human rights situation of agricultural labour in India is indeed dismal. The living and working conditions of agricultural labour is miserable. Even among the unorganised agricultural sector the worst sufferers are women and children. Women labour is discriminated against in disbursement of wages, working conditions, neglect of their health and maternity benefits. Similarly children are the worst exploited lot as they are made to work for longer periods, irrespective of nature of their employment. This goes against the mandates of Article(s) 15(3), 24, 39 and 45 of our Constitution. These provisions direct the State to take special measures to protect the rights of the children. Particularly it is the duty of the State to prevent the exploitation of children, physically, socially and mentally.

In today's world when the various human right forums both at national and international level are concentrating on creation of awareness of these rights, considerable attention needs to be paid to the basic human rights of labour in agriculture sector. The census 1981 indicates that nearly eighty percent population of the country dwells in villages. Various studies have clarified that nearly a quarter of agrarian population of India consists of agricultural labour and more than fifty percent of agriculture labour have no land.[5] Some specific problems of agricultural labour need a closer look to understand their real position.

Agriculture does not provide employment for the whole year. The average period of their employment is around six to eight months. The seasonal unemployment leads the agricultural labour to face evils of poverty, discrimination among men and women labour abounds and a situation of bonded labour has come to exist in this sector. Not surprisingly, the working paper prepared in the Planning Commission on the employment situation on the eve of the Eighth Five Year Plan shows a number of disturbing signs; more open unemployment, increasing casualization and growing dependence on unreliable and low productivity employment in the unorganised activities.[6]

The other prominent disadvantage is insecurity of job. There are hardly any growth of rural non-agricultural activities where these labour can be absorbed. Generally they are kept in an insecure position with a view to deprive them of certain social security benefits which they might derive once they are employed on permanent basis.[7] Here, the basic principle of equality i.e. equal means of livelihood are denied to agricultural labour.

Under the Minimum Wages Act of 1948, many states have fixed minimum wages to be paid to the agricultural labourer. But most of the provisions of the Act have remained on paper. The data on agricultural wages according to the nature of employment (casual or attached) of agricultural labour are not available on uniform basis from different states. The realization of administrative difficulties in minimum wages fixation in agricultural employment led the ILO to make the following remarks:

> "The enforcement of minimum wages in rural India is virtually impossible, given the structure of the village society and the mode of payment which is partly in kind and often in the form of a meal. Actual wage rates are affected by the relationship between the land owners and agricultural labourers which varies in every situation."[8]

Between 1971–72 and 1984–85 the real wages of agricultural labour in Bihar increased by 50.29 per cent and 73.64 per cent in case of male and female labourers respectively, though prices had increased by almost 200 per cent in the same period.[9]

Recently, the Centre for Labour Studies, Delhi made out a case for revision of minimum farm wages to Rs. 20.42 to make it subsistence wages.[10] Commendable is the move of Govt. of Bihar to increase the wages in the unorganised sector at the rate of 3 paise daily on the rise of every percent in the consumer price index. In West Bengal, Panchayats as elected bodies of rural people, Kisan Sabhas as a mobiliser of peasants and left wing political parties, all active at the grassroots level have seriously implemented minimum wage legislation and its revision.[11]

In other states also though the minimum Wages Act, 1948 is applicable with all its force, there is no machinery to enforce its proper application. In Haryana, there is a practice of keeping a 'Sajhi' (partner for helping in matters of agricultural production). He is generally a person who agrees to work for an agricultural year on a paltry sum and lives and dies with the master. This is no better than a bonded labour.

Gender differential has determined both work and wages in rural areas. This difference emanates from the ideology operating behind the evaluation of the work of male as compared to female agricultural labourers, their capacity to perform certain tasks and the awarding of this performance in terms of wages.[12]

The State is directed to ensure under Article 39(d) of the Constitution equal pay for equal work for both men and women. In this regard, the Parliament passed an Equal Remuneration Act 1976 which provides for equal pay for equal work to men and women for doing the same work or work of similar nature. But unfortunately this concept of equality does not find its fulfillment in actual practice. Poverty and illiteracy of agricultural labour, absence of knowledge of the existence of legislation, casual nature of employment, unorganised character of agricultural labour are the reasons in non-effective implementation of the Act in India. Majority of agricultural labourers are living below poverty line, which eventually result in their perpetual indebtedness. Like indebtedness, bondage is also becoming an acute problem in the agricultural labour sector. The Bonded Labour Abolition Act, 1976 was passed to abolish the evil system of engaging bonded labour which is the worst form of human bondage. However, this Act is hardly of any vital use to the agricultural labourers, because of reasons noted above.

The use of pesticides and insecticides in agriculture specially in rice regions of India, pose a serious threat to the health of the agricultural labour. Loevinsohu, 1987 reports; "There has been a 27 per cent increase in mortality among economically active farmers in rural areas of Philippines, most likely due to unsafe use of toxic chemicals and pesticides." On the basis of available statistics of various countries he argues, "that the currently accepted figure of 10,000 deaths annually all over the world due to accidental intoxification with insecticides is a substantial underestimate."[13]

In a country like India, where agricultural labour is illiterate and untrained as far as the use of pesticides is concerned the danger is substantially great. At the Indian Science Congress in 1985 Devika Nag and U.K. Misra of the King George Medical College Lucknow, said that workers who sprayed these agrochemicals reported visual impairment, dislike of bright light and night blindness and exposure to these pesticides led to mental disturbances, anxiety, insomnia and depression. A recent WHO study, which analysed cereals, pulses, milk, eggs and meat samples from across the country found that 59 per cent of the samples contained pesticide residues and in more than 30 percent of the samples, the residues were far in excess of tolerance limit.[14]

There is a need to provide social security to the agricultural labour. Our law has been extended only to organised agricultural farms by the judicial interpretation. With the mechanization of farming particularly in states like Punjab and Haryana, farming has become accident prone. Amputation of hands in threshers and crushers and other machines is a common feature in mechanized farming. There should be compulsory insurance to cover all risks of this nature. In India, Kerala is the only state which has provided comprehensive legislation for agricultural labourers. The Kerala Agricultural Workers Act 1974 provides for the welfare of agricultural workers in the state of Kerala; and also to regulate the condition of their work. Matters relating to disputes between the agricultural workers and their employers are fully covered by this Act. This Act provides for security of employment, hours of work, rest intervals and overtime, fixation and payment of wages, provident fund scheme and enforcement procedure for effective implementation of the Act. It has been suggested that the central legislature should enact a comprehensive measure to provide for security of service, safety of agricultural labour etc. If need be, the state govts. can pass acts to supplement the central provisions according to the peculiar conditions prevailing in their respective states.

The champions of human rights have made declarations and announcements about protecting rights of labour but they have confined to the plight and need of labour in the organised sector only. Not much attention has been paid to agricultural labourers, except a few ILO declarations. Similarly at the national level, Labour Welfare Ministry and various non-governmental organisations have tried to create awareness about violation of their rights but no concrete steps have been taken. A general lack of concern and indifference of administration has resulted in worsening of their condition.

What is most needed at present is not holding conventions and chalking out programmes for protecting the rights of agricultural labour but the implementation of various laws already available. The basic tenets of human rights aiming to maintain dignity of human life and human welfare becomes meaningless if the basic needs of labour are not provided for. Efforts should be made to provide good working conditions which would necessarily include providing adequate wages, removal of unemployment, partial and full, social security, health-care, special provisions for women and children as also for education of children.

REFERENCES

1. *Agriculture Labour Enquiry* 1956–57 consistent with the definition of agricultural employment contained in part II of the schedule appended to the Minimum Wages Act, 1948.
2. Report on National Commission on Labour, 1962.
3. *Rural Labour Enquiry* 1974–75, p. 6–7.
4. *Id.*
5. (a) The World Bank staff paper No. 320 published in 1979 entitled Small Farmers and Landless in South Asia.
   (b) Sixth Five Year Plan draft (1980–85), has also estimated 50 percent of the Agricultural Labour households have no land.
6. Report of Planning Commission. Eighth Five Year Plan 1990(a).
7. Srivastava M.K., *Agricultural Labour and Law,* 1993 p. 44–45.
8. *Id.*
9. Krishna Chaitanya, "Myth of Minimum Wages in the Organised Sector." *EPW* Dec. 14, 1991.
10. *Indian Express*, New Delhi, Feb. 17, 1990.
11. V.M. Rao, *EPW* June 27, 1992.
12. Chowdry Prem, "High Participation Low Evaluation: Women and Work in Haryana," *EPW* Dec. 25, 1993.

13. Loevinsohu, 1987, Quoted from Joan P. Mencher; "Agricultural Labour and Pesticides in Rice Region of India" *EPW* Sept. 28, 1991.
14. *Supra* note 12.

PART III

HUMAN RIGHTS AND JUDICIAL DISCOURSE

12

Constitutional Liability of the State: Erosion of Sovereign Immunity

*Mahendra P. Singh**

While the question of sovereign immunity of the state for the tortuous acts of its servants was and is still being debated, the courts have discovered a new route to bypass it. At the dawn of the last decade, in *Rudul Sah* v. *State of Bihar*[1] in a *habeas corpus* petition under Article 32 of the Constitution the Supreme Court not only ordered release of the petitioner from illegal detention but also granted him compensation of Rs. 30,000/- as an interim measure without prejudice to his right to file a civil suit for compensation. Relying upon the wide powers conferred on it in Article 32 for the enforcement of the fundamental rights and asking the general question whether in exercise of those powers it could pass an order for the payment of money if such an order was 'in the nature of compensation consequential upon the deprivation of a fundamental right,' the court held: 'One of the telling ways in which the violation of that right (right to personal liberty) can reasonably be prevented and due compliance with the mandate of Article 21 secured, is to mulct its violators in the payment of monetary compensation.' It added that 'the state must repair the damage done by its officers to the petitioner's rights.'

---

* Professor of Law and Dean Faculty of Law, University of Delhi-110007.

It is doubtful whether in the face of the dichotomy of sovereign and nonsovereign functions created in *P. & O. Steam Navigation Co.* v. *Secretary of State for India*[2] and carried upto *Kasturilal* v. *State of U.P.*[3] Rudul Sah could have succeeded in getting any compensation for his detention in prison. But ever since the grant of compensation to him, claims for such compensation have become a regular feature under Article 32 as well as under Article 226 and they have been invariably upheld. But it was being done without any refinement of the principles of liability or form of remedy until after a decade in *Nilbati Behera* v. *State of Orissa*[4] the Supreme Court found it necessary to make certain clarifications. The clarifications became necessary in view of the observations in Rudul Sah that 'the petitioner could have been relegated to the ordinary remedy of a suit if his claim of compensation was actually controversial' and that 'Article 32 cannot be used as substitute for the enforcement of rights and obligations which can be enforced efficaciously through the ordinary processes.' Because these observations could tend to raise a doubt that the remedy under Article 32 could be denied 'if the claim to compensation was factually controversial' and, therefore, not being a distinct remedy available to the petitioner in addition to the ordinary processes, 'the court thought it necessary to clear this doubt and to indicate the precise nature of this remedy which is distinct and in addition to the available ordinary processes, in case of violation of the fundamental rights.'

Drawing a distinction between the liability of the state for the violation of the fundamental rights and the liability in private law for payment of compensation in an action on tort, the Court laid down the following proposition in *Nilbati Behera*.

It may be mentioned straightaway that award of compensation in a proceeding under Article 32 by this Court or by the High Court under Article 226 of the Constitution is a remedy available in public law, based on strict liability for contravention of fundamental rights to which the principle of sovereign immunity does not apply, even though it may be available as a defence in private law in an action based on tort. This is a distinction between the two remedies to be borne in mind which also indicates the basis on which compensation is awarded in such proceedings.

This statement consists of at least the following propositions: (a) award of compensation under Article 32 and 226 is a public law remedy distinct from private law action in tort; (b) the distinction between the two kinds of remedies is also the basis for compensation; (c) the principle of sovereign immunity does not apply to the public law remedies; and (d) the liability of the state in these proceedings is strict. Explaining these propositions the Court said that *Kasturilal* is confined to the sphere of liability in tort, which is distinct from the State's liability for contravention of fundamental rights to which the doctrine of sovereign immunity has no application in the constitutional scheme. Again, relying upon an English precedent in support of public and private law distinction, it added.

> "It follows that 'a claim in public law for compensation' for contravention of human rights and fundamental freedoms, the protection of which is guaranteed in the Constitution, is an acknowledged remedy for enforcement and protection of such rights, and such a claim based on strict liability made by resorting to a constitutional remedy provided for the enforcement of a fundamental right is 'distinct from, and in addition to, the remedy in private law for damages for the tort' resulting from the contravention of the fundamental right. The defence of sovereign immunity being inapplicable and alien to the concept of guarantee of fundamental rights, there can be no question of such a defence being available in the constitutional remedy. It is this principle which justifies award of monetary compensation for contravention of fundamental rights . . . when that is the only practicable mode of redress available for the contravention made by the State or its servants in the purported exercise of their powers, and enforcement of fundamental right is claimed by resort to the remedy in public law under the Constitution by recourse to Articles 32 and 226 of the Constitution."

The Court buttressed these propositions with reference to its powers and obligations under Articles 32 and 142 and to the possibility of state officials extinguishing human lives if the only relief available was punishment for any resulting offence or recovery of damages under private law. It also emphasised the need of public law remedy being more 'readily available when invoked by the have-nots, who are not possessed of the wherewithal for enforcement of their rights in private law.' In his concurring opinion Justice Dr. Anand emphasised that in case of fundamental rights, particularly Article 21, the 'duty of care on the part of the State is strict and admits of no exceptions' and the public law remedies which ensure the rule of law and civilize public power must also protect and preserve the rights of the citizens. 'Law', he said, 'is in the process of development and the process necessitates developing separate public law procedures as also public law principles.'

While *Nilbati Behera* has made it clear that factual controversies and sovereign immunity cannot defeat a claim for compensation under Articles 32 and 226 for the enforcement of a fundamental right, it has introduced several other propositions viz. whether the claim for compensation can be upheld notwithstanding the principle of sovereign immunity because of the nature of remedy under Articles 32 and 226 or because the claim for the enforcement of fundamental rights is substantially different from the claim of enforcement of any other rights and therefore the principle of sovereign immunity cannot be invoked as a defence to it. Following *Rudul Sah* and its progeny as well as some foreign precedents in *C. Ramkonda Reddy* v. *State*,[5] the Andhra Pradesh High Court has held that the sovereign immunity is no bar to a private law suit for compensation for the violation of the fundamental right to life. An appeal against that decision is reportedly pending in the Supreme Court. It is of some interest to wait and watch whether the Supreme Court would like to decide the issue in terms of special nature of the proceedings under Articles 32 and 226 or in terms of the special position of the fundamental rights. If it follows the former course it will still be denying easy access to the courts to the have-nots to claim compensation for the violation of their fundamental rights at the district level and flooding its own and/or the High Courts already unmanageable docket with additional claims for compensation, some of which may be even factually controversial. If it follows the latter course then the emphasis shifts from remedy to substance. In that case the sovereign immunity defence is reduced to nonfundamental rights issues irrespective of the nature of proceedings. This course will strengthen and widen the enforcement network and mechanism of the fundamental rights which they richly deserve in view of the clear mandate of Article 13 as well as of Articles 32 and 226. It will also not conflict in any way with *Kasturilal,* though at the relevant time the appellant in that case could have claimed violation of his fundamental right to property. Again, it will also be consistent with the constitutional developments in many other common law countries some of which are also mentioned in *C. Ramkonda Reddy* and can be easily traced in judicial decisions and academic writings. Its logic may also be extended to other constitutional rights which have been put beyond the reach of the state in the same manner as the fundamental rights.

This approach is also consistent with the private law and public law distinction to which the Court has resorted in *Nilbati Behera*. The distinction is very important and given full practical effect in the civil law world. The principles of the public law of torts, for example, in France are very different from the principles of the private law of torts. The doctrine of strict or no fault liability which the Court has established in *Nilbati Behera* is justified only in the public law tort in France and not in the private law. Thus the very foundations and principles of public law are different from those of the private law though they may be influencing each other. The efforts to create a separate branch of public law of torts has, however, not been very successful in our law in so far as doubts have been cast on the principle of strict liability propounded by the Court [vide *M.C. Mehta* v. *Union of India*[6], and *Union Carbide Corpn.* v. *Union of India*[7]]. I do not see any apparent limitation on the courts in creating separate principles of liability in the sphere of public law. But will the courts be willing to create one in view of the unity of common law? Splitting that unity may have serious implications for our law and the legal system which require serious debate and discussion. A legislative effort in that direction will perhaps be more appropriate than the judicial.

Legislation can also take care of liability of public authorities generally and lay down principles which conform to the principles of justice and the rule of law as they operate and must operate in any civilized society. It can also fill the gaps with respect to the requirement of actual financial loss or injury, availability of compensation in addition to or in lieu of any other remedy, quantum and kind of damages, the forum for claiming such damages or compensation, etc. A useful discussion in this regard is provided in *Administrative Justice*,[8] from which help may be drawn in reforming our law.

Until, however, a comprehensive legislation is undertaken in this regard, the courts and the juristic deliberations should continue to refine and develop the law in the direction that ensures justice to the individual consistently with the efficiency of the administration. Fortunately it is now being realised day by day that assurance of justice to the individual also improves the efficiency of the administration. Therefore, the two goals instead of being contradictory are supplementary to each other. Moving in that direction the Supreme Court in *Lucknow Development Authority* v. *M.K. Gupta*,[9] in addition to holding that sovereign immunity cannot be claimed by statutory authorities from the liability to pay compensation for defective services and consequent harassment and suffering to the individual under the Consumer Protection Act, 1986, has also enforced the principle reiterated since *Rudul Sah* that the amount of compensation could be recovered from the erring officer or officers and ordered that the amount of Rs. 10,000 awarded by the Commission for mental harassment shall be recovered from such officers proportionately from their salary. The extension and application of this common law principle to state authorities is a very welcome development to ensure that there is no willful intent or gross negligence on the part of the individual functionaries in causing injury to the citizen. The German Constitution specifically provides for such course in Article 34.

It is a little enigmatic that the principle of sovereign immunity, a medieval and feudal remnant, which has long been discarded in the civil law system and was discarded even in England before our Constitution came into existence and which seemed to have been discarded under the Constitution in *State of Rajasthan* v. *Mst. Vidhyawati*[10] was resurrected in Kasturilal and is being preserved until this day. There are legal systems like the French which not only treat the state like any other master for the wrongs of its servants but also subject it to strict liability to which the other masters are not subject and also provide compensation for injuries caused not only by administrative measures but even by legislative measures. These principles of French law are fast entering English law through the European Union. *Rudul Sah* and its progeny are far away from the eventuality where the fundamental rights are violated under a law which is later on declared unconstitutional and still further from the eventuality of a law which though constitutional puts disproportionate burden on an individual. We cannot evade these questions for too long and must look for comprehensive solutions through legislation and judicial innovation.

REFERENCES

Reprinted with permission of the Author and Editor (Lawyer's Collective). The article was first published in May 1994 issue of Lawyer's Collective.

1. AIR 1983 SC 1086.
2. (1861) 5 Bom. BCR App 1.
3. AIR 1965 1039.
4. AIR 1993 SC 1960.
5. AIR 1989 A P 235.
6. AIR 1987 SC 1086.
7. AIR 1992 SC 248, 261.
8. Oxford Clarendon Press 1988, 331 ff.
9. (1994) 1 SCC 243.
10. AIR 1962 SC 933.

13

Compensation for Human Rights Violation and Judicial Policing of the Police

*Paramjit S. Jaswal**
*Nishtha Jaswal***

It is heart-rending to note that day in and day out we come across with the news of blood-curdling incidents of police brutality and atrocities, alleged to have been committed, in utter disregard and in all breaches of humanitarian law and universal human rights as well as total negation of the constitutional guarantees and human decency.[1] When the police becomes an irresponsible lot, the plight of the people becomes deplorable. No doubt that the horizon of human rights is expanding. But in the recent times too many cases of human rights violations by the police, in particular have been coming before the courts. These cases depict that the police acted not to uphold the law and protect the human rights of the citizens but in aid of a private cause and to oppress the citizen. The policemen stepping out of the legal boundaries is not new; but the frequency and the freedom with which they trample on the rights of the citizens are frightening. As the Supreme Court has said, the police has come to treat itself as law unto itself and sometimes even above the law.[2] It is a trend that bodes ill for the country and it must be promptly checked.[3]

* Reader, Department of Law, Panjab University, Chandigarh.
** Reader, Department of Law, Panjab University, Chandigarh.

Today, the most important question before us is: who will watch the watchman? In our country the judiciary has shown its activism and deep concern for the protection of human rights of the people. The courts, which are expected to intervene in exceptional cases, are having to do so on an almost daily basis. Judicial activism has not only protected the human rights of the people, but has also led to the granting of exemplary compensation to the victims of police atrocities, which result in human rights violation. The traditional view supported the theory that "arrest and detention" is a "sovereign function" of the State.[4] Thus, no liability of the state was considered if there was illegal arrest and detention. But the judicial grammar of interpretation of Article 21 has undergone a mutation particularly since Menaka Gandhi. One of the impacts of this new interpretation is that in some cases the courts have considered the question of giving monetary compensation to one who might have suffered unduly, detained illegally or was badly harmed.

Khatri v. *State of Bihar*[5] popularly known as *Bhagalpur Blinding* case, was the first case where the question of granting monetary compensation was considered by the Supreme Court. In this case, it was alleged that police had blinded certain prisoners and the state was liable to pay monetary compensation to them. Thus, an important question of constitutional importance was involved. *viz.*, if a person is deprived of his right to life or personal liberty in violation of Article 21 by the state, can the court grant monetary relief to such person? Bhagwati, J. (as he then was) speaking for the court observed:

> Why should the court not be prepared to forge new tools and devise new remedies for the purpose of vindicating the most precious of the precious fundamental rights to life and personal liberty.[6]

As regards the liability of the state to pay compensation for infringing Article 21, the court answered in the affirmative saying that if it were not so, Article 21 would be reduced to a nullity, "a mere rope of sand."[7] But since the matter as to the responsibility of the police officers was still under investigation, the court did not decide the issue. Belatedly though, justice has finally caught up with the perpetrators of the blinding in Bhagalpur. The three police officers who were involved in the shocking incident of blinding of the undertrials, were finally convicted for taking the law into their own hands.[8]

The Supreme Court brought about revolutionary breakthrough in the "Human Rights Jurisprudence" in *Rudul Sah* v. *State of Bihar*[9] when it granted monetary compensation of Rupees thirty five thousand to the petitioner against the lawless act of the Bihar government which kept him in illegal detention for over fourteen years after acquittal.

An important question to be determined by the court was whether it could grant some compensation or exemplary costs against the State under Article 32 of the Constitution for illegal detention in the jail. The Supreme Court observed:

> (T)he refusal of this court to pass an order of compensation in favour of the petitioner *will be doing mere lip-service to his fundamental right to liberty* which the State Government has so grossly violated.[10]

It was pointed out that Article 21 would be denuded of its significant content if the power of the court was limited to passing of orders of release from illegal detention. The Supreme Court further observed:

> *One of the telling ways in which the violation of that right can reasonably be prevented and due compliance with the mandate of Article 21 seemed, is to mulct its violators in the payment of monetary compensation.* Administrative sclerosis leading to flagrant infringements of fundamental rights cannot be corrected by any other method open to the judiciary to adopt. The right to compensation is some palliative for the unlawful acts of instrumentalities which act in the name of public interest and which present for their protection of powers of the state as a shield . . . . Therefore, *the state must repair the damage done by its officers to the petitioner's rights. It may have recourse against those officers.*[11]

Thus, the Supreme Court for the first time openly declared that compensation ought to be paid for the violation of basic human rights *i.e.,* right to life and liberty under Article 21 of the Constitution.

In *Sebastian M. Hongray* v. *Union of India*,[12] the Supreme Court in *habeas corpus* proceedings required the Government of India to produce two persons before it. These persons had been taken into custody by the military jawans in the military camp. The government failed to produce them in the court and also expressed inability to do so. The Court found that the explanation of the government was incorrect and untenable. In fact, the truth was that these two persons had met an unnatural death. The Court, in the circumstances, keeping in view the torture, the agony and mental oppression undergone by the wives of the persons directed to be produced, instead of imposing fine on the government for civil contempt of the court, required that "as a measure of exemplary costs as is permissible in such cases," the government must pay Rupees one lakh to each one of the aforesaid two women.[13]

In yet another important case of *Bhim Singh* v. *State of J&K*[14] the Supreme Court noted that the police officer acted in the most high handed way and it awarded Rupees fifty thousand as monetary compensation by way of exemplary costs to the petitioner so as to compensate him "suitably and adequately."[15] In this case, the petitioner, a member of Legislative Assembly of Jammu and Kashmir, was arrested by the police *malafide* and was not produced before the magistrate within the requisite period. The petitioner alleged that his fundamental rights under Articles 21 and 22(1) were violated.

The Supreme Court observed:

> When a person comes to us with the complaint that he was arrested and imprisoned with mischievous or malicious intent and that his constitutional and legal rights were invaded, the mischief or malice and the invasion may not be washed away or wished away by his being set free. *In appropriate cases we have the jurisdiction to compensate the victim by awarding suitable monetary compensation.* We consider this an appropriate case.[16]

In all the cases from *Rudul Sah* to *Bhim Singh*, in which the Supreme Court awarded the monetary compensation, no basis for quantification of the amount of exemplary costs was laid down by the court. And perhaps this was the reason that the amount of monetary compensation varied in all the above mentioned cases. In other words, the discretion to award monetary compensation for the gross violation of Article 21 was left to the individual judge who decided the case, which in our opinion is not a good law or good precedent.

The Supreme Court in *Peoples' Union for Democratic Rights* v. *State of Bihar*,[17] laid down the working principle for the payment of compensation to the victims of ruthless and unwarranted police firing. In the present case, about twenty one persons including children died and many more were injured due to the unwarranted firing of the police. The Supreme Court observed:

> Ordinarily in the case of death, compensation of Rupees twenty thousand is paid .... We may not be taken to suggest that in the case of death the liability of the wrongdoer is absolved when compensation of Rupees twenty thousand is paid. But as a working principle and for convenience and with a view to rehabilitate the dependants of the deceased such compensation is being paid.[18]

The Supreme Court further pointed out that without prejudice to any just claim for compensation that may be advanced by the relations of the victims who had died or by the injured persons themselves, for every case of death, compensation of Rupees twenty thousand and for every injured person compensation of Rupees five thousand shall be paid.[19]

From the above observations of the Supreme Court, it is evident that though it has evolved a working principle of awarding compensation to the victims of the police atrocities but it is not a good working principle. Where the life of the person was lost, his dependants were to be paid only the meagre sum of Rupees twenty thousand. The Supreme Court, while evolving the working principles of granting compensation, has also failed to differentiate between the major and minor injury to the limb or body of the person concerned. It appears that the Supreme Court evolved the working principle of awarding compensation with the primary object of rehabilitating the victims or their dependants. However, it might happen that the person might not die but with the police atrocities he might lose his eyes, limb and might become unable to earn his livelihood. Can we say that the suggested amount of Rupees five thousand to such a person would be sufficient to "rehabilitate" him. The obvious answer would be no. Therefore, it is suggested that if life and liberty is to have some meaning for the millions of Indians, then for rehabilitating these persons, who are often victims of police atrocities, some larger amount should be paid as compensation and not merely Rupees five thousand or so.

In *Rajasthan Kisan Sangathan* v. *State,*[20] it was held that it is now well settled that a person even during lawful detention is entitled to be treated with dignity befitting a human being and the mere fact that he has been detained lawfully does not mean that he can be subjected to ill treatment, much less any torturous beating. The right to be treated even during lawful detention in a manner commensurate with human dignity is a well recognised right under Article 21 of the Constitution and if it is found that the police has maltreated any person in police custody which is not commensurate with human dignity he is at least entitled to monetary compensation for the torturous act by the police.

In *R. Ramkonda Reddy* v. *State,*[21] it was held that where a citizen has been deprived of his life or liberty otherwise than in accordance with the procedure prescribed by law, it is no answer to say that the said deprivation was brought about while the officials of the state were acting in discharge of the "sovereign function" of the State. Suit for compensation against the State, when an undertrial prisoner in jail lost his life due to failure or neglect of its officers to perform their duties, will, therefore, be maintainable. The Court pointed out that indeed, this is the only mode in which right to life guaranteed by Article 21 can be enforced.[22]

In *Saheli, Women's Resources Centre* v. *Commr. of Police, Delhi,*[23] the Supreme Court once again considered the question of granting compensation in case of police atrocities. In this case, a 9 year old child died due to assault and beating by the police officer. The Supreme Court held that the State is liable to pay compensation in case of police atrocities and accordingly it directed State government to pay Rs. 75,000 as compensation to mother of victim.[24]

In *State of Maharashtra* v. *Ravikant S. Patil,*[25] an undertrial prisoner was handcuffed and taken through the streets in a procession by police during investigation. The Court held that Article 21 was violated. However, the Court further held that police officer responsible for the act, acted only as an official and cannot be made personally liable. The Court directed that compensation of Rs. 10,000 be paid by the State and authorities may, if consider necessary, hold an enquiry against the police officer and then decide whether any further action is to be taken against him or not.

It is submitted that when the complainant is entitled to compensation for violation of human rights or for physical or mental harassment, then an award of exemplary costs/damages can serve a useful purpose in vindicating the strength of law and promoting and protecting human rights. However, when the Court directs payment of damages/compensation against the State, the ultimate sufferer is the tax payer, because it is the tax payers' money which is paid for the wrong of public official. Therefore, it is suggested that the State should pay the complainant from the public fund but recover the same from those who are responsible for such unpardonable behaviour.[26]

Nilbati Behera v. *State of Orissa*,[27] is yet another case of custodial death where the deceased was taken in police custody and next day his body was found on railway track with multiple injuries. The Supreme Court once again reiterated that in case of violation of fundamental rights by State's instrumentalities or servants, Court can direct the State to pay compensation to victim or his heir by way of 'monetary amends' and redressal. The principle of "sovereign immunity" shall be inapplicable in such cases. Having regard to the age and income of the deceased, the State was directed in this case to pay Rs. 1,50,000/- as compensation to the deceased's mother. The Court further held that other liabilities of the respondents or any other person for custodial death remain unaffected. In other words, compensation in civil law or criminal law can still be claimed in addition to this. The Court clarified that "public law proceedings" are different from "private law proceedings" and the award of compensation in proceedings for the enforcement of fundamental right under Articles 32 and 226 of the Constitution is a remedy available in public law. It was rightly observed:

> The Court is not helpless and the wide powers given to the Supreme Court by Article 32, which itself is a fundamental right, imposes a constitutional obligation on the Court to forge such new tools, which may be necessary for doing complete justice and enforcing the fundamental rights guaranteed in the Constitution which enable the award of monetary compensation in appropriate cases . . . .[28]

To support the above observation, the Court rightly referred to Article 9(5) of the International Covenant on Civil and Political Rights, 1966 and held that the said provision indicates that an enforceable right to compensation is not alien to the concept of guaranteed right.[29]

Dr. A.S. Anand, J., while delivering a separate but concurring judgement in this case pointed out in sonorous terms that convicts, prisoners and undertrials also have the right under Article 21 of the Constitution and the State has strict duty to ensure that a person in custody of police is not deprived of his right except in accordance with law.[30]

In *Pratul Kumar Sinha* v. *State of Bihar*,[31] police atrocities led to the death of three young persons. One of them was a bachelor while the other two were married and left behind their young widows. The court issued directions for the ex-gratia payment of Rs. 25,000/- to the families of the deceased. The Court further held that if the State government so desires it would be free to take such action as it considers necessary to recover this amount from the tort feasors.

Whenever any case of human rights violation as a result of police atrocities has been brought before the Supreme Court, it has always taken a serious note of it and directed to make either judicial enquiry into the allegations of police atrocities or directed the Central Bureau of Investigation (CBI) to conduct an enquiry independently so as to fix the responsibility for violation of human rights.

In *Afzal* v. *State of Haryana*,[32] *habeas corpus* petition was filed for the release of two children alleged to have been taken away by some police officials, and not produced before any magistrate. The arrest and detention of children was denied by the police. However, the report of Director General of Police and affidavit of S.P. revealed that the said children had been taken away by some police officials from their residence. The Court, in order to ascertain the truth of the whole case and role played by each of the respondent, directed the District Judge to conduct a detailed enquiry into the matter.

Inder Singh v. *State of Punjab,*[33] is yet another case of human rights violation due to police atrocities. In this case seven persons ranging in age from 14 to 85 years were abducted by senior police officer (DSP) and sundry policemen used official machinery for this purpose. The State police acted leisurely and in most irresponsible manner in the whole case. The Supreme Court directed that the enquiry shall be conducted personally by the Director of the Central Bureau of Investigation (CBI). The investigation was to cover, *inter alia*—the circumstances of abduction of the said seven persons; their present whereabouts or the date and circumstances of their liquidation and whether there has been an attempt to cover up the misdoings of police officers and policemen involved in the abduction of the said seven persons and their subsequent incarceration or liquidation. The Court also made it clear that it shall be free to make such orders as are deemed necessary when the report of the Director, CBI is received, including the orders for payment of compensation by the respondents to the next of kin of the said seven persons.[34]

The Court once again took up this case after the receipt of the report of the Director, CBI. Thus in *Inder Singh* v. *State of Punjab,*[35] according to the Court, the report clearly established that the police was guilty of illegal abduction of the concerned persons and unlawfully kept them under detention.[36] The Court came heavily on the behaviour of the Panjab Police and directed the State of Punjab to pay to the legal representatives of each of the said seven persons an amount of Rs. 1.50 lakhs within 2 weeks.[37] The Court further directed that the guilty persons should be identified by the State and it should endeavour to recover the said amount which is the taxpayers' money. The Court further directed that disciplinary inquiries must be started against those police officials who were responsible for delaying the registration of the complaint earlier and the guilty officials must be proceeded against.

In *Charanjit Kaur* v. *Union of India,*[38] where an Army Officer died while in service in mysterious circumstances. On facts, authorities were found guilty of criminal omissions and commissions resulting in great mental agony and physical and financial hardship to the widow and children of the deceased. The Court granted to the dependants Rs. six lakhs as compensation and special family pension and children allowance.

Thus in cases of human rights violation the Supreme Court has gone beyond just awarding compensation to the victims and has even ordered unraveling of exact circumstances of disappearance and death.[39]

In *Khedat Mazdoor Chetna Sangath* v. *State of U.P.*,[40] where the tribals alleged the human rights violation and commission of inhuman atrocities on them by the police, the Supreme Court not only directed the Central Bureau of Investigation (CBI) to investigate the whole matter but also register cases and prosecute officers, however, high or low in the hierarchy of administration for these lapses. Further to ensure an independent trial, the Court directed that the trial of such cases should take place outside the district concerned.[41] These directions were given to uphold human values and protect the rights guaranteed by the Constitution.

Arvinder Singh Bagga v. *State of U.P.*,[42] is yet another case of police atrocities where police officers subjected a married woman to physical, mental and psychological torture calculated to create fright to make her submit to the demands of the police and abandon her legal marriage. Her husband and family members were also tortured. The Court took serious note of the human rights violation and directed the State to launch prosecution to pay compensation of Rs. 10,000/- to the victim women and her husband and Rs. 5000/- to each of the other victim. The Court further pointed out that upon such payment it will be open to the State to recover the amount of compensation from the police officers concerned.[43] It could have been better if the Supreme Court had made it obligatory for the State government to recover the amount of compensation from the guilty officials.

It is submitted that this new concept of "personal liability" of the police officials concerned for violating the human rights is a welcome feature of Indian judiciary on the path of protecting human rights of people. This will definitely have some deterrent affect on the police officials. However, in this case the amount paid to the victims was too less.[44]

Dhananjay Sharma v. *State of Haryana*,[45] is yet another case which shows the sorry state of affairs with the police department. In this case, the detenu, while going by taxi, was waylaid by the State Police, though not wanted in any case there, and detained in police station for two days along with the taxi driver. Pursuant to the *habeas corpus* petition, the senior police officials not only denied the waylaying and subsequent detention but also filed wrong affidavits in Court regarding the whole episode. The CBI report showed that the statements made by the police officials in their affidavits were wrong. The Court held that filing of false affidavits by the police officials amounted to contempt calling for stern action. Accordingly they were sentenced to imprisonment and were also fined. The Court rightly pointed out that "it would be a great public disorder if the fountain of justice is allowed to be poisoned by anyone resorting to filing of false affidavits or giving false statements and fabricating false evidence in a court of law."[46] The Court observed:

> The stream of justice has to be kept clear and pure and anyone soiling its purity must be dealt with sternly so that the message percolates loud and clear that no one can be permitted to undermine the dignity of the Court and interfere with the due course of judicial proceedings or the administration of justice.[47]

The Court also rejected the belated apologies of the police officials to escape the punishment.

It is submitted that this judgement of the court will serve as an eye opener to the entire police force that they cannot play with the human rights of the people at their sweet will or to please the politicians.

Regarding the liability of the State, the Court once again reiterated that "the State must be held responsible for the unlawful acts of its officers and it must repair the damage done to the citizens by its officers for violating their infeasible fundamental rights of personal liberty without any authority of law in an absolutely high-handed manner."[48] However, in the present case the detenus themselves were not fair before the Court and filed false affidavits and exaggerated the incident by involving persons who were not present at the scene. Therefore, the Court disentitled them from receiving any compensation as monetary amends for the wrong done by the police officials by violating their basic human right to liberty.[49]

It is submitted that the Court has evolved this new concept of disentitling the detenus from receiving compensation for violation of human rights in case they also try to mislead the courts which is fountain of justice. It is common knowledge that in recent times our administrative system is passing through a most critical phase, particularly the policing system which is not as effective as it ought to be and unless some practical correctional steps and measures are taken without further delay, the danger looms large when the whole orderly society may be in jeopardy.[50]

Thus, from the above cases it is evident that the Indian Judiciary has been very sensitive and live to protection of human rights of the people. It has served as an institution for providing effective remedy against the violation of human rights. The recent trends show that it has not only granted compensation to the victims or heirs of victims for human rights violation by the state officials, but also policing the police. The judiciary has no doubt provided justice in individual cases of human rights violation but if we want to make human rights a living reality for all, then some practical correctional steps and measures are required to be taken by the police force itself.

REFERENCES

1. See *Kartar Singh* v. *State of Punjab* (1994) 3 SCC 569 at 711.
2. See editorial, "Police Provokes Court", *The Tribune,* 10, Feb. 2, 1995.
3. *Inder Singh* v. *State of Punjab* (1995) 3 SCC 702 at 705.
4. See, for example, *Kasturi Lal* v. *State of U.P.,* A.I.R. 1965 S.C. 1039.
5. A.I.R. 1981 S.C. 928.
6. *Id.,* at 930.
7. *Khatri* v. *State of Bihar*, A.I.R. 1981 S.C. 1068 at 1074.
8. "Justice at Last", Editorial, *The Hindustan Times,* 3 Sept. 1987. See also *Sant Bir* v. *State of Bihar*, A.I.R. 1982 S.C. 1470 and *Veena Sethi* v. *State of Bihar*, A.I.R. 1983 S.C. 339. In these cases the Court raised the ques-

tion of granting compensation to the victims for their human rights violation but in the end left it open.

9. A.I.R. 1983 S.C. 1086.
10. *Id.*, at 1089 (emphasis added).
11. *Ibid.*
12. A.I.R. 1984 S.C. 571.
13. *Sebastian M. Hongray* v. *Union of India*, A.I.R. 1984 S.C. 1026 at 1028.
14. A.I.R. 1986 S.C. 494.
15. *Id.*, at 499.
16. *Id.*, (emphasis added).
17. A.I.R. 1987 S.C. 355.
18. *Id.*, at 356.
19. *Id.*
20. A.I.R. 1989 Raj. 10 at 16.
21. A.I.R. 1989 A.P. 235.
22. *Id.*, at 247.
23. A.I.R. 1990 S.C. 513.
24. *Id.*, at 516.
25. (1991) 2 SCC 373. See also *Sunil Gupta* v. *State of M.P.* (1990) 3 SCC 119; *Delhi Judicial Service Asson, Tis Hazari Court* v. *State of Gujarat*, A.I.R. 1991 S.C. 2176, Paramjit S. Jaswal and Nishtha Jaswal, "Right to Personal Liberty and Handcuffing: Some Observations", 33 *JILI* 246–253 (1991).
26. See *Lucknow Development Authority* v. *M.K. Gupta* (1994) 1 SCC 243 at 264.
27. A.I.R. 1993 S.C. 1960 (1993)2 SCC 746. See also *Dalip Singh* v. *State of Haryana*, 1993 Supp. (3) SCC 336; *Bhuwneshwar Singh* v. *Union of India* (1993) 4 SCC 327; *N. Narendra Rao & Co.* v. *State of A.P.* (1994) 6 SCC 205.
28. *Id.*, at 763–64.
29. *Id.*, at 764.
30. *Id.*, at 767.
31. 1994 Supp. (3) SCC 100. See also *R.S. Sodhi* v. *State of U.P.*, 1994 Supp(1) SCC 142 and 143.
32. (1994) 1 SCC 425.
33. (1994) 6 SCC 275.
34. *Id.*, at 281.
35. *Supra*, note 3.
36. *Id.*, at 704.
37. *Id.*, at 706.
38. (1994) 2 SCC 1. See also *R.S. Sodhi* v. *State of U.P.*, 1994 Supp.(1) SCC 142 and 143.
39. See *Arvinder Singh Bagga* v. *State of U.P.*, 1994 Supp(1) SCC 500; *Afzal* v. *State of Haryana* (1994) 1 SCC 425; *Inder Singh* v. *State of Punjab* (1994) 6 SCC 275.
40. (1994) 6 SCC 260. See also *Citizens for Democracy* v. *State of Assam* (1995) 3 SCC 743.
41. *Id.*, at 271.
42. (1994) 6 SCC 565; A.I.R. 1995 S.C. 117.
43. *Id.*, at 568.

44. In another case, the Supreme Court awarded compensation of Rs. 50,000/- to two brothers who were wrongly confined in a police station for seven days without any criminal case registered against them. The Court further held that the State can recover the amount of compensation from the guilty police officials. See "SC tells UP to pay compensation", 7 *The Tribune* (24 Jan. 1995). See also *State of Punjab* v. *Ajaib Singh,* J.T. 1995(1) SC 433 where the respondent was directed to deposit a sum of Rs. 5 lakhs which was to be paid to the dependants of the two victims.
45. (1995) 3 SCC 757.
46. *Id.,* at 777.
47. *Id.*
48. *Id.,* at 782.
49. *Id.,* at 783.
50. *Id.*

14

Custodial Violence and Human Rights— Indian Experience

*Subhash C. Raina**
*B.K. Raina***

Respect for human dignity while protecting the life and liberty of an individual is the cardinal principle of Indian Constitution[1] and International Covenants on Human Rights.[2] To be in conformity with basic law, the substantive and procedural laws in India also lay stress on observance of human rights in the administration of criminal justice.[3] It therefore, follows that an attempt has been made both through the Constitutional law of India and Criminal Procedure Code to ensure that human rights of the accused are assured in criminal justice system. Police being the primary agency of the criminal justice system is bound to follow the mandate of the law and protect the human rights of accused. It is due to the fact that custodians of law cannot be its transgressors.

Keeping this in mind it is endeavoured to analyse primarily the legal framework relating to the protection of human rights specifically in respect of those accused of crime and who are being kept under custody. Secondly an attempt has been made to highlight the extent of custodial violence vis-a-vis the violation of human rights in India and the role of

* Reader, Deptt. of Law, University of Jammu.
** Lecturer, Deptt. of Law, University of Jammu.

courts to protect the innocent and compensate the victims. Auxiliary to this the future action plan has been suggested to eliminate the problem of custodial violence.

Legal Frame Work

Arrest involves deprivation of liberty of an individual. From the time of arrest a person remains in custody of such authority (except where he is released on bail). Any use of force, threat or psychological pressure against such person by the authorities who hold him in custody is called 'Custodial Violence.'[4]

In quite unmistakable terms law prohibits the use of custodial violence. The Constitution *grundnorm* of all other laws in India provides that no citizen should be compelled to be a witness against himself.[5] Similarly Indian Penal Code makes it an offence to voluntarily cause hurt to extract confession or to compel restoration of property[6] as well as to wrongfully confine a person to extract confession or compel restoration of property.[7] The procedural laws too prohibit offering of threats, promises or inducements to extract information.[8] The law of evidence rejects any such confession as admissible evidence which has been made before a Police Officer in criminal trials.[9] The Indian Police Act under which the entire police organisation in India derives its legitimacy, while dealing with functions of police prohibits unwarranted personal violence by Police Officers to any person in police custody.[10] Further Indian Penal Code lays down punishment for rapes occurring in custody (Police Custody).[11]

The above law of the land receives vertibal support from international instruments of law relating to the protection of rights of an individual. It is in the light of this that UN General Assembly adopted a Code of Conduct for Law Enforcement Officials.[12] The said code emphatically states, that in the performance of their duty law enforcement officials shall respect and protect human dignity and maintain and uphold the human rights of all persons.[13] The use of force by law enforcement officials has been authorised in only exceptional circumstances.[14]

In unequivocal terms the above UN Code further declares that no law enforcement official may inflict, instigate or tolerate any act of torture or other cruel, inhuman or degrading treatment or punishment, nor may any law enforcement official invoke superior orders or exceptional circumstances such as state of war or a threat of war or threat to the national security, internal political instability or any other public emergency as a justification of torture or other cruel, inhuman or degrading treatment or punishment.[15] The above prohibition is also derived from the Convention against Torture and Other Cruel Inhuman and Degrading Treatment or Punishment.[16] The convention declares such an act as an offence against human dignity and shall be condemned as a denial of the purposes of the charter of UN and as violation of human rights and fundamental freedoms proclaimed in UDHR and other international instruments relating to human rights.[17] The above convention defines "torture" as 'any act by which severe pain or suffering whether physical or mental, is intentionally inflicted on a person for such purposes as obtaining from him or third person information or confession, punishing him for an act he or third person committed or is suspected of having committed or intimidating or coercing him or third person for any other reason based on discrimination of any kind, when such pain or suffering is inflicted by or at the instigation or with the consent or acquiescence of a public official or other person acting in an official capacity. It does not include pain or suffering arising only from, inherent in or incidental to lawful sanction to the extent consistent with Standard Minimum Rules for the Treatment of Prisoners.'[18]

The term cruel, inhuman or degrading treatment or punishment has not been defined by the General Assembly but should be treated to have an exhaustive meaning so as to provide maximum protection against physical or mental abuses.

In pursuance of these developments Ministry of Home Affairs, Govt. of India issued letters addressed to Chief Secretaries of all States and Union Territories and heads of C.P.O's containing Code of Conduct of Police. This code in addition to other rules provided strictly that, "in securing observance of law or in maintaining order the police should use as far as practicable methods of persuasion, advice and warning. When application of force becomes inevitable, only the irreducible minimum of force required in the circumstances be used."[19]

The above detailed discussion of laws makes it clear that the custodial violence is illegal and any law enforcement official (mainly Police) cannot indulge in such illegal acts. It is because of the fact that such violence against helpless victims (those who are in the custody) is barbaric and against all standards of human dignity. It is violative of the laws of land and of international conventions relating to human rights. Unabated custodial violence shakes the faith of people from institution of justice and exposes the law and order agency.

Inspite of these warning bells the custodians of law in India indulge in custodial violence. In absence of a broad based study on the magnitude of this problem one cannot be sure about its statistics. However, the frequent reports which have appeared in press during last couple of years can be said to be the mirror images of the magnitude of custodial violence in India.

Magnitude of Custodial Violence

Incidents of custodial deaths due to torture are increasing even when the police continues to paint a human face of their actions. According to statistics for 1991–94 at least 285 deaths have been reported from various jails and police lock-ups in the country. In 1994 at least 80 people were killed in custody. There were 76 custody deaths in 1993, 70 in 1992 and 59 in 1991.[20] In Delhi alone in the high security Tihar Jail there were 69 deaths during 1992–93 and in 1994 only as many as 22 have been reported.[21]

The above quoted figures on custodial deaths are in no way insignificant, the figures indicate the steep rise of such cases during last couple of years. The magnitude of the problem has led a Chief Minister of a State in India to comment:

> "The instances of violence perpetrated upon detenus while in custody are ugly incidents that tarnish the name of the Govt. and the image of the police . . . such instances raise the basic question of who shall guard the guards themselves."[22]

With the collapse of probity in public life the police inevitably gets an upper hand. They seem to take it for granted that they will not be touched since those in authority are often inclined to cover their misdeeds.[23] Without flooding this paper with instances of custodial deaths in India a glance of the reports[24] by persons interested in this area of study makes it crystal clear that the police in India are the violators of human rights of those who are in their custody. Police by using different methods of torture and without any respect for human dignity have flouted all the rules of international convention on human rights to which India is a signatory. The latest case in sequence is the death of business tycoon Rajan Pillai.[25]

Judicial Approach

This abuse of power by police has been during last few years seriously dealt with by judiciary in India. The judicial institution has once again proved that nobody can be above the law of land. Furthermore the grant of compensation to the victims of abuse of power (in custodial death cases) by various high courts and the apex court has strengthen the belief that victimological jurisprudence in India is on the march.

The role of judiciary against police torture has been broadly laid down as early as 1980 by Justice Krishna Iyer in his observations as follows:

> "The grim scenario burns into our judicial consciousness, and the moral emerging from the case being that if today freedom of one forlorn person falls to the Police somewhere, tomorrow the freedom of many may fall elsewhere with none to whimper unless the Court process invigilates in time and polices the police before it is too late."[26]

Similarly the extent of responsibility of protecting human life by those in whose custody the detenu may be was laid down by apex court in the following observations:

> "There can be no second opinion that the preservation of human life is of paramount importance. That is so on account of the fact that once life is lost the status-quo ante cannot be restored. Whether he be an innocent per-

son or a criminal liable to punishment under the law, it is the obligation of those who are in charge of the patient to preserve his life so that the innocent may be protected and guilty may be punished. Social laws do not contemplate death by negligence to be tantamount to legal punishment."[27]

The apex court has not restricted itself with observations only in cases of custodial violence, resulting into custodial deaths but has also asked the concerned Government to pay compensation. As recently as on third of February 1995 the Supreme Court directed the Haryana Govt. to pay an ad-hoc relief of Rs. 2,00,000/- to the dependents of a 22 year old youth a resident of Delhi who allegedly died as a result of torture by Gurgaon Police during March 1993. The court further directed the Central Bureau of Investigation to enquire into the matter expeditiously.[28]

Similarly in August, 1994 Madras High Court unhesitatingly granted a compensation of Rs. 1,00,000/- to the mother of a youth who was assaulted by police to the extent that it resulted into his death.[29] In a landmark judgement Rajasthan High Court ordered the relief to the dependents of persons killed in police custody since 1990. The relief was an amount of Rs. 50,000/- to each case. The Govt. was authorised to charge the amount from those personnel found responsible for such deaths. Further court directed that one dependent of every killed person should be given a Govt. job. In case the dependent is not eligible or does not want a job the family should be provided with agricultural land. Court also directed to provide training to police regarding treatment to be meted out to persons in their custody.[30]

The judicial activism with respect to victims of custodial deaths was exhibited as recently as June 1995 when in a case involving the violation of human rights by police the Karnataka High Court ordered the payment of compensation of Rs. 2,00,000/- to the next of kin of deceased who died in the lockup eight years ago allegedly due to torture.[31] Directions to give compensation in custodial death cases have been given by other High Courts too.[32]

Apart from the grant of compensation the courts have moved a step further and have even suspended and convicted the policemen found guilty of custodial violence. Thus on April 12, 1994 Metropolitan Session's Judge of Vijayawada (A.P.) convicted a Sub-Inspector and four other police men in the sensational case of lock-up death of Navy man (T. Murlidhar) in police station in 1986.[33] In a landmark judgement the apex court has made custodial violence (including handcuffing without Magistrate's permission) an offence punishable not only under penal laws but also under Contempt of Courts Act.[34]

On analysing judicial pronouncements one clear inference can be drawn that custodial violence by the police is always subjected to very tight judicial scrutiny in India. In other words, the judicial institutions in India are safeguarding the human rights of all including the detenus under the law. This judicial guarantee of protection of human rights, in India has further been strengthened by establishment of "National Human Rights Commission." This observation is supported by the fact that NHRC was able to get Rs. 50,000/- sanctioned as compensation to the next of kin of Hellen Kuki (a rebel) who died in Army custody during 5th/6th March, 1994. In another case of custodial death in Assam of Mr. Sariful Hussain Alias Babul Hussain, NHRC recommended to State Govt. to take action against the erring police constable under Section 302 of IPC.[35]

Future Action Plan

There may be difference of opinion on the magnitude of custodial violence among various researchers, however, unanimity prevails among them regarding its existence. The need of the hour, therefore, is to chalk out a future plan, so that positive steps are taken to eliminate this practice in police force. It is an established fact that no plan of action can be sustainable unless the etiology of problem is known.

The primary cause seems to be the enactment of numerous social and other laws whereby the powers of the police to arrest have been widened beyond imagination. It is here that the phrase "power corrupts and absolute power corrupts absolutely" fits in. Thus under this absolute power the scope of police misbehaviour is increasing. It is submitted that it is necessary to review the existing laws providing unbridled powers of arrest to police so that suitable corrective steps are taken in time.

Performance of police in India is judged by two factors; (a) rate of conviction and (b) quantum of property recovered from criminals. It is under this stress that police resort to harsh methods to obtain confession and to recover property. Equally to maintain the rate of convictions of their unit, they arrest and torture innocent people. It is therefore, submitted that a resetting of goals and levels of performance of police may help considerably to change their behaviour.

The recommendations of the last Police Commission to establish monitoring units under the guidance of responsible and senior officers should be implemented in letter and spirit. This will lead to an inbuilt mechanism of checks and balances and any deviation should be dealt in time and strictly before it is too late.

The police training colleges and national institutes set up to impart training orientation to police personnel should include human right subject in their curriculum. This will create necessary awareness among police personnel about human rights and consequences of their violation.

Last but not the least National Human Rights Commission, may undertake an intensive research either directly under its control or may sponsor some independent team of researchers or an agency on custodial violence in India. This will help in bringing out exact magnitude of the problem and will be the basis to evolve a strategy to eliminate it. The proper course would be to set up a full time broad-based multi-disciplinary research unit attached to NHRC which will undertake research on topics of contemporary importance, including the present one. Such researches will serve as a feed back to the agencies concerned to keep their records straight in as much as they will augur well to the prohibition of custodial violence, by such continuous monitoring.

REFERENCES

1. See Article(s) 20, 21, & 22(1) & (2) of Constitution of India.
2. Article(s) 9 and 14(2) of International Covenant of Civil and Political Rights 1966; Article 11(2) of Universal Declaration of Human Rights

(1948); See also Convention against Torture and Other cruel, Inhuman or Degrading Treatment or Punishment (1984).
3. See for details Section 57 and 167(2) (a) (i) (ii) & (2) (b) of Criminal Procedure Code of 1973.
4. S. Subramanian, *Human Rights and Police* (1992) p. 21.
5. Article 20(3).
6. Section 330.
7. Section 331.
8. Section 163 of Criminal Procedure Code of 1973.
9. Section 25 read with Section 24 of Indian Evidence Act 1872.
10. See in detail Indian Police Act 1860 specifically Sections 20 and 23.
11. Section 376(2) (a).
12. Article 1 of U.N. Code of Conduct of law Enforcement officials 1979. Law Enforcement officials "includes officers of the Law whether appointed or elected, who exercise police powers specially the powers of arrest and detention."
13. *Id.*, Art. 2.
14. *Id.*, Art. 4.
15. *Id.*, Art. 5.
16. Convention against Torture and other Cruel, Inhuman or Degrading Treatment or Punishment 1984 (Enforced from 1987).
17. See *supra* n. 2.
18. Part 1 Article 1 of the Convention on Torture . . . (1984).
19. Letters No. VI-24021/97/84-GPA-I dated 4.7.85 & 10.7.85 Quoted in S. Subramanian; *supra* note 4, p. 94.
20. *Indian Express,* New Delhi, 19.1.1995.
21. Highlights of the Programme "*Tonight*" on DD 2, 13th July 1995.
22. *The Hindu* 26.7.1994. Excerpts from Inaugural Speech of Miss Jai Lalita to the 3 days Conference on Distt. Administration from 25.7.94 to 27.7.94 at Madras.
23. Nikhil Chakravarthy, 'Cops as Criminals' *Economic Times*, 31.5.94.
24. See in detail the newspapers quoted by the Author.
25. Rajan Pillai who was in custody in Tihar Jail died due to negligence of Jail Authorities. As reported that he was refused proper medical facilities inspite of his repeated requests and clear cut proof of his chronic liver disease. This was in contravention to Jail Rules.
26. *Prem Shanker Shukla* v *Delhi Administration* A.I.R. 1980 S.C. 1535 at 1536.
27. *Pt. Parmanand Katara* v *Union of India and others* A.I.R. 1989. S.C. 2039.
28. *Indian Express,* New Delhi, 4.2.1995.
29. *The Hindu* 25.8.94.
30. *Indian Express,* New Delhi, 3.5.94.
31. *The Hindu* 8.6.1995.
32. Andhra Pradesh High Court on 19.9.94 provided Rs. 1,00,000/- to parents of Basheer Ahmad who died on account of beating and torturing by police while in custody at Nadanapalli. See *The Hindu* 20.4.94.
33. *The Hindu* 13.4.1994. Similarly in Delhi (North-West Distt.) an S.H.O., two Sub-Inspectors and 3 Constables were suspended and booked under Section 304 of I.P.C.

34. *Indian Express* 2.6.1995.
35. *News Letter* of N.H.R.C., Vol. (2) No. 4, April 1995.

15

Expanding Role of Judiciary in the Protection of Environment: An Environmental Concern as a Human Right

*Sudesh Kumar Sharma**

The goal of the Indian Constitution is a "welfare idealism" covering a wide range of socio-economic aspirations of its people. The founding fathers believed that the utility of the state would be best judged from its effect on the common man's welfare. They pledged the country to the task of securing "to all its citizens, justice—social, economic and political."[1] The fundamental rights and directive principles impose an affirmative duty upon the state to raise everyone to a minimum acceptable standard of living.[2] For the life and development of its citizens the Indian Constitution is very categorical. Article 21 guarantees right to life and personal liberty. Article 47 imposes a primary duty upon the state to improve public health. Article 48-A mandates the state to protect and improve the environment and safeguard the forests and wildlife of the country. Article 51A(g) imposes a fundamental duty on every citizen of India to protect and improve the national

* Reader, Faculty of Law, University of Jammu, Jammu-180 004.

environment including forests, lakes, rivers and wild life, and to have compassion for living creatures.[3] Every citizen possesses the right to approach the Courts as a part of this duty. There is a general acceptance that protection of environment and keeping it free of pollution is an indispensable necessity for life to survive on earth.[4] Thus both the state and citizens are under a fundamental obligation to protect and improve the environment, including forests, lakes, rivers, wild-life and to have compassion for living creatures.

There are number of legislations dealing with environmental pollution. Most prominent are—Water Pollution Act, 1974, Air Pollution Act, 1981 and the Environment (Protection) Act, 1986.[5] Apart from these Acts, there are many other provisions scattered in various statutes—the civil and criminal as well as in the uncodified common law dealing with environmental pollution.[6]

The problem of environmental pollution is of high degree and becoming acute day by day. Most of the legislations have proved ineffective. For various reasons the people are not able to raise their voices and have learnt to live in environmentally degrading conditions. Poverty and ignorance has made them silent sufferers. For long the environmental conditions has been no body's concern in India. However, the judiciary as a champion of social justice and a sentinel on the *qui vive* has maintained a balance between the social justice and justice to the nature. It has played an important role in protecting the environment and nature through a number of pronouncements.

The Courts have held that the right to live in a healthy environment is a component of fundamental right to life and personal liberty and hence enforceable. With this cue, the thrust of this paper is to examine the concern expressed by Indian judiciary on environmental pollution and citizens' right to live in a healthy environment. The industrial development causing ecological imbalances and the liability of the industrial units polluting the environment has also been discussed. Directions given by the judiciary on environmental education to create mass awareness are also examined.

Judicial Response

Indian judiciary is an embodiment of judicial activism. It has been taking a keen interest in environmental matters. A brief review of some of the judgements having a bearing on environmental pollution is taken here.

1. *Fundamental Right to Live in Healthy Environment—Lack of Funds no excuse*

In *Municipal Council Ratlam* v. *Vardhichand,*[7] residents of Ratlam municipality tormented by stench and stink caused by open drains and public excretion by nearby slum dwellers filed a complaint under Section 133 Criminal Procedure Code. The magistrate ordered the municipality to provide amenities to abate public nuisance by constructing drain pipes and flush them with water to wash the filth etc. He further directed that failure to comply with would entail prosecution under Section 188 of the Indian Penal Code.

This order of the magistrate was reversed by the Sessions Judge, but upheld by the High Court. The municipality by way of special leave contended before the Supreme Court that because of financial difficulties, the construction of sanitation facilities was not possible. Dismissing the special leave petition, Court observed that financial incapacity is no defence and on the basis of this the municipality cannot be exonerated from its statutory liability under Section 133 of Criminal Procedure Code. Court further remarked: "The Criminal Procedure Code operates against statutory bodies and others regardless of cash in their coffers, even as human rights under part III of the Constitution have to be respected by the State regardless of budgetary provision. . . . Otherwise a profligate statutory body or pachydermic governmental agency may legally defy duties under the law by urging in self-defence a self-created bankruptcy or perverted expenditure budget."[8]

Stressing upon the preservance of public health, the municipality was directed to take steps to stop effluents flowing from an alcohol factory into the *Nallah* and spreading the obnoxious smell and to construct within a period of six months, a sufficient number of public latrines and also to provide water supply and scavenging service. The municipality was also directed to fill up cesspools and other pits of filth and use a sanitary staff to keep the place free from accumulation of filth. The court also empowered the Sub-Divisional Magistrate to prosecute the officers concerned, if they fail to comply with these directions.[9] The Court remarked, "industries cannot make profit at the expense of public health."[10].

In *M.C. Mehta* v. *State of Orissa*[11] a writ was filed seeking mandamus to protect the health of thousands of innocent people living in Cuttack and adjacent areas who were suffering from pollution being caused by Municipal Corporation Cuttack and the SCB Medical College Hospital Cuttack by discharge of sewage. It was alleged that the several acts of aforesaid authorities and state of Orissa were in violation of Article 21 of the Constitution of India, the National Healthy Policy, the Environment (Protection) Act, 1986 and the Water (Prevention and Control of Pollution) Act, 1974. Survey report by the Prevention Board revealed health injuries caused by the use of water. The Court directed the authorities to take immediate action to prevent and control water pollution. Court remarked: "the health of large number of people is at stake. Therefore, no amount of plea of helplessness or passing the buck to the other wings of the department will be of any assistance."[12]

In *Ganga Water Pollution Case*[13] the Supreme Court directed the owners of tanneries to establish the primary treatment plants so as to prevent the pollution of water of Ganga. The Supreme Court observed that the polluted water affected the health and life of large number of people of the country and hence the financial capacity of the tanneries is irrelevant to be considered for the establishment of treatment plants.

In a subsequent case[14] filed by Mr. M.C. Mehta on the above said issue the Supreme Court issued certain directions by way of affirmative action to the Kanpur municipal corporation and other concerned authorities. The Court observed that the water in river Ganga has become so much polluted that it can no longer be used by the people either for drinking or bathing, the High Court should not ordinarily grant orders of stay of criminal proceedings to prosecute the industrialists or other persons who pollute the water in river Ganga. However, if an order of stay is issued in an extra-ordinary case the concerned High Court should dispose of the case within a short period of two months from the date of institution of such case.[14a]

In *Charan Lal Sahu* v. *Union of India,*[15] the validity of Bhopal Gas Leakage Disaster (Processing of Claims) Act, 1985 was involved. Justice K.N. Singh while upholding the validity of the Act observed: "In the context of our national dimensions of human rights, right to liberty, pollution free air and water is guaranteed by the Constitution under Articles 21, 48-A and 51A(g). It is the duty of the State to take effective steps to protect the guaranteed constitutional rights.[16] In *Chhetriya Pradhushan Mukti Sangarsh Samiti* v. *State of U.P.*[17] the petitioner had sought directions from the Supreme Court to check the pollution and ecological imbalance caused by two industrial units at Sarnath, Varanasi, thereby exposing the population to health hazard and risk to life. The court discovered *prima facie*, the provisions of the Air (Prevention and Control of Pollution) Act, 1981 and the Water (Prevention and Control of Pollution) Act, 1974 had been complied with by the industrial units as indicated by the Pollution Control Board. The Court discovered a long history of ugly rivalry between the parties in the instant case. Rejecting the petition as constituting an abuse of PIL, Mukerjee CJ, remarked, "Article 32 is a great salutary safeguard for preservation of fundamental rights of citizens. Every citizen has a fundamental right to have the enjoyment of quality of life and living as contemplated by Article 21. . . . Anything which endangers or impairs by conduct of any body either in violation or in derogation of laws, that quality of life and living by the people is entitled to be taken recourse of Article 32." This judgement shows that the Supreme Court is conscious of citizens' right to live in a healthy environment and has upheld the same provided the petitioner is a person interested genuinely in the protection of society or acts on behalf of the society or community.

In *Subash Kumar* v. *State of Bihar*[18] the Supreme Court upheld the right of a citizen to go to court of law under article 32 of the Constitution for removing the pollution of water or air. The court observed that right to live included the right to pollution free water and air.

In *K.C. Malhotra* v. *State of M.P.*,[19] it was observed that the inhabitants of the locality may be belonging to backward class or weaker sections of society, they have got a fundamental right under Article 21 of the Constitution entitling them to live as human beings in the area which is in the limits of the Municipal Corporation. In this case, the health and security of the inhabitants of the locality was endangered by open drainage. The court passed directions that the drainage must be covered and there should be proper lavatories for public conservancy which should be regularly cleaned. That the pipe line of drinking water is not contaminated at the places where they are joined in the pipe lines. There shall be vaccination against cholera and other epidemic diseases, distribution of chlorine tablets and other medicines to keep up the health and safety of the inhabitants above board and free from cholera and other similar types of diseases. Court pointed out that public health and safety cannot suffer on any count and all steps are to be taken as Article 47 makes it a paramount principle of government for the improvement of public health as among its primary duties. Court also directed that it shall be the duty of the state and its instrumentalities to educate not only the inhabitants of the locality, but the members of the society to live with appropriate awareness and to take all measures so that water and environment may not be polluted.

2. *Ecological Balance, Industrial and Social Development*

Lime Stone Quarries[20] is the first case of its kind involving issues relating to environment and ecological balance. It brings into sharp focus the conflict between development and conservation and serves to emphasise the need for reconciling the two in the larger interests of the society.

Supreme Court ordered for the closure of certain *Lime Stone Quarries* as they were proving hazardous to the health of workers and people putting up in the Mussoorie Hills. Court expressed its concern over the hardship its order would cause to the owners and observed: "It is a price that has to be paid for protecting and safeguarding the right of the people to live in healthy environment with minimal disturbance of ecological balance and without avoidable hazard to them and to their cattle, homes and agricultural land and undue affectation of air, water and environment."[21] Court also directed the state government to take immediate steps for reclamation of the areas forming part of such lime stone quarries with the help of already available Eco-Task Force and to give priority to all those workers who were thrown out of employment in the afforestation and soil conservation programmes to be taken up by the state.[22]

Subsequently in *R.L. and E. Kendra* v. *State of U.P.*[23] the question which remained to be considered was whether the schemes submitted by mine *lessees* to the Bandopadhyaya Committee under the earlier Supreme Court order had been rightly rejected or not by the Bandhopadhyaya Committee and whether under those schemes, the mine lessees can be allowed to carry on mining operations without in any way adversely affecting environment or ecological balance or causing hazards to individuals, cattle and agricultural lands. It was pleaded that the lime-stone quarries in this area satisfy about three per cent of the country's demand for raw material for special kind of steel. Rejecting the plea Court observed:

> It is for the Government and the Nation and not for the Court to decide whether the deposits should be exploited at the cost of ecology and environmental considerations or the industrial requirement should be otherwise satisfied. It may be perhaps possible to exercise greater control and vigil over the operation to strike a balance between preservation and utilisation that would indeed be a matter for expert body to examine and on the basis of appropriate advice, Government should take policy decision and formally implement the same.[24]

Realising the disastrous consequences of interference in ecology and environment by man, the court remarked that it was not oblivious of the fact that natural sources have got to be tapped for the purpose of social development but it should not be forgotten that tapping of resources have to be done with requisite attention and caution so that ecology and environment may not be affected in any serious way. There must be long term planning with regard to national wealth.

It is always to be remembered that natural resources are permanent assets of whole mankind and these are not to be exhausted in one generation. Court also directed that preservation of environment and keeping the ecological balance unaffected is a task which not only governments but also every citizen must undertake. It is a social obligation and constitutional duty.

Shri Sachidanand Pandey v. *State of W.B.*[25] is another case where ecological imbalance was brought to notice of the Court. The government of West Bengal had given on lease a plot of four acres out of land of Zoological Gardens, Calcutta to Taj Group of Hotels for the construction of a five star hotel. It was this giving away of land that was challenged by two citizens of Calcutta. The main question before the Court from ecological point of view was about disturbance to be caused to the birds of zoo from vehicular traffic and lights of hotel. The Supreme Court while considering the point of development and ecological disturbances observed: "Today society's interaction with nature is so extensive that the environmental question has assumed proportions affecting all humanity. Industrialisation, urbanisation, explosion of population, over-exploitation of resources, depletion of traditional sources of energy and raw materials and the search for new sources of energy and raw materials, the disruption of natural ecological balances, the destruction of a multitude of plant and species for economic reasons and sometimes for no good reason at all are factors which have contributed to environmental deterioration. While the scientific and technological progress of man has invested him with immense power over nature, it has also resulted in the unthinking use of the power, encroaching endlessly on nature. If man is able to transform deserts into oases, he is also leaving behind deserts in the place of oases. In India as elsewhere in the world, uncontrolled growth and consequent environmental deterioration are fast assuming meaning proportions and all Indian cities are afflicted with this problem."[26] Despite such observations, expressing concern over the environment protection, no relief was granted in this case. Perhaps the court was swayed by legal technicalities and observed: "where an administrative action or order of the Government involves the problem of environment and the

Government is alive to the various considerations regarding thought and deliberation and has arrived at a conscious decision after taking them into account, it may not be for the Court to interfere in the absence of malafides."[27]

In the instant case, in order to encourage tourism, the Government intended to establish Five Star Hotels at Calcutta. The court found that the intention was well publicised and made known to the public and the Government had taken into account the relevant considerations and thus the decision was not based on malafides.

3. *Liability of Enterprises Engaged in the Manufacture of Hazardous Products*

In *Shriram Foods and Fertiliser Industries*,[28] there was a leakage of oleum gas in one of the units of Shriram Foods and Fertilisers Factory at Delhi. As a result several persons were affected and it was alleged that one advocate practising in Delhi died. Delhi Municipal Corporation ordered the closure of the factory. A public interest petition was filed in the Supreme Court for determining the liability of large enterprises engaged in the manufacture of hazardous products in populated areas. It was realised that science and technology involves risks and hazards as inherent elements. But these industries are essential for progress and development. What is to be done is to minimise hazard and risk to mankind. The Supreme Court observed:

> We cannot possibly adopt a policy of not having chemical or other hazardous industries merely because they pose hazard or risk to the community. If such a policy were adopted, it would mean the end of progress and development. . . . We can only hope to reduce the element of hazard or risk to the community by taking all steps for locating such industries in a manner which would pose least risk or danger to the community and minimising safety requirements in such industries. We would, therefore, like to impress upon the Government of India to evolve a national policy for location of chemical and other hazardous industries in areas where population is scarce and there is little hazard to the community.[29]

Supreme Court directed reopening of the factory subject to certain conditions. A committee was to inspect the plant at least once a fortnight and the company was ordered to deposit Rs. 30,000/- in the court to meet the expenses of the committee. The Chief Inspector of Factories was directed to pay surprise visits to the factory at least once a week and report back to the court as well as to the Labour Commissioner. The Trade Unions were also empowered to report on any default or negligence to the management and if the management did not concede to their requests then to report the matter to the Labour Commissioner. The Court further directed that workers, representatives be given adequate training in this regard. The Central Board for Water Pollution was also directed to make surprise visits at least once a week and submit its findings to the court. The Court directed the Chairman and Managing Director of the company to give an undertaking holding themselves personally responsible to pay compensation for any death or injury in case of escape of chlorine gas. The company was also directed to deposit Rs. 20 lakh as security for satisfying compensation claims for leakage of oleum gas and also give a bank guarantee of Rs. 15 lakhs to be encashed by the Registrar of the court in case of an escape of chlorine gas resulting in death or injury.

M.C. Mehta v. *Union of India*[30] is a significant pronouncement. The apex court observed that where an enterprise is engaged in a hazardous or inherently dangerous activity and harm results to any one on account of an accident in the operation of such hazardous or inherently dangerous activity resulting, for example, in escape of toxic gas the enterprise is strictly and absolutely liable to compensate all those who are affected by the accident and such liability is not subject to any of the exceptions which operate *vis-a-vis* the tortuous principle of strict liability. In such a case, the measure of compensation must be correlated to the magnitude and capacity of the enterprise because such compensation must have a deterrent effect. The larger and more prosperous the enterprise, the greater must be the amount of compensation payable by it for the harm caused on account of an accident in the carrying on of the hazardous or inherently dangerous activity by the enterprise.[31]

In *Bhopal Gas Leak Case*,[32] there was leakage of poisonous gas resulting into the pollution of environment affecting the life of the people. Supreme Court directed the government to immediately provide the interim relief to the victims of the gas tragedy.

In *Union Carbide Corporation* v. *Union of India*,[33] the Supreme Court directed the Union Carbide Corporation to pay a sum of 470 million US dollars to the Union of India in full settlement of all claims and liabilities related to and arising out of Bhopal Gas disaster. The Court emphasised the need to evolve a national policy to protect national interest from ultra hazardous pursuits of economic gains. The Court observed that there are certain things that a civilised society simply cannot permit to be done by its members, even if they are compensated for their resulting losses.[34]

4. *Environmental Education and Mass Awareness*

M.C. Mehta v. *Union of India*[35] is another public interest petition relating to environment and pollution. The reliefs claimed were for issuing of appropriate directions to cinema exhibition halls to exhibit slides containing information and messages on environment free of cost; directions for spread of information relating to environment in national and regional languages and for broadcast thereof on the All India Radio and exposure thereof on the television in regular and short term programmes with a view to educating the people. It was also prayed that the environment should be made a compulsory subject in schools and colleges in graded system so that there would be a general growth of awareness.

Court accepted in principle the prayers made by the petitioner and observed: "We are in a democratic polity where dissemination of information is the foundation of the system. Keeping the citizens informed is an obligation of the Government. It is equally the responsibility of society to adequately educate every component of it so that social level is kept up."[36] The Court issued the following directions:

1. That the Respondents were directed to issue appropriate directions to the state governments and union territories to invariably enforce as a condition of licence of all cinema

halls, touring cinemas and video parlours to exhibit free of cost at least two slides/messages on environment in each show undertaken by them. The Ministry of Environment was also directed to bring out within two months appropriate slide material which would be brief but efficiently carry the message home on various aspects of environment and pollution.[37]

2. The Ministry of Information and Broadcasting was directed to produce without delay information films of short duration on various aspects of environment and pollution. Court directed that one such film should be shown, as far as practicable in one show everyday by the cinema halls and the central government and state governments were to ensure compliance of this condition from February 1, 1992.[38]
3. The Court suggested to the programme controlling authorities of the Doordarshan and the All India Radio to take proper steps to make interesting programmes and broadcast the same on the radio and exhibit the same on television. The national network as also the State Doordarshan centres were required to immediately take steps to implement this direction so that from February 1, 1992, regular compliance could be made.[39]
4. Court accepted in principle that through the medium of education awareness of the environment and its problems related to pollution should be taught as a compulsory subject. The University Grants Commission was directed to take appropriate steps i.e. requiring the universities to prescribe a course on environment and consider the feasibility of making this a compulsory subject at every level in college education. Court directed every state government and every education board to take steps to enforce compulsory education on environment in a graded way so that in the next academic year there would be compliance of this requirement.[40]

The Supreme Court in one of its earlier decisions namely *M.C. Mehta* v. *Union of India*[41] had directed the central government to get the text books on environment written and distributed to the educational institutions free of cost. Court also suggested the introduction of short term courses for training the teachers who will teach this subject.[42] Government of India and the government of states and union territories were required to organise "keep the city/town/village clean" week in every city, town and village falling under their jurisdiction at least once a year.[43]

It was suggested that the organisation of the week should be entrusted to the Nagar Mahapalikas, Municipal Corporations, Town Municipalities, Village Panchayats or such other local authorities having jurisdiction over the area in question. During that week all the citizens including the members of the executive, members of the parliament and state legislatures, members of the judiciary may be requested to co-operate with the local authorities and to take part in the celebrations by rendering free personal service. This would surely create a natural awareness of the problems faced by the people by the appalling all round deterioration of the environment. Ministry of Environment, Government of India was requested to give serious consideration to this suggestion.[44]

Conclusion

It is unfortunate that although Parliament and State Legislatures have enacted laws imposing duties for the prevention and control of environmental pollution, many of these provisions have just remained on paper without any adequate action being taken pursuant thereto. On the other hand whenever a problem of environmental pollution is brought before judiciary, it has kept in mind the constitutional mandates contained in Articles 21, 48-A and 51-A(g) and discharged its responsibility most conscientiously. The courts have given directions and never shifted the responsibility by telling that environmental priorities are a matter of policy. The judiciary emphasised "an environmental concern as a human right." Such a right the courts have held encompasses the entire community in common against the environmental pollution. Judiciary never caged this right in procedural webs rather encouraged the public spirited persons in most deserving cases to approach the court as a part of their fundamental duty.

REFERENCES

1. See the Preamble of the Indian Constitution.
2. See Sudesh Kumar Sharma, *Directive Principles and Fundamental Rights: Relationship and Policy Perspectives* 11 (1990).
3. Arts. 48-A and 51A(g) were incorporated by the Constitution (Forty-Second Amendment) Act, 1976.
4. *M.C. Metha* v. *Union of India* A.I.R. 1992 S.C. 382 at 385.
5. Reference may also be made to Forest Act, 1927; The Water (Prevention and Control of Pollution) Rules, 1975; The Water (Prevention and Control of Pollution) Cess Act, 1977; The Water (Prevention and Control of Pollution) Amendment Act, 1978; The Water (Prevention & Control of Pollution) Cess Rules, 1978; and Air (Prevention and Control of Pollution) Rules, 1982 etc. The object of these legislations is to maintain ecological balances among natural forces and to provide for protection and improvement of environment. These laws aim to control water and air pollution effectively.
6. See Mihir Desai, "Environmental Pollution", *The Lawyers Collective* pp. 52–55 (July 1986). Reference may be made to Ss. 269, 277, 278 and 426 of Indian Penal Code, 1860, S. 133 of Criminal Procedure Code, 1973 and S. 91 of Civil Procedure Code, 1908.
7. A.I.R. 1980 S.C. 1622 at 1629–30 and 31.
8. *Id.*, at 1628.
9. *Id.*, at 1630.
10. See Krishan Mahajan, "Environment and the Poor," *Indian Express* Chandigarh, Sunday, December 29, 1991, p. 7. Mr. Mahajan has analysed the judgement delivered by Mr. C.K. Chaturvedi, Sub-Judge Delhi in *Suresh Kumar* v. *Pooran Chand and the Municipal Corporation of Delhi* (dated 26.11.1991). This judgement enunciates the people's right to clean environment, in the context of slaughtering of animals, shows that even the subordinate judiciary in India is conscious of an environmental concern as a human right.
11. A.I.R. 1992 Orissa 225.
12. *Id.*, at 231.
13. *M.C. Mehta* v. *Union of India* A.I.R. 1988 S.C. 1037.
14. A.I.R. 1988 S.C. 1115.

14a. *Id.*, at 1127.

15. (1990) 1 S.C.C. 613.
16. *Id.*, at 717. See also M/S *Shantistar Builders* v. *Naryan K. Tomate* (1990) 1 S.C.C. 520. In this case Supreme Court once again observed that the right to life would include within its sweep the right to decent environment and reasonable accommodation to live in.
17. (1990) 4 S.C.C. 449.
18. A.I.R. 1991 S.C. 420.
19. A.I.R. 1994 M.P. 48.
20. *Rural Litigation and Entitlement Kendra Dehradun* v. *State of U.P.* A.I.R. 1985 S.C. 652.
21. *Id.*, at 656.
22. *Id.*, at 657.
23. A.I.R. 1987 S.C. 359.
24. *Id.*, at 363.

25. A.I.R. 1987 S.C. 1109.
26. *Id.*, at 1114.
27. *Id.*
28. *M.C. Mehta* v. *Union of India* A.I.R. 1987 S.C. 965.
29. *Id.*, at 981.
30. A.I.R. 1987 S.C. 1086.
31. *Id.*, at 1099.
32. A.I.R. 1989 S.C. 1069.
33. A.I.R. 1990 S.C. 273.
34. *Id.*, at 283.
35. A.I.R. 1992 S.C. 382.
36. *Id.*, at 384.
37. *Id.*
38. *Id.*
39. *Id.*, at 385.
40. *Id.*
41. A.I.R. 1988 S.C. 1115.
42. *Id.*, at 1127.
43. *Id.*, at 1128.
44. *Id.*

16

Prisoners' Right to Socialisation

*Naresh Kumar**
*A.S. Dalal**

Law is to protect liberties. But the State's authority and its duty to maintain law and order at any cost are always in conflict with the human feelings and liberty of the people. Liberty, as history has shown, is the basic thing that goes to make up the ethos of man and civilisation, and without it no one can attain happiness which is the ultimate objective of all human beings. But liberty has to be regulated so that all may enjoy it equally. Absolute liberty is neither possible nor exists in any civilized society.

Crime, repression and injustice have always been parts of the human conditions. So are the prisons wherein the persons condemned for their anti-social and unlawful acts are lodged. Traditionally, prisons and prisoners have been considered as somewhat violent, mysterious and frightful entities by the society. The history of prisons and its use as a place of detention for the condemned persons is not of recent origin but is very old. The outlawed inmate of a prison, till the beginning of the century, was never considered fit to claim any right enjoyed by law-abiding persons of the society. He was put in jail only to realize his folly and to pay for it through his sufferings.

* Lecturer, Law Deptt., M.D. University, Rohtak.

After World War II, radical changes were brought in the system of Prison Administration due to the effect of Human Rights Movement at the international level. The idea of reformation and rehabilitation along with the fact that a prisoner has to come outside and to live in the society from which he was expelled due to his unlawful conduct, were given recognition by the courts and the prison administration agencies.

Standard Minimum Rules for Prisoners[1]

The importance of this document framed by the Amnesty-International has been certainly increased due to the reason that the document contains certain provisions supporting the reformative aspect of punishment. Undoubtedly and undisputedly, the purpose of punishment is not to torture a person but to reform him and ultimately making him a good citizen. So going on his line of thinking there are a number of provisions regarding the social relations of a prisoner and his after-care.

The purpose and justification of a sentence of imprisonment or a similar measure deprivitive of liberty is ultimately to protect the society against crime. This end can only be achieved if the period of imprisonment is to ensure so far as possible, that upon his return to society, the offender is not only willing but able to live in law abiding society and self supporting life.[2]

Rule 60 (2) states:

> Before the completion of the sentence it is desirable that the necessary steps should be taken to ensure for the prisoner a gradual return to normal life in society. This aim may be achieved, depending on the case by a pre-release regime organised in the same institution or in other appropriate institution or by release on trial under some kind of supervision which must not be entrusted to the police but should be combined with effective social aid.

Moreover, the treatment of prisoners should not emphasize their exclusion from the community but should emphasize their continuing part in it. Community agencies, should therefore, be enlisted wherever possible to assist the staff of the institution in the task of social rehabilitation of the prisoner.

One of the good methods prescribed by this document for continuing and resuming the social relations of a prisoner is that special attention should be paid to the maintenance and improvement of such relations between a prisoner and his family as are desirable in the best interest of both.[3]

Summarily, it can be stated that these are simply certain principles of criminal justice incorporated in the form of rules. But as there is no effective implementation, hence, these rules have been considered by the courts as well as states as guidelines for interpretation and legislation. But in this decade these rules have been highlighted and maximum protection has been given to the persons behind the bars.

Constitution of India, other Statutes and Prisoners

There is no specific guarantee of prisoner's rights in the Constitution of India. However, certain rights which have been enumerated in part III of the Constitution are available to prisoners too because a prisoner remains a 'Person' in the prison. Besides the Constitution, there are certain other statutes like the Prison Act, 1894, Prisoners Act, 1900 and Prisoners (Attendance in Courts) Act 1955, where certain rights are conferred upon the prisoners. Prison and Police manuals, which also have certain rules and safeguards for the prisoners also cast an obligation on the prison authorities to follow these rules.

Rule 26. 21A[4] declares:

> Undertrial prisoners are divided into classes based on previous standard of living. The classifying authority is the trying court subject to the District Magistrate, but during the period before a prisoner is brought before a competent court, discretion is to be exercised by the officer-in-charge of the Police Station concerned to classify him as either 'better class' or 'ordinary'.
>
> Only those prisoners are to be classified provisionally as 'better class' who by social status, education or habit of life have been accustomed to a superior mode of living.

> The fact for the commission of any particular class of offence is not to be considered. The possession of a certain degree of literacy is in itself not sufficient for 'better class' classification and no undertrial prisoner shall be so classified whose mode of living does not appear to the police officer concerned to have been definitely superior to that of the ordinary run of the population, whether urban or rural.

The above rule speaks of the category of prisoners on the basis of social status and other habits.

Meeting with Family Members and Friends

Punjab Jail Manual provides that the undertrial prisoners shall be allowed to contact his family members and friends twice in a week.[5]

Other rule provides that the convicted prisoners shall be allowed to meet the family members and friends once in a week.[6]

The rules are silent so far as 'detenues' under preventive detention are concerned and have created a lot of confusion regarding the facility of visits with friends and family members.[7]

Parole

Parole is considered as a useful tool for the social rehabilitation of the prisoner because it provides him an opportunity to meet his family members and hence, can realise his responsibility towards his family.

Section 58A[8] provides that the appropriate government should make provisions for parole depending upon the nature and conduct of the criminal and gravity of the offence committed by him.

Temporary Release of the Prisoners

It is provided in the Prisons Act that prisoners should be temporarily released subject to certain conditions for a period not exceeding ten days in a year excluding the time required for journeys and the days of departure from, and the arrival at the prison.[9]

However, no prisoner is to be released under above provision, unless:

(a) he has, at the time of his release, served one-half of his release including remission or a period of not less than two years of his sentence including remission, whichever is less;[10]
(b) his conduct in prison has been good;
(c) twelve months have elapsed from the date of the expiry of the period of his previous release, if any under this provision.[11]

Judicial Activism

The prisons during the last three centuries or so, have evolved to the status of an institution of social control. In today's versions when death penalty, banishment and life transportation are generally called as inhuman and cruel, the institution of prison is certainly more influencing and correct. It not only carries the bearings of the ideals of the period but is also impregnated with the expediencies of organisational science.

However, one of the major defects in the prison custody is that it provides frustration to the prisoners by shielding and cutting him completely from the outer world. So, in order to change the behaviour of the prisoner, it is not only necessary but compulsory for the State that it should provide the maximum attention to the social and cultural norms of a prisoner.

For the purposes of socialisation of the prisoners it must be seen that the relations of the prisoner should not be wholly cut off from the outer world. The prison authorities should give due consideration to the maintaining and improving the healthy relations between a prisoner, his family members and friends.

The ultimate purpose of imprisonment is to make a prisoner a good citizen. So, keeping in view this object of imprisonment special attention should be paid from the beginning of a prisoner's sentence regarding his after-release prospectives. More so, the prison authorities should allow the outer agencies to contact the prisoner which will ultimately be useful for the social rehabilitation of the prisoner concerned.

The adverse effects of the non-socialisation were stated by Shri Jawahar Lal Nehru on the Naini Prison[12] in the following words:

> For years and years, many of these 'lifers' do not see a child or woman, or even animals. They lose touch with the outside world completely and have no humane contacts left. They brood and wrap themselves in angry thoughts of fear and revenge, hatred, forgot the goods of the world, the kindness and joy, and live only wrapped up in the evil, till gradually even hatred loses its edge and life becomes a soulless thing, a machine-like routine. From time to time the prisoner's body is weighed and measured. But how is one to weight the mind and the spirit which wilt and stunt themselves and while this was the terrible atmosphere of fear and oppression, people argue against the death penalty and their arguments appeal to me greatly. But when I see the long drawn out agony of a life spent in prison, I feel that it is perhaps better to have that penalty rather than to kill a person slowly and by degrees.[13]

The Supreme Court of India recently considered the aspect of socialisation of prisoner. In the *Francis Coralie*[14] case, the honourable court considered the scope of Article 21 for all the category of prisoners, viz, detenue, undertrials and convicts. In this case the petition was filed by a British national under Article 32 of the Indian Constitution, raising a question in regard to the right of a detenue to have meetings and interview with his lawyer and members of her family.

The petitioner was arrested and detained in the Central Jail, Tihar, under an order dated November 23, 1979 under section 3 of the COPEPOSA Act. She preferred writ of *habeas corpus*, challenging her detention but her petition was rejected by the Supreme Court. The petitioner experienced grave difficulty in having interview with her lawyer and the members of her family. Her daughter aged about 5 years and her sister, who was looking after her daughter were permitted to meet only once in a month. The petitioner also wanted to meet the lawyer regarding a criminal proceeding which was pending against her. The procedure for obtaining the interview was very tedious as it required the prior permission of district magistrate and the lawyer can meet only in the presence of custom officer. The petitioner was thus, substantially denied the facility of interview with her lawyer and meetings with her kids except once in a month.

This restriction on interview and meetings was imposed by the prison authorities under the prison rules. The principal ground on which the constitutional validity of these rules was challenged was that these provisions were violative of the Articles 14 and 21 of the Indian Constitution in as much as they were arbitrary and unreasonable. It was contended on behalf of the petitioner that allowing interviews and meetings with the members of her family only once in a month was discriminatory and unreasonable, particularly when the undertrials were granted the facility of interview with family and friends twice in a week[15] and convicted prisoners were permitted to have interviews with their relatives and friends once in a week.[16]

The petitioner further argued that a detenue was entitled under Article 22 of the Constitution to consult his lawyer.

After going through a detailed discussion on the scope of Article 21 and the prison rules, the Supreme court laid down that the 'right to life' enshrined in Article 21 can not be restricted to mere animal existence. It means something more than just physical survival. The right to life includes the right to live with human dignity and all that goes along with it, namely, the bare necessaries of life such as adequate nutrition, clothing and shelter over the head and facilities for reading, writing and expressing oneself in diverse forms, freely moving about and mixing and commingling with fellow human beings.[17]

The Supreme Court further opined that there is a vital distinction between 'Preventive detention' and 'Punitive detention'. Punitive detention is intended to inflict punishment on a person who has been found guilty for certain offence, while preventive detention is not by way of punishment at all, but it is a preventive measure taken by the state as to restrain the detenue from indulging in the activities which are likely to disturb the peace of society. Considering these objectives, the detenues are supposed to be treated with more humanity and dignity. More so, when an undertrial prisoner is granted the facility of interviews with relatives and friends twice in a week and a convicted prisoner is permitted to have interviews with his relatives and friends once in a week, the restriction on the detenues to be interviewed or meet with family members once in a month can not be regarded as reasonable and non arbitrary, particularly when a detenue stands on a higher pedestal than an undertrial or a convict.[18]

The decision of the Supreme Court in this case can be taken as a landmark as it not only tried to minimise the adverse impact of imprisonment by allowing socialising to a prisoner but also made three categories of the prisoners in order of their treatment in jails. The right to meet with family members can be easily extended to attend the family functions. Prisoners should be allowed to attend these functions by prior permission from the authorities and after furnishing a reasonable security bond, if otherwise it is not objectionable. No doubt that a prisoner is no more a free man, yet he must, as far as possible and practicable, be allowed to meet the family members because it will ultimately help in the social rehabilitation of the prisoner after release.

Conclusion and Suggestions

The prison manuals do allow the prisoner to have meetings inside the prisons with their family members and friends as regulated by the prison authorities. Meeting with family members and friends have special humanising effect on the prisoner. These meetings, therefore, should not depend entirely on the whims and fancies of the prison authorities, but should be allowed as a matter of right. This privilege authorised by law to the prisoners should not be allowed to be used by the prison authorities as a means of exploitation but only as a step towards his rehabilitation with his kith and kins.

Parole and temporary releases are allowed to prisoners by the prison authorities in deserving cases to meet some of their essential social or family obligations. The paroles are sparingly granted. It is submitted that in proper cases, the parole is an important and timely step in allowing the prisoner a chance for readaptation in his social surroundings. The parole should be granted not only on essential functions such as sowing or harvesting the crop, visiting a near or dear one on his or her death bed or to attend the funeral procession of the same but should also be granted to discharge the conjugal obligations.

Discharge of conjugal obligation will help the prisoner for changing his attitude and thinking towards life. Moreover, it will be useful for the other partner who is an innocent sufferer. It is, however, possible that the very liberal use of parole particularly for the exercise of conjugal rights may minimise the impact of the imprisonment on other inmates. It is submitted that these methods, without being a right, should be applied in appropriate cases with necessary care and caution. Parole is delicate but essential instrument for the social rehabilitation of the prisoner after his release. Parole ultimately helps the prisoner in development of his personality as it keeps him in touch with the outer world and thereby minimises the corrosive effects of imprisonment on human qualities.

It is, however, reported that the State of Punjab is facing a lot of hardships in the process of rehabilitation of a number of persons detained under TADA and the National Security Act. Due to long detention periods and almost complete isolation, these prisoners have developed psychological disorders. The problem has been further aggravated due to their disowning by their respective families.

REFERENCES

1. Amn. International—U.N. DOC./A/CONF./6/1(1955).
2. *Id.,* rule 58.
3. *Id.,* rule 61.
4. Punjab Police Rules, 1934.
5. Rule 559A, Punjab Jail Manual.
6. *Id.*, rule 550.
7. *Francis Coralie* v. *U.T. Delhi,* AIR 1981 SC 746. It was laid down by the Supreme Court that detenues should be considered on a higher footing so far as right to visits and to be interviewed is concerned.
8. The Prisons Act, 1894.
9. *Id.,* Section 31A (1).

10. *Id.,* Section 31A (2).
11. *Id.,* Section 31A (3).
12. Quoted by Justice Krishna Iyer in the *Sunil Batra* v. *Delhi Administration*, AIR 1978 SC 1675.
13. *Id.,* at 1713.
14. *Francis Coralie Mullin* v. *U.T. Delhi,* AIR 1981 SC 746.
15. Rule 559A, Manual for the Superintendence and Management of Jails in Punjab.
16. *Id.,* rule 550.
17. *Supra* n. 13 at 747.
18. *Id.,* at 747.

PART IV

HUMAN RIGHTS AND THE CHILD

17

Rights of the Child and Judicial Activism— A Critical Appraisal

*K.P.S. Mahalwar**
*Shahabuddin Ansari***

Children are the foundation of a nation and future course of its progress and development will be determined by their mental and physical well being. Realising this, the Government of India adopted a policy for welfare of children, which inter-alia enunciates the following approach:

> "The nation's children are a supremely important asset. Their nature and solicitude are our responsibility. Children's programmes should find a prominent part in our national plans for the development of human resources, so that our children grow up to become robust citizens, physically fit, mentally alert and morally healthy, endowed with the skills and motivations needed by society. Equal opportunities for development to all children during the period of growth should be our aim, for this would serve our larger purpose of reducing inequality and ensuring social justice."[1]

* Reader in Law, M.D. University, Rohtak, Haryana.
** Lecturer in Law, K.G.K. College Moradabad, U.P.

In recognition of the universally accepted norms of human dignity and of equal inalienable rights of the civilized society, the Universal Declaration of Human Rights (1948) too deals with welfare and development of children. Apart from it, the UN Commission on Human Rights drafted the Convention on the Rights of the Child, which was subsequently adopted by the General Assembly on 20 November, 1989. This document also recognises the exceptional vulnerability of children and proclaims that childhood is entitled to special care and assistance. Understandably, it places a moral and legal obligation on the State to ensure that children get a fair deal in the society. The convention basically draws attention to their right to survival, protection, development and to participation thus providing a legal basis for punitive action against its violation by society. The above convention simply reiterates what has already been embodied in the Constitution of India.

The Constitution of India enshrines our basic philosophy in its Preamble and lays down certain invaluable directive principles of governance recognising the child and his well being as an important matter of concern in the entire process of policy planning and its implementation. Article 15(3) of the Constitution casts a duty on the State to give special treatment to the children. Article 24, guarantees another important fundamental right to the child below 14 years for protection against exploitation in the form of child labour in factories, mines and other hazardous occupations. Article 45 directs the State to provide for universal free and compulsory education upto the age of 14 years. Further, according to Article 39, the State shall, in particular, direct its policy towards securing:

> "(e) that the health and strength of workers, men and women, and the tender age of children are not abused and that citizens are not forced by economic necessity to enter vocations unsuited to their age or strength;
>
> (f) that children are given opportunities and facilities to develop in a healthy manner and in conditions of freedom and dignity and that childhood and youth are protected against exploitation and against moral and material abandonment."

Our National Policy for Children (1974) lays down, "It shall be the policy of the State to provide adequate services to children, both before and after birth and through the period of growth to ensure their full physical, mental and social development." But alas, the blatant misuse of technique of amninocentesis for sex determination and selective abortions still continue at an accelerated pace inspite of legislative prohibitions. The scenario speaks of the pseudo-concern of the State for the welfare and rights of helpless children. Female foeticide has already disturbed the sex ratio in many parts of our country and may assume monstrous proportions if hard steps to deal with this shameful practice are not taken post haste.[2] In order to achieve our own lofty constitutional, goals all the three wings of the State, i.e. Legislature, Executive and Judiciary have been seemingly striving hard and a plethora of laws have been enacted to achieve these goals. In the more recent past, rights of the child have certainly become a subject of grave concern for all and have drawn attention universally. However, despite so much hue and cry over the child welfare schemes, programmes, policies and laws the situation continues to remain grave. Incidence of child delinquency, prohibited forms of child labour, servitude, sexual abuse, vagrancy are still grim realities of our society forcing innocent millions to live inhuman and substandard existence in utter disregard of the UN Convention on Rights of the Child (1989) and clear constitutional mandates to the State.[3] Unconcerned about the legal prohibition on child labour, fire cracker manufacturers still continue to employ them with absolute impunity.[4] Heart rending plight of bonded children was brought to limelight by the Bonded Labour Liberation Front in the Supreme Court in 1984 through Bandhua Mukti Morcha case. Today we have over a whopping 55 million children living in servitude because of grinding poverty, unemployment, illiteracy, abominable caste system, ethnic discrimination and above all lack of political will, all of which in varying degrees have been responsible for this scourge.[5] Efforts have been made to regulate child labour ever since 1981, through various legislations in various aspects such as laying down of minimum age, working hours, ordering total prohibition in certain specific industries and so on. The latest such legislation is The Child Labour (Prohibition & Regulation) Act, 1986, wherein the child labour has been recognised as a necessary evil and a slightly more determined bid is made to regulate this social and economic malady. Various trade unions like INTUC and CITU have also launched campaign to fight this menace.[6] After the Protection of Human Rights Act, 1993 having come into force and after the establishment of National Human Rights Commission, NHRC has seriously taken up the cause of thousands of children engaged in glass factories making bangles and miniature bulbs. NHRC has announced some welfare scheme for organised and unorganised sectors covering such industries in Firozabad and Shikohabad in U.P.[7] Right under the nose of Government of India in Delhi, employment of children as bonded labour was brought to notice of the NHRC and in response to NHRC's notice, the Government of National Capital Territory of Delhi confirmed that 7 children duly covered under the Bonded Labour System (Abolition) Act, 1976 were employed by a contractor and that an order for their release had been made by the Deputy Commissioner. After considering the response of Government, the NHRC in its meeting on 24.1.95 recorded their dissatisfaction over the fact that no action was taken to prosecute the contractor who had employed these children and the person who procured them for employment. Such apparent callousness and apathy of the Government allows the malady to persist and successfully frustrate all efforts.

We often come across shocking reports in the newspapers highlighting the incidents of inhuman treatment being meted out to such hapless children at their places of work. Though child labour is legally prohibited in every walk of life, we find children at work unsuited to their age and strength because conditions of absolute poverty have made them a vast source of cheap labour. What to talk of their wages and rights, these innocent and poor creatures have no voice even to express their pains, sufferings and agonies while their tormentors thrive.[8] They have no dignity and present the spectre of a slavish existence. There are children, wading through smelly garbage and scouring it for food and salable waste. Food thus collected from waste bins is mostly their meal.[9] Similarly, they sell industrial and domestic waste such as paper, tin, bottles, plastic, etc; at the rates varying according to the quality of material sold (e.g. paper or glass is sold at 50 paisa per kg) and that farthing is their proud earning for the family.[10] Their day begins at 5.00 A.M. and they have to walk for miles in sun, rain and cold and move from one dustbin to another. Many of them die a premature death resulting from malnutrition, hunger and lack of care and concern on the part of society. Law prohibits child labour, but this is sadly viewed as "self-employment" hence there is no law to protect these kids from unimaginable agonies. There are also other forms of such "self-employment", like shoe shine boys, vendors in trains, buses and theatres, dish washers in hotels and dhabas, street hawkers, etc. The most risky "self-employment" which has come to light is collecting metal scrap and pellets from military firing ranges, where poor children often become the target resulting in either death or serious injury maiming them permanently. Children collect scrap from these danger zones and sell at very low rates in the market, just to keep their body and soul together.[11]

In bidi and match industries, the work is usually got done through labour contractors who in turn engage poor women and children to do it at their dwellings and, therefore, provisions of law do not apply to them. Law is applicable to industrial premises only and not to private dwelling houses and thus it fails to protect such women and children from inhuman exploitation.[12] In hotels, restaurants and dhabas the plight of child labour is horrible. Poor and feeble boys start at 5.00 a.m., clean the premises, collect water, milk and other necessities at work place and remain engaged throughout the day like robots without break or rest. Not only this, they are often abused, maltreated and beaten like beasts.[13] Their work much exceeds the maximum working hours fixed by Shops and Establishment laws.

The inhuman conditions in which they work goes on unquestioned. Sheela Barse, a journalist, surveyed the working conditions of children working in glass factories of Firozabad in Agra district of U.P. and she found thousands of boys of tender age working in glass factories where furnaces hold tonnes of smouldering coal with the temperature maintained at 140°C. Child workers of 7–12 years are made to handle the burning loams of glass, the basic material used in the process of manufacturing bangles. What boggles the mind all the more is the fact that they are paid as little as Rs. 7–10 for a shift of 8 hours (may be day or night). Atmosphere in the factory is polluted with intolerable heat, unbearable chemical fumes, soot and coal dust while particles of broken glass cover the floor.[14] Children are forced to work in such hazardous conditions to earn their livelihood or to supplement their parents' meagre income. Understandably, no parent will send his children to such factories except under extreme conditions of poverty and deprivation.

In different parts of our country, a large number of children are working in zari work, embroidery and carpet industry. Little children of tender age (7–10 years) are brought to carpet industry in Bhadoi near Varanasi (U.P.) from Palamau in Bihar whose parents are paid a paltry sum of about Rs. 500/- as consideration thereof. Such children are forced to work in abominable conditions in carpet industry.[15] The laws prohibiting child labour are grossly ineffective to deal with the malady. Similarly, in brass industries of Moradabad, numerous children are working in unhygienic conditions. They commute from adjoining villages to earn not more than Rs. 5/- a day. The industrial processes there emit fumes and gases which cause tuberculosis among the children.[16] Such is the miserable plight of these born slaves. The only thing they know and understand is to be ready at the call of their master. Their elders have spent their lives working and ultimately retired passing their debt liability to their siblings. The wrought is perpetuated because of illiteracy, poverty, meagre wages and exorbitant interest charged by unscrupulous money lenders. Their offsprings are born burdened with huge debt, interest and fines. The spectre of children being subjected to severe beating and filthy abusive language for absence from work and sometimes even being branded with hot iron in such work places is not uncommon. Agonies do not end there; many times they are thrown in the hands of another master to clear debts, interest and fines. This cycle of miseries is the life cycle of these unfortunate buds. They are born in slavery, live in slavery and die in slavery. Labour laws and Constitution have no meaning for them.

Apart from the instances discussed above, a big chunk of children are working in the countryside also engaged in farming or domestic work.[17] Majority of children in villages are deprived of education and made to work in the fields or for pasturing cattle. During the formative years they are employed to work in the farms by the wealthy farmers. This is another independent class of exploited children in that they are denied the normal enjoyment of childhood life and proper opportunities for growth and development.

Many deprived children of tender age in our country are found working day and night under inhuman conditions. After all why? Ours is a poverty ridden society and parents send their children for work or pledge their labour when economic conditions compel them. Children at work contribute to the income of family and if prohibited from work, it would lead to vagrancy, starvation in addition to so many other social evils and even crimes. Since child labour is an economic problem, employers claim to employ children on sympathetic grounds so that the poor child can at least earn something for survival.[18] It is said that it is because of this compelling consideration that the Inspectors to prevent child labour do not take action. It is argued that strict enforcement of law will throw the poor child workers out of job and deprive them of their livelihood. In carpet industry, zari work, etc; employers justify employment of children of tender age with the logic that it is at this state only that they can be trained as perfect artisans.[19]

A sizeable number of children mostly from labour class or small artisans do not go to school because sending them to school works as a double edged weapon for their parents. Firstly, they forgo the earnings that otherwise come to them from child labour or at least lose a member to look after the siblings when mother is out to work. Secondly, they also have to spend money on uniform, books, stationery, etc; though amount of tuition fee may be negligible. In view of these inhibiting factors, a large number of parents prefer to send their kids to work.[20] Tall claims of the Government to eradicate child labour, constitutional guarantees and U.N. Convention on Rights of the Child notwithstanding, any degree of success on this point continues to remain the proverbial mirage in

India and our unfortunate children continue to suffer an undignified existence even as we boast of preparing to enter the 21st century with a bang. Sometime back a study conducted on child labour employed in hazardous fire and match industries in Sivakasi revealed that 45000 children have been engaged in these factories since long.[21] In *M.C. Mehta* v. *State of Tamil Nadu*,[22] the Supreme Court dealt with a PIL concerning the child labour in Kamraj District of Tamil Nadu in various match factories. The horrifying state of the children engaged in these factories in blatant violation of various laws sensitized the Hon'ble court to issue directions to the State of Tamil Nadu to properly enforce the provisions of Factories Act and to provide for facilities for recreation, medicare, proper working environment and basic diet during working hours besides minimum facilities for their education. Court also suggested a scheme for compulsory insurance cover for children employed in hazardous factories and thus played a significant role to ameliorate the worsening condition of youth.

Eradication of child labour can be possible only by removal of economic disparities and a multipronged scheme for abolition of poverty. Taking into account the basic requirements for a proper mental and physical development of our children on the one hand and the poor economic condition of their parents on the other hand, it becomes the duty of State to ensure that children at work get proper education, nourishment and hygienic conditions for a steady development of their faculties so that they can enjoy life normally and be useful citizens of tomorrow. Sadly the employer lacks a sense of natural human compassion and, therefore, callously ignores the sufferings and pains of these children at work in tender age. He exploits the child as much as possible, therefore, children mutely prefer to work only in those spheres where they are away from health hazards, cruel eyes of their employers or where they can work with their parents and get parental care, love and affection which is essential for their growth. If they work under the supervision of parents, at least parents will take care of their affordable minimum basic requirements. Many a times there is abuse of youth or childhood by parents themselves when they ignore the basic requirements for nurturing children into healthy, robust and useful citizens and attach greater importance to the temporary economic gains to serve selfish motives because they live life merely from day to day. Wherever child labour is necessary predominantly to overcome economic constraints, it must be properly regulated. No laxity ought to be tolerated in this area of governmental responsibility.

Need of the hour, therefore, is sincere implementation of the laws and greater commitment on the part of the Government to launch a decisive offensive to wipe out this evil. Human right activists and voluntary groups can also play a vital role with the help of provisions in the new law under which any one can move the court for its enforcement. Recognising child labour as a necessary evil, the Government has now come up with a policy of its regulation which promises strict enforcement of provisions relating to the welfare measures for working children and their families, rehabilitations, etc. The Government must also relentlessly endeavour to gradually rehabilitate the children at work in self employment so that the energy of these children of tender age can be gainfully utilised for their own development.[23]

In 1991, the famous Ameena's case rendered a great service to the society by exposing once again the rot in our social fabric, wherein ten years old Ameena was forced to marry a rich Arab of 60 years who had paid a handsome amount to Ameena's father. Working on a tipoff the man was nabbed at the airport while trying to take her away to Riyadh without her consent. Further reports revealed that this case was not an isolated event but only a tip of the ice-berg. It became evident that over the years hundreds of unfortunate minor girls like Ameena have been sold in similar circumstances from the single locality of Hyderabad.[24] Abysmal poverty is again said to be at the root of this shameful practice. Greedy parents and relatives of these girls have sold them abroad in the guise of adoption. It turned to be a lucrative trade for many racketeers, pushing innocent children of tender age into life long slavery, prostitution or various other forms of inhuman existence. According to investigations, instances of minor girls being offered to temples whence they are ultimately drawn into flesh trade. Metropolitan towns have in fact seemingly become the breeding places for child prostitution.[25]

Grim spectre of the child prostitution[26] and their living in inhuman conditions in brothels have been exposed through PIL writs being filed before the apex court. In *Vishaljeet* v. *U.O.I*[27] Ratnavel Pandian J. recalled that parents owing to poverty sold their daughters for paltry sums hoping that they would be engaged in household duties but subsequently pimps and brothelkeepers inveigle them into flesh trade. The court observed,—"The malady is not only social but also a socioeconomic problem and, therefore, the measures that are to be taken in that regard should be more preventive than punitive."[28] In order to prevent such child abuse, the government departments have been directed to take measures to uproot child prostitution and to implement the social welfare programmes for the cause of protection, proper treatment, development and rehabilitation of the young victims namely the children engaged in hazardous occupations and girls recovered from brothel houses, etc. Vishaljeet's case has brought into sharp focus the miseries of many more victims being exploited by the highly organised sex industry and the Hon'ble court had issued some very important remedial and preventive directions to the State Governments but the extent of their compliance is extremely disheartening. Through PIL many more cases of child abuse have come to light in the past few years wherein the Supreme Court has laid down similar principles and issued directions to the Government.[29] Feeling aghast at the miseries of the female child and the manner of their being traded like commodity, Supreme Court gave a precious piece of judicial legislation for evolving a procedure to prevent illegal sale of babies in the garb of adoption by the agencies in *Laxmikant Pandey* v *U.O.I.*[30] In this landmark case the court issued various valuable directions regarding adoption of Indian children by foreigners with a view to evolve a genuine procedure. The instant purpose however, was to lay down proper norms to be followed in giving a child in adoption to a foreigner and to prevent incidence of illegal sale of babies.[31] Once again in 1991, the Supreme Court was called upon to issue fresh directions on the matter of adoptions in *Laxmikant Pandey* v. *U.O.I.*[32] This case is the most symptomatic example of legislative adhocism in India and through it was exposed the apathy of State in matters relating to prevention of oppression and exploitation of adopted Indian children in foreign countries. The Supreme Court had to perforce resort to judicial legislation exercising its epistolary jurisdiction. This landmark action of our apex Court at once became an apostle of judicial activism of our superior judiciary.

Many social-scientists have observed and our Government also feels that illiteracy and ever increasing population lead to all conceivable social evils and at the same time retard our development and growth as a nation. Universalization of primary education is once again made one of the basic objectives in the 8th Five Year Plan (1992–97). Despite a clear mandate to the States under Article 45 of the Constitution providing for free and compulsory education for all children, India has already earned the dubious distinction of being one of the very few countries in the world where primary education has not been made compulsory and hence remains a distant goal. Everybody has a right to live with dignity, which if understood holistically, includes right to education, growth and development also. Though not explicitly guaranteed as a fundamental right under part III of the Constitution, but it is unequivocally and unambiguously clear from Constituent Assembly Debates that framers of our Constitution made it obligatory for the State to provide for universal free education upto age 14. However, in our poverty ridden society, State has not so far succeeded in achieving the goal. Nonetheless, we woke up to a happy development recently in the form of a Supreme Court decision in *Mohini Jain* v. *State of Karnataka*[33] and *Unni Krishnan* v. *State of Andhra Pradesh*[34] holding the right to free education upto the age of 14 years as a fundamental right by further expanding the scope of Article 21. The Supreme Court has thus recognised that the right to life and personal liberty guaranteed under Article 21 of the Constitution means right to live with human dignity and that education is the key to that, State's plea of lack of financial resources rightly did not convince the Court. In many ways the above decisions are eye-openers for our legislators and policy makers and are expected to go a long way in ensuring universally accepted minimum rights to the children and thus usher in a new era of development of the individual and of the nation. Want and deprivation will ultimately give way to plenty and affluence all over though the pace of progression of changeover may be tardy.

Another evil, affecting our child's right to development, dignity, expression, health and protection from all forms of violence, injury or abuse, neglect, exploitation, etc; is the maltreatment of juvenile offenders in which the State has to share the blame. The matter has, of course, been steadily gaining attention of social activists, voluntary organisations and courts as well since long. Tiny kids, who being entrapped by various socio-economic factors are coerced into doing underworld activities, can not be treated like hardened criminals. Nor can they be kept in jails sharing professional offenders, because most juvenile offenders are still found to be in their formative stage and can be easily moulded into useful and law abiding citizens provided due care is exercised and right efforts in right directions made. Horrifying tales of little kids languishing in jails in the company of hardened criminals, inhuman treatment given to them by the police are quite common in India.[35] Justice V.R. Krishna Iyer has rightly remarked while speaking on our juvenile justice system: "the law, in the past, has lashed the child, not loved it, whatever it's pretensions . . . corrections informed by compassion, not incarceration leading to degeneration, is the primary aim of juvenile justice. . . . Regrettably our juvenile justice system still thinks in terms of terror, not cure; of wounding, not healing, and sort of blindmen's buff is the result." Sheela Barse, has also rightly observed, "a law that is meant to help the most helpless of the helpless must have meticulously framed rules to protect children from the implementors, to provide safeguards against a negative, oppressive, coercive, even destructive operation of the laws.[36] She filed a petition in the Supreme Court under Article 32 of the Constitution seeking a writ or order for release of children below 16 years serving jails in different states of the country, demanding complete information of children lodged in jails, borstals, remand homes and other reformatories and for issuance of a direction that District Judges should visit jails and sub jails within their jurisdiction to ensure that children are properly looked after when in custody. The petition sought a further direction to the State Legal Aid Boards to appoint duty counsels to ensure availability of legal protection for children as and when they are involved in criminal cases and are proceeded against.[37] Supreme Court in its historical judgement directed the Union of India that, "where a complaint is filed or FIR is lodged against a child below 16 years for an offence punishable with imprisonment of not more than 7 years, the investigation shall be completed within 3 months and if the investigation is not completed within this time the case against child must be treated as closed. If chargesheet is submitted within 3 months, the case must be disposed of within next 6 months."[38] Realising the gravity of the problem caused by shabby conditions in our prisons generally, the Hon'ble Judges further observed that, "if a child is a national asset, it is the duty of the State to look after the child with a view to ensuring full development of its personality. . . . Incarceration in jail would have the effect of dwarfing the development of child, exposing him to the baneful influences, coarsening his conscience and alienating him from the society. . . . It is also no answer on the part of the State to say that it has not got enough number of remand homes or observation homes or other places where children can be kept and that is why they are lodged in jails. . . . It is the atmosphere of the jail which has a highly injurious effect on the mind of the child, estranging him from the society and breeding in him aversion bordering on hatred against a system which keeps him in jail."[39] Their Lordships further impressed upon the state governments that they must set up necessary remand homes and observation homes where children accused of an offence can be lodged pending investigation and trial. On no account should the children be kept in jails and if a state has not got sufficient accommodation, the children should be released on bail instead of being subjected to incarceration in jail.[40] The judges were firmly of the view that every state government must take necessary measures for the purpose of setting up adequate number of courts, appointing requisite number of judges and providing them the necessary facilities for expeditious disposal of cases. They expressed the urgency to set up an institute or academy for training of judicial officers so that their efficiency may be improved.[41]

Emphasizing the need for implementation of law they said, "it is not enough merely to have legislation on the subject, but it is equally, if not more important to ensure that such legislation is implemented in all earnestness and mere lip sympathy is not pleaded on the ground of lack of finances on the part of the State. The greatest recompense which the State can get for expenditure on children is the building up of a powerful human resource ready to take its place in the forward march of the nation."[42]

In yet another case, *Sheela Barse* v. *The Secretary, Children Aid Society*,[43] the apex court further stressed the need of proper care of children in a healthy atmosphere. The court observed "a problem child is indeed a negative factor. Every society must, therefore, devote full attention to ensure that children are properly cared for and brought up in a proper atmosphere where they could receive adequate training, education and guidance in order that they may be able to have their rightful place in the society when they grow up."[44] Juveniles being a class in themselves require different kind of treatment by judicial officers and others dealing with them. Therefore, the officers at different levels called upon to perform statutory duties by exercising powers need to be given proper training and it should be only after they are equipped with such training that they can be safely called upon to handle the delicate juvenile offenders.[45] Aforesaid remarkable decisions of the Supreme Court establish that through innovative approach it has not only redressed the grievances of petitioners but has also played a truly dynamic role by suggesting a central legislation to remove diversities in different states in different areas in specifying a definite time-frame to ensure speedier disposal of cases of juvenile offenders, in instructing the states to establish juvenile courts, remand homes, etc; manned by professionally skilled personnel to handle juveniles and to provide proper facilities for education and vocational training to children lodged in various reformatories. Though Government of India seriously thought over the valuable suggestions of the Supreme Court and the Parliament enacted the above suggested uniform law i.e. The Juvenile Justice Act, 1986, the situation has not yet visibly improved. State is under obligation to ensure a healthy development of youth and their protection from being spoiled due to environmental maladies over which State has control. Juvenile deviance is a delicate problem which can be tackled with persistent and sincere efforts and not by the indulgence of judiciary and enactment of law alone. The matter should be a cause for deep concern to each individual, each school, each official and all parents and any improvement can be possible only when all of these sections understand the gravity of the problem and put their heads together to identify the factors that aggravate it. Means of mass communication like radio, T.V., press, etc. can play a vital role in educating the masses about the menace and methods of its prevention. Juvenile's activities need individual attention so that each slight deviance is immediately diagnosed and cured appropriately. In the end, the foremost thing to address the problem is wholehearted implementation of laws dealing with social problems with particular attention to juvenile delinquency so that dreams may be translated into reality and children may grow into healthy, useful and good citizens of the society and are able to shoulder due responsibilities in their town.

In the light of the above discussion, there is sufficient evidence of our judiciary's dynamic role in recognising, protecting and even imparting greater meaning to the definition of human rights of the children through various directions to the States. But unfortunately there have been countless instances to substantiate the charge of inaction against the Government machinery and pronounced lack of will against our body politic, which together have been busy advancing alibis and winking over the implementation of enactments and valuable judicial initiative in such an important area. No wonder then the situation has defied solution and continues to assume even greater and more ominous proportions day by day and bacons every responsible citizen to respond to the dictates of his soul. Otherwise the sacred concept of human rights will have no meaning to the very future of our society.

REFERENCES

1. National Policy for Children, Govt. of India (Resolution of 22 Aug. 1974).
2. Pandharinath, R.R., "Fighting Female Foeticide." *The Lawyer,* Vol. 6, No. 8 (1991) pp. 4–11.

3. Mahalwar, K.P.S., "Children at work—A Socio-Legal Conspectus" *Law Review* Vol. VI (1987) pp. 37–45.
4. On 25 May 1995 about two dozen children died in a cracker factory at Rohtak a district headquarter at the periphery of National Capital New Delhi.
5. Swami Agnivesh, "Child Slavery in India", paper presented in International Conference on Shaping the Future by Law at Vigyan Bhawan New Delhi on 21–25 March 1994.
   Sharma, Pawan, "Child labour—A socio-legal study" *JILI* (2)36 (1994) pp. 221–220.
6. "Trade Unions Open Front to Fight Child Labour", *Times of India*, New Delhi 8.1.95.
7. "Employment of Children as bonded labour Condemned," *Human Rights News Letter*, February 1995.
8. Article 18 of the Convention on Rights of the Child (CRC) states,
   "States parties shall take all appropriate legislative, administrative, social and educational measures to protect children from all forms of physical or mental violence, injury or abuse, neglect or negligent treatment, maltreatment or exploitation including sexual abuse . . ."
9. 'Children of the dustbin,' *Link* N. Delhi 9th Nov. 1980 p. 24.
   Also see Article 24 (CRC) which states,
   "State parties shall . . . take appropriate measures . . . to combat disease and malnutrition, including the framework of primary health care thoroughly . . . the provision of adequate nutritious foods and clean drinking water. . . ."
10. "Scouring garbage for daily bread" *Indian Express*, N. Delhi, 16/17 April 1986.
11. *Indian Express* 4th June 1986.
12. Art. 32 of CRC states,
    "State parties recognise the right of the child to be protected from economic exploitation and from performing any work that is likely to be hazardous or to interfere with the child's education or to be harmful to the child's health or physical, mental, spiritual, moral or social development."
13. *Supra* note 8.
14. Sheela Barse, "Children Playing with Fire" *Indian Express*, New Delhi 5/6 April 1986.
15. Hutokshi, R., "Of nimble Fingers and broken backs" *The lawyer*, Vol. 10 No. 1 & 2 (1995) pp. 4-17.
16. *Ibid.*
17. Mahalwar, K.P.S., "Agriculture labour—A need for uniform legislation" *JILS* Vol. VII 1987.
18. "Poverty, illiteracy root cause of child labour: Study" *Times of India*, N. Delhi, 30 January 1995.
19. *Supra* note 15.
20. "Child labour in the country"; A series of 11 parts appeared in *Times of India*, N. Delhi, Nov. 1994.
21. Kothari, S., "There is blood on those match sticks" in Upendra Baxi (ed.) *Law & Poverty–Critical essays* (1988) pp. 322–40.
22. AIR 1991 SC 417.

23. Dogra Bharat & Pankaj, H.S., "More Broadbased Efforts against Child Labour are needed" *Legal News & Views*, Vol. 9, No. 2 (1995), p. 21.
24. Gopal. R, "Child Welfare—A Far Cry in Ameena's Case" *The Lawyer* October 1991.
25. Art. 34 of CRC states,
    "States parties undertake to protect the child from all forms of sexual exploitation and sexual abuse. For these purposes, States parties shall in particular take all appropriate national, bilateral and multilateral measures to prevent:
    (a) the inducement or coercion of a child to engage in any unlawful sexual activity;
    (b) the exploitative use of children in prostitution or other unlawful sexual practices;
    (c) the exploitative use of children in pornographic performances and materials."
26. Rozario, M. Rita, *Trafficking in Women & Children in India* (1988) p. 117.
27. *Vishaljeet* v. *Union of India* AIR 1990 SC 1412.
28. *Ibid.*, at 1416.
29. *Gaurav Jain* v. *Union of India* (1990) Supp S C C 709 *Bholanath Tripathi* v. *State of U.P.* (1990) Supp S C C 151.
30. (1987) 1 S C C 67.
31. *Ibid.*, at 70–79.
32. (1991) 4 S C C 33 decided on 14 Aug. 1991.
33. 2 *Scale* (1992) 90.
34. 1 *Scale* (1993) 290.
35. Mahalwar, K.P.S., "Juvenile delinquency—Prisons and role of police" *Lawyer* July 1987 pp. 1–7.
36. Sheela Barse, "Children and the Courts" *Indian Express*, New Delhi, 6 January, 1985.
37. *Sheela Barse* v. *Union of India* 2 *Scale* (1986) p. 184.
38. *Ibid.*
39. *Sheela Barse* v. *U.O.I.* AIR 1986 SC 1773 per J. Bhagwati.
40. *Ibid.*, para 10.
41. *Ibid.*, para 12.
42. *Ibid.*, para 13.
43. AIR 1987 SC 656.
44. *Ibid.*, para 11.
45. *Ibid.*, para 5.

18

Sexploitation of Minors–Some Socio-legal Aspects

*P.S. Lathwal**

The future, bright and hopeful belongs to children everywhere. These are the real assets of society. The concept of global children's rights, proposed at the league of Nation in 1924, has taken many decades to germinate and grow. International year of the child in 1979 could not provide them love and care they deserve, the food they need to grow and opportunity to earn and develop. All this caused a major rethinking about children's rights, the protection of which is the most fundamental duty of the civilised society.

The convention adopted by U.N. general Assembly on the Rights of the child on November 20, 1989 also sets international standards and measures intended to protect and promote the well-being of the children in the society. Vienna Convention of 1993 emphasises upon special care and assistance for children and a need to create an environment in the society conducive to healthy growth and development of children so that the children are able to live securely and realise their full potential in life. The Convention draws attention for the following rights[1] of the children:

1. Right to Survival—including right to life, health, nutrition and adequate standard of living.

* Lecturer in Law, M.D. University, Rohtak, Haryana.
Paper presented at XVIII Indian Social Science Congress held at M.S. University, Baroda from 27–30 August, 1994.

2. The Right to Protection—freedom froms all forms of exploitation, abuse, inhuman and degrading treatment and right to special protection in case of emergency and armed conflicts.
3. The Right to Development which includes the right to education, support for early childhood, development and care, social security and right to leisure, recreation and cultural activities.
4. The Right to Participation—includes respect for the views of children, freedom of expression, access to appropriate information and freedom of thought, conscience and religion.

All these rights are included to secure a better quality of life and freedom of people in general and children in particular. The Convention advocates these measures for harmonious protection and development of the child.

The efforts of the UNICEF, to promote respect for rights of the children, are also underlined.

U.N. declaration in 1959 emphasised to protect child against all forms of neglect, cruelty and exploitation. He shall *not be subject* of traffic in any form, the declaration stated. Our Constitution is committed to secure protection and well being of children through fundamental rights and Directive Principles of State Policy.

Art. 23 prohibits traffic in human beings. Art. 39(f) provides that the State shall direct its policy towards securing that children are given opportunity to develop in a healthy manner and in conditions of freedom and dignity and that childhood and youth are protected against exploitation and against moral and material abandonment.

Also "we as a people have given expression in our Constitution to certain concepts at the care of a great heritage of thought that belongs not just to the people of India but to all community," rightly observed Dr. S.D. Sharma, the President of India.[2]

In spite of all such concern, the children/minors are facing inhuman and degrading situation. Instead of protecting their rights for their well being, they are being even sexually abused at their tender age. Even fathers, brothers, social workers, police and others who are supposed to protect their female relatives, wards etc. turn out to be their exploiters.

According to one of the girls, her father had been criminally. assaulting her for the past five years as a result of which she had undergone two abortions. Her mother was beaten badly if she protested against his atrocities, the girl added.[3]

Also a self proclaimed godman, Ram Avtar Shastri, has been charged with raping his teenage daughter. The girl's mother reportedly told the police that her husband had intimidated them into silence and that he had often slept with the girl in the past two years. Interestingly, Mr. Ram Avtar had been running a one man party called '*Rashtriya Chetna Manch*' of which he was the president.[4]

The another instance of such sin is where sexual deviant's sister was his first victim. Ram Parsad did not spare his daughter in law. Even he was caught in a compromising position with a woman by the people in vicinity. In the last couple of years Ram Prasad, however, turned to young blood. In July 1993, he lured 10 year old Virender, sodomised and then strangled him. Another victim of his sexual hunger was a 10 year old girl when he raped and murdered her. He claimed to be involved in 19–20 murder cases when police interrogated him.[5]

The 'Protector' police is also not lagging behind in such horrendous acts. Recently a trainee police officer, Pramod Pawar, attached to Nagpur's Lakkad-Ganj Police Station, has been remanded to police custody till August 6 by a Malegaon Court on charges of raping a minor girl from Ballarshah in Chandrapur district last month. Surprisingly he offered to marry her and still he handed over the girl to his friends.[6]

A case of serious negligence and carelessness of police is accounted for when an under-trial who is reported to be involved in a case of kidnapping and rape of a teenage (13 year old) girl in a jhuggi cluster of Laxmi Nagar, in East Delhi, made a daring escape from Tihar Jail on 18-8-94 night dodging security men at four points. He scaled four walls ranging from 12 feet to 16 feet in height and crossed barbed wire fence in jail compound and a nallah beyond the perimeter wall. The I.G. Prison, Mrs. Kiran Bedi said the security men had switched off powerful search lights installed on the boundary walls and did not fire at Sagar.[7] It shows how careless the police is in controlling such injurious persons put behind bars.

Even in jails[8], observation homes[9] and protective homes, sexual exploitation of children/teenagers is taking place.[10] Not only this but even in Devdasi system and Jogin tradition prevailing in the society, minor girls are also subjected to sexual abuse.[11] One daily has narrated such stories. It revealed that one 14 year old girl was given to goddess. Later on she was sold to a businessman and eventually she was brought to Bombay red light area. She could no longer work there because she contracted AIDS there. She had to attend 4–5 clients a day in a brothel house. She is not the only victim of this system but there are 80,000 brothel based sex-workers in Bombay. Of those 20,000 live in Kamatipura Lane. 50 per cent of sex workers are infected. 50,000 taxi drivers alone are staying away from their families. Infection generally passes on to their wives in villages also when they come back home. The lady thus carries her husband's curse. Maximum clients are not willing for sex with condoms. Hence government intervention through distribution of condoms does not seem to have work. Poverty also cannot allow the girls to insist sex with condoms. Moreover they are not bothered of getting diseases. They are not even leaving now, uttered young girl from Nepal.

Most of the brothels are tiny structures. Even the children/minors of the sex workers live within this space. Lack of family support from their villages does not permit them to send their children there.[12] Sooner or later they all fall in the profession of their parents i.e. in prostitution.

There are more intricate problems of women infected by their husbands and then ostracised in their middle class milieu, of babies and children with HIV. Because AIDS (Acquired Immuno Deficiency Syndrome) comes from the Human Immuno Deficiency Virus (HIV) which can lie dormant for years but it finally leads to the breaking down of the body's defences against infection. It has assumed epidemic proportions in the parts of Africa. In India and rest of sub-continent official figures read 742 cases of full blown AIDS and 15399 HIV infections.[13]

The poverty and helplessness of the parents are of such a grave nature that it may compel their minors even to be unwilling victim of sexual exploitation. Very horrible and amazing situation can be visualised when the sounds of trucks trundling into Bandarsindri village sends 15 year old Rani rushing to the door of her hut, not out of childish awe for the mammoth vehicles, but to pose for the drivers who will bid for her immature body. She has even to drop her price when the customer threatens to move on.[14]

What a pity, the parents are living at the earning of their daughters indulged in sexual abuse. Though living on the earning of the prostitution is punishable.[15]

Such a state of affairs ridicules the ancient Indian philosophy which propagated the maxim यत्र नार्यास्तु पुज्यते रमणते तत्र देवता. Man is said to be a social animal but it appears that he has reduced himself to mere animal or even lower than that because the animals have a season whereas the men do not have any. He is eveready for having sex.

Moreover the mass tourism has increased this abuse even in countries surrounding India, Pakistan, Bangladesh, Sri Lanka, Indonesia, Thailand, Laos and Philippines.[16] Even in India (in Goa) the same practice is flourishing.

Forty per cent of child prostitutes have been condemned to death having contracted the HIV (Human Immuno deficiency Virus). Every year million of children fall in the hands of brothel keepers and unscrupulous business. It is one of the most abominable form of modern slavery involving about 10 millions boys and girls. The brothel keepers are hardly pursued by Thai Prison but held only prostitutes.[17]

No doubt the child prostitution in Asia, Africa and Latin American Nations has steeply risen along with increasing foreign tourism. Vice rings started kidnapping girls from China and Myanmar to be delivered at their brothels.[18] Often the children would be kept imprisoned in massage parlours, often totally drugged. For the girls there is hardly any escape from the brothels. The younger the girl the more vulnerable she is. The sex tourists in U.S., Western Europe, Japan and Australia may no longer get away unpunished. Germany have had laws since 1993 to this effect. Other countries also have made law stricter or there are proposals to do so.[19]

In India also there is sufficient legislation to curb this problem. Section 361 of I.P.C. contains provisions against kidnapping. Section 366A (dealing with offence to procure minor girls for illicit intercourse), 366B (against importation of girls from foreign country for illicit intercourse) and Section 372 (dealing with the offence of selling of minors for purpose of prostitution) of I.P.C. are there to overcome this abuse. Section 373 I.P.C. is against buying minor for purpose of prostitution. But the girls, minor or otherwise are still being sold for paltry sum for their sexual exploitation. Offence of 'rape' is covered under section 375 I.P.C. The following section i.e. Section 376 I.P.C. contains the provisions for severe punishment for committing rape.

The SITA (the Suppression of Immoral Traffic in Women and Girls Act) 1956 as amended in 1986 as PITA (Prevention of Immoral Traffic Act) does not aim at abolition of prostitution and prostitutes. A prostitute can carry on her trade whenever she desires as long as it is not within 200 metres of a public place. The punishment for such an offence is imprisonment for 3 months. In case of a child or minor the person committing the offence may be imprisoned for not less than 7 years or for life or for 10 years and fine. If the place where such offence is committed in respect of a child/minor is a hotel, such licence shall also be liable to be cancelled.

Thus the aim of PITA, 1986 is to abolish prostitution (sexual exploitation or abuse) of person for commercial purpose.

What we need is the strict compliance of law. Proper check and administration may control the abuse. NGOs participation will bring good results in this regard.

Our Judiciary has also shown great concern for the children of the victims of sexual abuse. In *Gaurav Jain* v. *Union of India*,[21] the Apex court directed the State to separate the children of the prostitution from their parents because if it is not done, these children will lead to sexploitation there, in following the footsteps of their parents. The main requirement, it is submitted, is to rehabilitate, educate and to make them self sufficient to lead a dignified life.

The Supreme Court in *Vishal Jeet* v. *Union of India*[22] found the children unwilling and involuntary victim of compelled circumstances, indulged in sexual exploitation. Severe and speedy legal action against pimps, brokers and brothel keepers can minimise the problem.

Even there is huge cry for protection of children's rights, their sexual exploitation is at rampage. At one time Judiciary has also turned its face away from the protection of minors. *The Bombay High Court* recently[23] reduced the sentence on a father who had raped his minor girl on the ground, that the father was a poor widower who fell to temptation but was otherwise a good father.

Severe punishment is essential for such offences. Criminal/rapist must be disarmed of the weapon of this offence, suggested B. Lentin rightly. Because human rights are intended for human beings and not for sub-humans and brutes.[24]

Though various national and international organisations are fighting against this sin, yet effective results are not attained. The commitment of Government, Judiciary and specially that of society is the main requirement. May be sufficient law, but having law and sleeping over it does not fulfil the purpose. Until we are basically/mentally prepared to voice against such vice there is hardly any scope of improvement. The women shall have to be alert, serious, and stronger instead of being depressed, angry and sad.

Universal Humanitarian outlook is required at the official and the individual levels of the society at every stage otherwise the law, be it municipal or international, devoid of morality, will have no claim to regulate the human behaviour. Then the question is: are we heading towards lawless society that progressively moves towards immorality?

REFERENCES

1. "The Right to be a Child", UNICEF India Back-ground Paper, March 1994–UNICEF, 73 Lodi Estate, New Delhi, 110 003 India.
2. Inaugural Speech of Dr. S.D. Sharma, President of India at the International Conference on "Shaping the Future by Law–Children, Environment and Human Health" at Vigyan Bhawan, New Delhi, 21-3-94.
3. See, *The Times of India*, New Delhi, July 29, 1994, p. 3 Col. 1.
4. See, *The Times of India*, New Delhi, August 3, 1994.
5. See, *The Times of India*, New Delhi, August 18, 1994, p. 3.
6. See, *The Times of India*, New Delhi, July 29, 1994, p. 4, Col. 8.

7. See, *The Times of India*, New Delhi, August 20, 1994, p. 7, Col. 1.
8. *Muna* v. *State*, AIR 1982, SC 806.
9. *Sheela Barse* v. *Secretary, Children Aid Society*, AIR 1987 SC 656.
10. See, *Dainik Tribune*, Chandigarh, March 25, 1993, p. 6 Col. 4.
11. *Dainik Tribune*, Chandigarh (Sunday, Magazine) January 10, 1993.
12. Kalpana Jain, "Devadasi in Bombay's temple of doom," *The Times of India*, New Delhi, August 8, 1994 p. 1, Col. 2.
13. See, *The Times of India*, August 5, 1994, p. 1, Col. 2.
14. *Ibid.*
15. Sec. 4 of The Immoral Traffic (Prevention) Act, 1986.
16. *Employment Federation of India, Bulletin*, Vol. 13 (Oct. 1-15, 1992) p. 49 at 49–50.
17. See, *The Tribune*, Chandigarh, November 20, 1993.
18. *The Times of India*, New Delhi July 4, 1994, p. 8. Col. 4.
19. *The Times of India*, New Delhi July 6, 1994, p. 8, Col. 4.
20. *Jan Satta*, Chandigarh Dec. 11, 1993 p. 5, Col. 1.
21. AIR 1990 SC 292.
22. AIR 1990 SC 1412.
23. B. Lentin, "Judging the Judiciary—Continuing search for the Ideal", *The Times of India*, New Delhi, July 15, 1994.
24. *Ibid.*
    See also Sonora Jha Nambiar, "It cannot happen to my daughter." *The Times of India*, New Delhi, July 24, 1994. p. 1.